The Philosophy of the Brahma-sūtra

Bloomsbury Introductions to World Philosophies

Series Editor:
Monika Kirloskar-Steinbach

Assistant Series Editor:
Leah Kalmanson

Regional Editors:
Nader El-Bizri, James Madaio, Sarah A. Mattice, Takeshi Morisato, Pascah Mungwini, Omar Rivera and Georgina Stewart

Bloomsbury Introductions to World Philosophies delivers primers reflecting exciting new developments in the trajectory of world philosophies. Instead of privileging a single philosophical approach as the basis of comparison, the series provides a platform for diverse philosophical perspectives to accommodate the different dimensions of cross-cultural philosophizing. While introducing thinkers, texts, and themes emanating from different world philosophies, each book, in an imaginative and path-breaking way, makes clear how it departs from a conventional treatment of the subject matter.

Titles in the Series:

A Practical Guide to World Philosophies, by Monika Kirloskar-Steinbach and Leah Kalmanson

Daya Krishna and Twentieth-Century Indian Philosophy, by Daniel Raveh

Māori Philosophy, by Georgina Tuari Stewart

Philosophy of Science and the Kyoto School, by Dean Anthony Brink

Tanabe Hajime and the Kyoto School, by Takeshi Morisato

African Philosophy, by Pascah Mungwini

The Philosophy of the Brahma-sūtra, by Aleksandar Uskokov

The Philosophy of the Brahma-sūtra

An Introduction

Aleksandar Uskokov

BLOOMSBURY ACADEMIC
LONDON • NEW YORK • OXFORD • NEW DELHI • SYDNEY

BLOOMSBURY ACADEMIC
Bloomsbury Publishing Plc
50 Bedford Square, London, WC1B 3DP, UK
1385 Broadway, New York, NY 10018, USA
29 Earlsfort Terrace, Dublin 2, Ireland

BLOOMSBURY, BLOOMSBURY ACADEMIC and the Diana logo are trademarks of Bloomsbury Publishing Plc

First published in Great Britain 2022

Series design by Louise Dugdale
Cover image © Liyao Xie / Getty Images

A catalogue record for this book is available from the British Library.

A catalog record for this book is available from the Library of Congress.

ISBN: HB: 978-1-3501-5001-0
PB: 978-1-3501-5000-3
ePDF: 978-1-3501-5002-7
eBook: 978-1-3501-5003-4

Series: Bloomsbury Introductions to World Philosophies

Typeset by Deanta Global Publishing Services, Chennai, India

To Kalina and Angel, my two birds

Contents

Preface

The introductions we include in the World Philosophies series take a single thinker, theme, or text and provide a close reading of them. What defines the series is that these are likely to be people or traditions that you have not yet encountered in your study of philosophy. By choosing to include them you broaden your understanding of ideas about the self, knowledge, and the world around us. Each book presents unexplored pathways into the study of world philosophies. Instead of privileging a single philosophical approach as the basis of comparison, each book accommodates the many different dimensions of cross-cultural philosophizing. While the choice of terms used by the individual volumes may indeed carry a local inflection, they encourage critical thinking about philosophical plurality. Each book strikes a balance between locality and globality.

The *Brahma-sūtra of* Bādarāyaṇa, a major text in Indic intellectual history, systematizes the philosophy of the first principle—the Brahman—for select adepts. In *The Philosophy of the Brahma-sūtra,* Aleksandar Uskokov reconstructs aspects of the commentarial accord that are salient to understanding this systematization. Uskokov foregrounds one theme in the commentaries of Śaṅkara, Bhāskara, Rāmānuja, Nimbārka, and Śrīnivāsa: the intricate relation between grasping Brahman's being, becoming conscious of this first principle, and the bliss that sets in by becoming conscious of this understanding. This fine guide to the *Brahma-sūtra* promises to open up the text's esoteric teaching to a reader who is ready to join Uskokov on the journey from metaphysics to bliss, and back.

Acknowledgments

This volume started in the research for my doctoral dissertation at the University of Chicago and contains elements of its Introduction and Chapters 1 and 4. I am most thankful to Gary Tubb, my doctoral advisor, as well as Wendy Doniger and Dan Arnold, my committee members, without whose kind guidance that project would not have seen the light of day.

The scope of this volume, however, is different, and the bulk of the dissertation is yet to come out in a published form. Much more research went into writing this book, for which I am most thankful to the institutional support of the MacMillan Center for International and Area Studies at Yale University and to the Yale Library System. At Yale I am particularly thankful to Phyllis Granoff. I see my academic career so far as consisting for the most part of two serendipitous and most beneficial encounters, the first with Gary and the second with Phyllis. I hold both of them in my heart.

Viktor Ilievski was my sounding board throughout writing this volume, particularly for Chapters 4 and 5, and he remains the best companion both in *pāṇḍityam* and *bālyam*.

A thread that ties the book together is the Upaniṣadic idea about two souls that are like two friendly birds occupying the same tree. I don't know if this Upaniṣadic image has been purposely depicted in art heretofore, but it is now by Kalina Uskokova, whose *Two Birds* graces the back cover of the book. I am most thankful to her for that. She and Angel are the light of my life, and my wife Jasna—the ground on which I stand.

I have used and thoroughly reworked some material published previously in two entries—on "Brahman" and on "Brahma Sūtras (Vedānta Sūtras)"—in Springer's *Encyclopedia of Indian Religions: Hinduism and Tribal Religions* edited by Jeffery D. Long, Rita D. Sherma, Pankaj Jain, and Madhu Khanna. The introduction to Chapter 3 is informed by part of the first, and elements of the second are included in the Introduction and in Chapter 6. The revised portions are printed here with the kind permission of Springer Nature.

I am, finally, most thankful to the people at Bloomsbury Academic whose initiative and good work made the book possible. James Madaio kindly invited me to write a *Brahma-sūtra* volume for the Bloomsbury Introductions to World Philosophies series, Monika Kirloskar-Steinbach saw the manuscript proposal through the review process, the anonymous reviewer helped me improve many elements of the book, and Colleen Coalter was a most helpful and supportive editor. To them all: thank you!

Note on Sanskrit Transliteration and Translation

Sanskrit terms are transliterated in accordance with the International Alphabet of Sanskrit Transliteration (IAST), except for the *anusvāra*: whereas IAST requires ṃ, I use instead ṁ. Within words, I represent the *anusvāra* before the stops by their homorganic nasal; that is, Śaṅkara, not Śaṁkara.

All translations from Sanskrit are mine, unless stated otherwise.

Abbreviations

Works are referred to by abbreviations only in the notes. In the main body of the text, full titles are used instead. Likewise, in the main body of the text the various Upaniṣads are referred to just by their name. To illustrate, *Taittirīya* always means *Taittirīya Upaniṣad*.

AA	Pāṇini's *Aṣṭādhyāyī*
ĀDhS	*Āpastamba Dharma-sūtra*
ĀŚ	Gauḍapāḍa's *Āgama-śāstra*
ĀŚBh	Śaṅkara's commentary (*bhāṣya*) on Gauḍapāḍa's *Āgama-śāṣtra*
BĀU	*Bṛhad-āraṇyaka Upaniṣad*
BĀUBh	Śaṅkara's commentary (*bhāṣya*) on the *Bṛhad-āraṇyaka Upaniṣad*
BĀUBhVAB	Sureśvara's commentary (*vārttika*) on the *Aśva-brāhmaṇa* section of Śaṅkara's commentary (*bhāṣya*) on the *Bṛhad-āraṇyaka Upaniṣad*
BDhS	*Baudhāyana Dharma-sūtra*
BGBh	Baladeva's *Govinda-bhāṣya* commentary on the *Brahma-sūtra*
Bhāmatī	Vācaspati Miśra's *Bhāmatī* commentary on Śaṅkara's *Brahma-sūtra-bhāṣya*
BhBSBh	Bhāskara's commentary (*bhāṣya*) on the *Brahma-sūtra*
BhP	*Bhāgavata Purāṇa*
BrS	Maṇḍana Miśra's *Brahma-siddhi*
BS	*Brahma-sūtra*
Bṛhatī	Prabhākara's *Bṛhatī* commentary on Śabara's commentary on the MS
ChU	*Chāndogya Upaniṣad*
ChUBh	Śaṅkara's commentary (*bhāṣya*) on the *Chāndogya Upaniṣad*
GDhS	*Gautama Dharma-sūtra*

KauU	*Kauṣītaki Upaniṣad*
KKP	Keśava Kāśmīrī's *Kaustubha-prabhā* commentary on the *Brahma-sūtra* inspired by Śrīnivāsa's *Vedānta-kaustubha*
Manu	*Manu-smṛti*
MBh	*Mahābhārata*
MBSBh	Madhva's commentary (*bhāṣya*) on the *Brahma-sūtra*
MS	*Mīmāṁsā-sūtra*
MSBh	Śabara's commentary (*bhāṣya*) on the *Mīmāṁsā-sūtra*
MU	*Muṇḍaka Upaniṣad*
NBhV	Uddyotakara commentary (*vārttika*) on Vātsyāyana's commentary (*bhāṣya*) on the *Nyāya-sūtra*
NVPS	Nimbārka's *Vedānta-pārijāta-saurabha* commentary on the *Brahma-sūtra*
RŚBh	Rāmānuja's *Śrībhāṣya* commentary on the *Brahma-sūtra*
ṚV	Śālikanātha's *Ṛju-vimalā* commentary on Prabhākara's *Bṛhatī*
RVD	Rāmānuja's *Vedānta-dīpa* commentary on the *Brahma-sūtra*
RVS	Rāmānuja's *Vedānta-sāra* commentary on the *Brahma-sūtra*
ŚBSBh	Śaṅkara's commentary (*bhāṣya*) on the *Brahmas-sūtra*
ŚBhGBh	Śaṅkara's commentary (*bhāṣya*) on the *Bhagavad-gītā*
SK	Īśvarakṛṣṇa's *Sāṅkhya-kārikā*
ŚKBSBh	Śrīkaṇṭha's commentary (*bhāṣya*) on the *Brahma-sūtra*
SŚP	Sudarśana Sūri's *Śruta-prakāśikā* commentary on Rāmānuja's *Śrībhāṣya*
ŚU	*Śvetāśvatara Upaniṣad*
ŚV ĀV	Kumārila's *Śloka-vārttika*, chapter *Ātma-vāda*
ŚV SĀP	Kumārila's *Śloka-vārttika*, chapter *Sambandhākṣepa-parihāra*
ŚVK	Śrīnivāsa's *Vedānta-kaustubha* commentary on the BS, following Nimbārka's commentary
TU	*Taittirīya Upaniṣad*

TUBh	Śaṅkara's commentary (*bhāṣya*) on the *Taittirīya Upaniṣad*
TUBhV	Sureśvara's commentary (*vārttika*) on Śaṅkara's commentary on the *Taittirīya Upaniṣad*
VABh	Vallabha's *Aṇu-bhāṣya* commentary on the *Brahma-sūtra*
VAS	Rāmānuja's *Vedārtha-saṅgraha*
VNM	Bhāratītīrtha's *Vaiyāsika-nyāya-mālā*
VP	*Viṣṇu Purāṇa*
VPBK	Bhartṛhari's *Vākyapadīya, Brahma-kāṇda*
VVABh	Vijñānabhikṣu's *Vijñānāmṛta* commentary (*bhāṣya*) on the *Brahma-sūtra*

Chronological Table of Commentaries

The following chronology includes only the commentaries and versified summaries that are mentioned in the book. It is a representative but not an exhaustive list of works on the *Brahma-sūtra*. All dates CE. The dates will not be mentioned again in the body of the text.

Author	Date	Work
Śaṅkara Bhagavatpāda	ca. 750	*Brahma-sūtra-bhāṣya*
Bhāskara	ca. 750–800	*Brahma-sūtra-bhāṣya*
Padmapāda	ca. 750–800	*Pañca-pādikā* on the first 4 *sūtra*s of Śaṅkara's *Brahma-sūtra-bhāṣya*
Vācaspati Miśra	late 10th century	*Bhāmatī* on Śaṅkara's *Brahma-sūtra-bhāṣya*
Prakāśātman	late 10th century	*Vivaraṇa* on Padmapāda's *Pañca-pādikā*
Sarvajñātman	late 10th century	*Saṅkṣepa-śārīraka* inspired by Śaṅkara's *Brahma-sūtra-bhāṣya*
Rāmānuja	ca. 1077–1157	*Śrībhāṣya* *Vedānta-dīpa* *Vedānta-sāra*
Madhva	ca. 1238–1317	*Brahma-sūtra-bhāṣya* *Anu-vyākhyāna* *Aṇu-bhāṣya* *Nyāya-vivaraṇa*
Nimbārka	13th century	*Vedānta-pārijāta-saurabha*
Śrīkaṇṭha	13th or 14th century	*Brahma-mīmāṁsā-bhāṣya*
Śrīnivāsa	13th or 14th century	*Vedānta-kaustubha* inspired by Nimbārka's *Vedānta-pārijāta-saurabha*
Sudarśana Sūri	late 13th early 14th century	*Śruta-prakāśikā* on Rāmānuja's *Śrībhāṣya* *Śruta-pradīpikā* on Rāmānuja's *Śrībhāṣya*
Vedāntadeśika	ca. 1269–1370	*Adhikaraṇa-sārāvalī* inspired by Rāmānuja's *Śrībhāṣya*

Author	Date	Work
Bhāratītīrtha	14th century	*Vaiyāsika-nyāya-mālā* inspired by Śaṅkara's *Brahma-sūtra-bhāṣya*
Jayatīrtha	ca. 1365–88	*Nyāya-sudhā* on Madhva's *Anu-vyākhyāna*
Keśava Kāśmīrī	15th/16th century	*Vedānta-kaustubha-prabhā* inspired by Śrīnivāsa's *Vedānta-kaustubha*
Vallabha	ca. 1479–1531	*Aṇu-bhāṣya* up to 3.2.33
Viṭṭhalanātha	ca. 1516–86	*Aṇu-bhāṣya* from 3.2.34 to the end
Appayya Dīkṣita	ca. 1520–93	*Śivārka-maṇi-dīpikā* on Śrīkaṇṭha's *Brahma-mīmāṁsā-bhāṣya*
Vijñānabhikṣu	2nd half of 16th century	*Vijñānāmṛta*
Baladeva Vidyābhāṣaṇa	ca. 1700–93	*Govinda-bhāṣya*

Introduction

Situating the *Brahma-sūtra*

The *Brahma-sūtra* or "Thread of Statements about Brahman" is one of the most important works in Indian intellectual history. It is the foundational text of the tradition of Vedānta, one of the premier brands of philosophy and theology on the subcontinent, and since early modernity it has become closely associated with Hindu doctrinal identity. Sawai Jai Singh II (1688–1743 CE), the ruler of Amber who founded Jaipur and fashioned himself as a religious king (*dharmarāja*) in the later days of the Mughal Empire by reintroducing ancient rituals and actively promoting Brahmanical social and moral norms, required religious communities seeking royal patronage in his domain to have an authoritative commentary on the *Brahma-sūtra*.[1] In the Sacred Books of the East series that was produced in the heyday of Orientalism, the *Brahma-sūtra* was included as the only systematic work of Indian philosophy, allotted three full volumes in the total of fifty, and represented by two of its greatest commentaries. Sarvepalli Radhakrishnan, the second president of India, produced an English translation-cum-commentary in his normative selection of four texts that best represent "the spirit" of Indian philosophy, along with the Upaniṣads, the *Bhagavad-gītā*, and the *Dhammapada*.[2]

What is the *Brahma-sūtra*? In short, it is a systematization of the Upaniṣads around its two central concepts of Brahman, the first principle of the world, and of meditation on Brahman, the means of attaining the highest good. But what are the Upaniṣads, then? They are part of the Vedas, "the holy books" of Brahmanism, one of the oldest doctrinal communities on the Indian subcontinent. Composed in Sanskrit and with their oldest parts stemming from the middle second millennium BCE, the Vedas are a collection of liturgical texts, myths, ritual prescriptions, and philosophical speculation concerned, in broadest terms, with the aspiration toward "immortality" or the attaining of a permanent world, a heaven (*svarga*), in the hereafter, by means of performing rituals that harness hidden causal relations and involve recitation of mantras. It is difficult to state what constitutes the Upaniṣads as a subgenre of the Vedas, indeed impossible in a single sentence, but to my mind closest to succeeding has come Śaṅkara their most celebrated commentator, who sees two genre-defining characteristics in them: (1) they are esoteric works that originated and were taught in seclusion, out of the public eye; and (2) they pertain to anything in the Vedas that is *mental*, that is, not *recited* or physically *enacted* in a ritual.[3] Much more on this in Chapter 6.

The gist of the *Brahma-sūtra* can be stated as follows. There is Brahman, the first principle from which all created things come, by which they exist, and into which they return upon destruction. It is known only from the Upaniṣads. This Brahman is a conscious principle, and bliss is its defining characteristic. It is also the efficient cause of the world, an omniscient and omnipotent being: Brahman is "it," neuter in Sanskrit grammatical gender, but in all classical commentaries it is also Īśvara, "he," a creator God, masculine in grammatical gender, an ambiguity that I will not attempt to avoid in the text. Brahman transforms itself into the world without being ontologically exhausted in the process, that is, remaining beyond its creation. There are also individual souls (*jīvātman*) who are in some sense identical, yet also distinct from it. Crucially, whenever Brahman creates, it enters every created thing, a body, and it does so along with an individual soul; it enters this soul as well. In fact, it is precisely this entry into and residence within created things that accounts for the oldest name of the *Brahma-sūtra*, the *Śārīraka-sūtra* or "Thread of Statements about the Embodied."[4] This makes Brahman—as the *Taittirīya* says—present "in the heart and in the highest heaven" simultaneously.[5]

The individual souls are eternal yet transmigrating beings: they have never been created but move from one body to another through a process of rebirth. Ontologically they are "parts" of Brahman, not in a partitive sense but through exhibiting only a fraction of their Brahman-ness: in embodiment, their essential nature is concealed. They can be liberated from this embodiment, however, and achieve what the *Brahma-sūtra* describes as "no return," that is, the end of rebirth, and as "manifestation of essential nature." Some interpreters understand this manifestation of essential nature to mean merging into Brahman, a loss of individuality, but a more plausible reading is that the soul becomes Brahman in kind, achieving an ontological apotheosis. In positive terms, liberation means attaining the "world of Brahman," a place of heavenly delights, along a meticulously mapped path called "the course of the gods," absolute freedom of motion, and the power of unrestricted enjoyment.

How does one achieve liberation? By meditating on Brahman as one's self: Brahman's entering and residence in created things and individual souls is not only an element of cosmology but a most important soteriological feature of the text as well. Meditation on Brahman is the Upaniṣadic counterpart of ritual. Crucial in its exercise is the description of Brahman as the meditational object, in which a pan-Upaniṣadic notion of Brahman is combined with Brahman's characteristic stated in a particular Upaniṣadic text. The prolonged, indeed lifelong, practice of such meditation is supposed to culminate in a direct vision of Brahman, which, once attained, would make the present embodiment final: at death, one would take "the course of the gods" leading to the "world of Brahman," never to return to transmigration.

Purpose of the Book

The book that follows has a dual purpose. First and foremost, it is envisioned as an introduction to the philosophy of the *Brahma-sūtra*, as its title explicitly says: it is not written primarily for philologists and scholars but, to use Wendy Doniger's delightful turn of phrase, "for people."[6] Its main objective is to introduce the *Brahma-sūtra* to students of philosophy, religious studies, and South Asian studies, and to that mythical creature called "general reader" who might wish to make the work's acquaintance, as much as it is possible in the confines of a short volume. It is hoped, nevertheless, that philologists and scholars will benefit from the book, as I strongly believe that new insights are brought to the old work and that the reconstruction provided here is the closest approximation to its meaning. To read the *Brahma-sūtra* afresh is the book's second purpose.

In terms of presentation, it is slanted toward the non-specialist audience, although there will be much material to entertain philologists in the notes, including quotations and translations of the original *sūtra*s, brief quotations from the commentaries, and occasional discussions of the views of scholars who have written on the *Brahma-sūtra* before me.[7] Several scholars have produced studies of the entire *Brahma-sūtra* or its parts, and particularly prominent are Thibaut (1890), Telivala (1918), Karmarkar (1919–20, 1920–21), Ghate (1926), Modi (1943, 1956), Nakamura (1983: 425–532), Sharma (1986), and Adams (1993).[8] Beyond that, much has been written on the composition history of the *Brahma-sūtra*, its relationship with the *Mīmāṁsā-sūtra*, the question of authorship, and so on, issues that fill the remainder of this Introduction as we try to flesh out the "identification card" of our work but are not discussed in the main body of the text.

Authorship, Composition History, and Date

Who wrote the *Brahma-sūtra*? The short answer is, we do not know. The commentaries most commonly call the author by the common noun "the aphorist," *sūtrakāra*. In the oldest preserved commentary, that of Śaṅkara, this aphorist is identified with "the venerable Bādarāyaṇa," and traditionally Bādarāyaṇa is considered the author of the *Brahma-sūtra*. Very little is known about Bādarāyaṇa, however. The name itself is a patronymic: according to the rules of Sanskrit grammar, "Bādarāyaṇa" would be "the grandson of Badara" or anyone in Badara's lineage after the grandson. Additionally, while Śaṅkara's student Padmapāda and younger contemporary Bhāskara still talk about Bādarāyaṇa as the author, already for Vedāntins at the turn of the first millennium Bādarāyaṇa is identical with Vyāsa, the legendary seer of the *Mahābhārata* and editor of the Vedas.[9] (Please bear with the proliferation of names of various works in this heading: they will be briefly introduced in the next.)

Both identifications are, nevertheless, problematic. The structure of the *Brahma-sūtra* is such that the text has likely undergone several redactions before assuming the form on which the commentaries were written, and such a text cannot have *an* author, except in the sense of whoever gave the work its final shape, a *redactor*. Bādarāyaṇa is, in fact, quoted several times in the *Brahma-sūtra* along with a number of other teachers: Jaimini, Bādari, Āśmarathya, Ātreya, Auḍulomi, Kārṣṇājini, and Kāśakṛtsna. While Bādarāyaṇa's views are generally conclusive, this at the least suggests that the final text could have been put together after him. Śaṅkara's student Sureśvara (ca. 750 CE), in fact, attributed the *Brahma-sūtra* not to Bādarāyaṇa but to Jaimini, with whom the related *Mīmāṁsā-sūtra* is associated, and Asko Parpola had argued convincingly that Bādarāyaṇa reworked Jaimini's earlier composition.

As for the attribution of the *Brahma-sūtra* to Vyāsa and Vyāsa's identification with Bādarāyaṇa, I have argued elsewhere that this was probably driven by another classic, the *Bhāgavata Purāṇa*, and its self-presentation as a work of Vedānta and a continuation of the *Brahma-sūtra*.[10]

Be that as it may, here I will talk about the author as "Bādarāyaṇa," for two related reasons. First, the final shape of the *Brahma-sūtra* is not a mere accretion of elements through time, but a finely redacted work that embodies a coherent worldview and interpretation of the Upaniṣads. In that more general sense, the *Brahma-sūtra is* a work of a single author: after all, no philosopher whose name is not Ludwig Wittgenstein ever starts from scratch. And such being the case, second, I want to place front and center the personal agency of our author, easily hidden behind common names as "the aphorist" or "the redactor," at the pain of replicating the cult British sitcom "Only Fools and Horses," where Trigger, one of the supporting characters, consistently addresses the main character Rodney Trotter as "Dave," blissfully ever unaware of the folly.

With this caveat, nevertheless, what more can be said about the *Brahma-sūtra* composition history? It has since long been recognized that the

Brahma-sūtra looks very much like a systematization of the *Chāndogya Upaniṣad*. Paul Deussen was probably the first to notice that in section one of the first chapter, twelve of the twenty-eight topical passages were from the *Chāndogya,* while no other Upaniṣad supplied more than four. Further, the passages from each Upaniṣad were discussed in the order as they appear in their texts, which prompted Deussen to suggest that Bādarāyaṇa or a follower of his inserted sixteen passages from other Upaniṣads into an earlier work that systematized the *Chāndogya*, keeping the principle that the original order of the extracts should be maintained.[11] The dominance of the *Chāndogya* appears even more striking in other parts of the book. For instance, the whole first section of the third chapter is based on the doctrine of five fires as discussed in the fifth book of the *Chāndogya*. The third section of the same chapter, further, deals with five passages of the *Chāndogya*, again in the order in which they appear in the Upaniṣad itself.[12] S. K. Belvalkar went farthest in proposing that there could have been a *Chāndogya-brahma-sūtra*, a *Bṛhad-āraṇyaka-brahma-sūtra*, and so on. The *Brahma-sūtra* that became the normative was the *Chāndogya* one, written by Jaimini, in which Bādarāyaṇa or his students introduced passages from the other Upaniṣads as side illustrations or supporting evidence. A third and final recension, Belvalkar suggested, included refutation of the doctrines of other schools of philosophy.[13]

While this is an appealing proposition, it is not one without difficulties, the chief one being the all-important role of the *Taittirīya*, which supplies the definition of Brahman as the topic of the treatise, the paradigmatic meditation on Brahman, and many of the other key doctrines. While the *Chāndogya* core can hardly be questioned, the *Taittirīya* is so structural to the text that it is hard to imagine that the *Brahma-sūtra* was not a novel undertaking predicated on the view that *all* Upaniṣads form a coherent corpus and should speak in a single voice.[14]

Since the *Brahma-sūtra* comes in line of an already established tradition, citing along with Bādarāyaṇa seven other teachers as we have seen in the previous paragraphs, it is likely that these teachers were authors of earlier *sūtra* compositions on which Bādarāyaṇa drew and which he in effect replaced. This process can be compared to the composition of another great *sūtra* work, the *Aṣṭādhyāyī* Sanskrit grammar of Pāṇini, whose genius drew on and replaced a number of earlier works.[15] This argument can be further supported by considering the relationship of the *Brahma-sūtra* with another canonical Vedānta work, the *Bhagavad-gītā*. In verse four of chapter thirteen, the *Bhagavad-gītā* refers to "words that form threads about Brahman," *brahma-sūtra-padaiḥ*. On the other hand, topical passages from the *Bhagavad-gītā* are discussed in the *Brahma-sūtra*: *sūtra* 2.3.44 refers to *Bhagavad-gītā* 15.7, and 4.2.20 discusses *Bhagavad-gītā* 8.23–7. From this, several scholars have suggested that the *Bhagavad-gītā* verse refers to multiple older *brahma-sūtra*s, perhaps by the teachers cited in the *Brahma-sūtra*, which were used by Bādarāyaṇa to produce his own treatise.[16]

It has been proposed that the final text of *Brahma-sūtra* postdates the early fifth century CE and the time of the Buddhist philosopher Vasubandhu, the exponent of idealism, since *Brahma-sūtra* 2.2.28–32 seems to refute precisely his doctrine.[17] This is likely, although not universally accepted, and the final date of the text will likely remain a "cold case" forever.[18] Be that as it may, the *Brahma-sūtra* could not have been finalized much later than the fifth century because we know for a fact that several prominent Vedāntins wrote commentaries on it before the eighth century Śaṅkara.

Sources of the *Brahma-sūtra*

It is important to note that the Upaniṣads are the doctrinal source of Vedānta, and in the oldest Vedāntic works "Vedānta," lit. "end of Veda," simply means "an Upaniṣad." While various explanations of this semantic identity are possible, it is likely due to the final position of those works that have become Upaniṣads in a collection of Vedic texts, and due to their being last in the sequence of study.[19] The details of this need not bother us here, except to appreciate that under "a Veda" a collection of various texts is meant, some of which have been labeled "Upaniṣads."[20] There are four such Vedas—Ṛg, Sāma, Yajur, and Atharva—and each of them has several texts that go by the name "Upaniṣad." Arranging them by their Veda, the classical Upaniṣads are the following:

Ṛg Veda	1) *Aitareya*
	2) *Kauṣītaki*
Sāma Veda	3) *Chāndogya*
	4) *Kena*
Yajur Veda	5) *Bṛhad-āraṇyaka*
	6) *Īśā*
	7) *Taittirīya*
	8) *Kaṭha*
	9) *Śvetāśvatara*
Atharva Veda	10) *Muṇḍaka*
	11) *Praśna*
	12) *Māṇḍūkya*

The oldest among them are predominantly in prose, whereas the later tend to be versified, although most are mixed in style.

Three other texts have a strong association with a Veda: *Jaiminīya-upaniṣad-brāhmaṇa* (of which, in fact, *Kena* is a part) to the Sāma Veda and *Mahānārāyaṇa* and *Maitrī* to the Yajur Veda. Many later works claim a status of an Upaniṣad, attached to the Atharva Veda, but even this list of twelve is a bit wide for the *Brahma-sūtra*, which never references the *Māṇḍūkya* and, arguably, the *Kena*. Most important among these are the *Chāndogya*, which provides the core of Bādarāyaṇa's systematization; the *Taittirīya*, from which the definition of Brahman and many other key doctrines are derived; the *Bṛhad-āraṇyaka*, important in virtue of its sheer size and prestige; and the *Muṇḍaka*, which is referenced surprisingly often for its relative shortness and probably represented state-of-the-art Upaniṣadic thinking in Bādarāyaṇa's time.

There are occasional references to other Vedic texts, and the Vedas in general, collectively called *śruti* or "hearing," are the first layer of the Brahmanical canon from which Bādarāyaṇa draws. Another set of Brahmanical texts called *smṛti* or "memory" is also very important. We will unpack the epistemological significance of "hearing" and "memory" in Chapter 2, but in the *Brahma-sūtra* the second is represented by the epic *Mahābhārata* and its part the *Bhagavad-gītā*; by the texts on *dharma*, roughly translatable as "Brahmanical law," primarily the *Manu-smṛti*; and very sparingly by works called "Purāṇas" that are difficult to define as genre and mostly consist of myths, stories, cosmologies, and doctrine.

A third important source is the so-called *Mīmaṁsa-sutra*, "Thread of Deliberation Sentences." Attributed to one Jaimini, it is in structure entirely like the *Brahma-sutra*, but its focus is on the Brāhmaṇas, another kind of Vedic texts. Its central idea is *dharma*, in a different (but related) sense from the abovementioned "Brahmanical law." Here *dharma* means Brahmanical ritual that leads the ritualist to "heaven" (*svarga*), which is defined simply as a state of felicity or pure happiness in the hereafter. So closely is the *Mīmāṁsā-sūtra* tied to the *Brahma-sūtra* that the two are both called "a *Mīmāṁsā-sūtra*," with the qualifier "prior" (*pūrva*) for the first and "posterior" (*uttara*) for the second. While the exact relationship between them has been hotly debated, Asko Parpola's argument that they were originally a single work that was later split and redacted into two is closest to the mark. The *Brahma-sūtra* refers to the *Mīmāṁsā-sūtra* often and in a self-referential manner, and more generally its interpretation is impossible without presupposing rules stated in the *Mīmāṁsā-sūtra*.[21]

Even without textual continuity, however, there is a minimal, ideological sense in which the *Brahma-sūtra* and the *Mīmāṁsā-sūtra* are related: indeed, the respective traditions of their interpretation go by the names of

Pūrva-Mīmāṁsā, the "Prior Deliberation," what I call here just "Mīmāṁsā," and Uttara-Mīmāṁsā or "Posterior Deliberation," here simply "Vedānta." We shall unpack this minimal relation in the conclusion of Chapter 2. Here we should note, though, that Mīmāṁsā is not only a major source but occasionally a foil as well, especially in the second part of the *Brahma-sūtra* where issues such as the independence of meditation on Brahman from ritual and the nature of the attainment are discussed.[22]

A second foil is the philosophical tradition of Sāṅkhya, whose place in Brahmanical philosophy is complicated and liminal between the Vedas and heterodoxy: its ontology thoroughly informs the *Mahābhārata* and the *Bhagavad-gītā*, but in its classical formulation as a philosophical school, known to us from Īśvarakṛṣṇa's (ca. 350 CE) *Sāṅkhya-kārikā* (SK), it rejects the Upaniṣadic Brahman as the first principle in favor of what it calls "prime matter" (*mūla-prakṛti* or *pradhāna*). The world emerges from the evolution of prime matter into secondary principles of creation. Along with prime matter, there are individual souls (*puruṣa*s) that undergo transmigration, like in the *Brahma-sūtra*, yet they are not essentially in touch with the world, nor are they agents with moral freedom for soteriological pursuits. Liberation from transmigration is the highest good, but as a state, it is describable as total "isolation" of the souls from prime matter. This doctrine is Bādarāyaṇa's main opponent for the entire first part of the *Brahma-sūtra*, and most of his ontology is developed through constant dialogue with it.[23]

Bādarāyaṇa briefly considers the philosophies of all other doctrinal communities prevalent in his time. They go by the names of Nyāya-Vaiśeṣika, Buddhism, Jainism, Pāśupata, and Pañcarātra. Only the first will appear occasionally in the following pages. Nyāya-Vaiśeṣika is a competing Brahmanical system in which the first principles of the world are atoms or infinitesimal particles of matter, and a God who is coeval with them. Unlike Brahman, the God of Nyāya-Vaiśeṣika is not the origin of the world but only its efficient cause: things do not *come* from God, but God makes the world and its natural products by arranging atoms in composite objects and by governing the law of karma. This God is not known from the Upaniṣads, but from analogical inference.[24]

Genre, Method, Themes, and Structure

As its name makes clear, the *Brahma-sūtra* is a *sūtra* work, part of a genre of texts that systematize various aspects of Vedic learning and serve as teaching manuals. *Sūtra* works are the canonical texts for knowledge systems such as ritual and rites, law, phonetics, grammar, prosody, and so on. Some of them are directly related to Vedic texts, such as the Śrauta-sūtras that treat Vedic injunctions on public rituals, or the *Brahma-sūtra* itself, which systematizes the doctrine of Brahman from the Upaniṣads, whereas others deal with issues auxiliary to the Vedas, for instance rules concerning the recitation of Vedic mantras and pronunciation in general. The *sūtra* works are not uniform in style or method, but are invariantly based on the "sūtra," a short sentence or an aphorism, as their vehicle of expression. "Sūtra" literally means "thread," and it describes both the entire work—the running thread—and its individual sentences, "the rosary" and "the beads" as it were. Śaṅkara emphasizes the first aspect: "The purpose of the *sūtra*s is to knit the flowers that are Upaniṣadic passages; for, it is these passages themselves that are examined through the *sūtra*s."[25]

In later Brahmanical literature, two definitions of "sūtra" are common in particular:

> The thoughtful describe *sūtra*s as sentences that are brief, whose meaning is indicated (*sūcitārthāni*), expressed in few words and syllables, and essential in all respects.[26]

> The knowers of *sūtra*s describe a *sūtra* as what is stated in few syllables, is clear, essential yet comprehensive, without embellishments, and irreproachable.[27]

The expression "whose meaning (*artha*) is indicated (*sūcita*)" has a double meaning in Sanskrit, suggesting that *sūtra*s work through "indication" or indexing of their topic, which is why they are brief, but also by "stitching" them together in a string. Brevity of expression but completeness of the system, thus, is the characteristic feature of the genre, and *sūtra*s are particularly averse to using verbs. The existential verb "to be" is almost never stated in any of its uses, unless bearing the emphasis, as in the shortest of all sentences in the *Brahma-sūtra* itself (2.3.2): "But, there *is*," *asti tu*.

The *Brahma-sūtra* consists of four chapters (*adhyāya*), each divided into four sections (*pāda*), the *sūtra*s in which are organized in headings (*adhikaraṇa*). The headings can consist of a single *sūtra*, though commonly they are longer. The number of *sūtras* is not uniform across the commentaries—for instance, in Śaṅkara's commentary there are 555 *sūtra*s, whereas in Rāmānuja's 545—nor are the *sūtra*s read uniformly: occasionally the different commentaries read different words, join two *sūtra*s in one, or split a single *sūtra* in two. That said, the text is relatively coherent across the main commentaries.

The *adhikaraṇa*s are headings in which a single topic is discussed, such as a particular Upaniṣadic passage, and they are inherently dialogical and argumentative. In later accounts, the structure of an *adhikaraṇa* is said to consist of five steps: (1) positing of a topic, *viṣaya*, which is generally an issue discussed in an Upaniṣadic passage, *viṣaya-vākya*, and often comes in the form of a preliminary thesis; (2) doubt, *saṁśaya*, with respect to the topic; (3) prima facie view, *pūrva-pakṣa*, that will be eventually overturned; (4) conclusion, *siddhānta*, affirmation of the thesis through clarifying the doubt and overturning the prima facie view; and (5) coherence, *saṅgati*, of the topic, which is its pertinence for Brahman, the theme of the knowledge system, and appropriateness for the chapter and the section. What *sūtra*s constitute an *adhikaraṇa* is also not uniform across the commentarial tradition: Śaṅkara's commentary, for instance, has 191 *adhikaraṇa*s, whereas Rāmānuja's 156.

In practice, Bādarāyaṇa's headings tend to consist of presenting a thesis and supporting it with arguments, which is covered entirely by step four, and it is left to a commentator to supply many of the five as implied but not expressed, in a structure that does not always conform to the idealized sequence. Here is an illustration of such a typical heading taken from *Brahma-sūtra* 1.2.19–21:

> [*sūtra* 1.2.19] Brahman is the inner ruler in the divine and other domains, because its characteristics are mentioned.
> [*sūtra* 1.2.20] The inner ruler is not prime matter, because characteristics that are not proper to it are mentioned.
> [*sūtra* 1.2.21] It is not the individual soul either, because both understand it as different.[28]

The topic here is the so-called *antaryāmin*, the inner ruler, which for any reader educated in the Upaniṣads points directly to *Bṛhad-āraṇyaka* 3.7. The "both" in the last *sūtra* refers to two traditions of transmission of the *Bṛhad-āraṇyaka*, the so-called "Kāṇva" and "Mādhyandina," the readings in which occasionally differ. Bādarāyaṇa begins with the thesis directly, which in the formal argument is a combination of steps one and four, so it is left for the commentators in their lead to the first *sūtra* to reference the said topical passage explicitly and thus state the topic; to present the prima facie view, that the inner ruler is prime matter or the individual soul; in virtue of not being clear that Brahman is the said inner ruler, which constitutes the doubt. The item of coherence comes in play in the commentaries at juncture points, such as the beginning of a new chapter or section, and only rarely in the text itself, for instance when it needs to be clarified why certain issues that have already been settled are taken up for discussion again.

As part of the argument, another text may be referenced, typically from the *smṛti* corpus or from the *Mīmāṁsā-sūtra*, and in both cases formulaic expressions are used, for instance "and, it is remembered" (*api ca smaryate* and related variants) for the first, and "this has been said" (*tad uktam*) for the second. Some of the longer *adhikaraṇa*s do begin with the prima facie view in any number of *sūtra*s, so one can say that Bādarāyaṇa tackles only elements of steps three and four. However, it is not that the tradition has invented this five-step procedure out of thin air, since the same structure of argument is evident in Vedic texts when they talk about *mīmāṁsā*, deliberation on the esoteric aspects of ritual.[29] This suggests that the *Brahma-sūtra*, along with its counterpart the *Mīmāṁsā-sūtra*, were embedded in a context of interpretation, which initially would have been oral and instructional, from their very inception.

It is in virtue of this specific method that the *Brahma-sūtra* is called *uttara-mīmāṁsā*, "posterior deliberation," and *brahma-mīmāṁsā*, "deliberation on Brahman." Related in meaning is the idea that the *Brahma-sūtra* is the so-called *nyāya prasthāna* or the "argument departure point" of Vedānta, which becomes prominent later in the tradition. Briefly, Vedānta as a knowledge system is said to have three departure points, *prasthāna*, loci on which the entire system is based and with respect to which it develops. The first is the *śruti-prasthāna* or the Vedas, more restrictedly the Upaniṣads; the second is the *smṛti-prasthāna* or the second layer of the Brahmanical canon, later zeroed in on the *Bhagavad-gītā*. It is precisely the *adhikaraṇa* or heading structure of argument that makes the *Brahma-sūtra* Vedānta's *nyāya-prasthāna*. Particularly clear about this was the Vedāntin Bhāratītīrtha, whom we shall encounter in Chapter 1.

The content of the *Brahma-sūtra* is generally said to consist of three topics across the four chapters: *tattva* or ontology, the nature of Brahman and its relation to the world and the individual souls, covered in the first two chapters; *sādhana* or the means to liberation, discussed in chapter 3; and *phala*, result, or *puruṣārtha*, liberation from rebirth as the highest human good, treated in the fourth chapter. While this structure is roughly justified, we should note two things. The real topic of the first chapter is not so much a positive definition of Brahman or ascertainment of Brahman's nature—indeed, we learn more about the essential characteristics of Brahman in chapter 3, when there appears the need to standardize the idea of Brahman across the Upaniṣadic meditations—but the argument that Brahman rather than prime matter or the souls of Sāṅkhya is the topic of individual Upaniṣadic texts. The second chapter is all about Brahman *in its causal role*, in the context of which the various Upaniṣadic creation accounts are standardized; a pan-Upaniṣadic doctrine of the individual soul is developed, occasioned by the fact that the soul is not created but spoken as such metaphorically; Sāṅkhyan objections to Brahman's being both the material and the efficient cause are answered, and so on. While in the first two chapters Sāṅkhya is throughout the dialogue partner, in the second section of chapter two all the other contemporary rival doctrines of causality are discussed.

Based on this, the traditional names of the four chapters of the *Brahma-sūtra* are: (1) *samanvayādhyāya*, the chapter on Brahman as the common meaning of all Upaniṣads; (2) *avirodhādhyāya*, the chapter on absence of contradiction, in the Upaniṣads internally and by opposing doctrines; (3) *sādhanādhyāya*, the chapter on the means; and (4) *phalādhyāya*, the chapter on the result.

Methodology

Although *sūtra* works are definitionally pithy, a good number of them are relatively easy to read.[30] The *Brahma-sūtra* is different, however, and it has been said that it is impossible to understand even a single *sūtra* without the help of a commentary.[31] We may seek the reasons for this in the intersection of two observations, made by Hajime Nakamura and Asko Parpola.[32] The *Brahma-sūtra* was not conceived as a public text. It was an esoteric teaching restricted to elite members of Brahmanism who were initiated in the study of the Vedas, and to whose mind outsiders did not have the privilege to do ritual or to study Brahman. The brevity of the text, then, presupposed unbroken oral instruction and served as a means of exclusion. It was also a result of composition practices within the *sūtra* genre, where later authors customarily reused material from their predecessors in fewer words than the original. The present *Brahma-sūtra* comes last in the line of similar works on Brahman that it replaced but also condensed. This too requires the context of oral instruction.

The claim that it is impossible to understand even a single *sūtra* without a commentary is overstated: a good portion of chapter 1 is quite formulaic, the references to Upaniṣadic passages are transparent, and the arguments are clear and somewhat repetitive, albeit succinct to the extreme. This notwithstanding, anyone proposing to write an interpretation of the *Brahma-sūtra* will fancy oneself a Robert Langdon by necessity. I should like to clarify, therefore, the principles of interpretation that inform my method of reading Bādarāyaṇa, which can be subsumed under three points.

The first concerns understanding Bādarāyaṇa without dependence on commentaries. As mentioned earlier, there are *sūtra*s that can be read without a commentary, and often they are of crucial importance. Their meaning is clear either directly, or because their reference to a topical passage is unambiguous. Let me illustrate both scenarios.

The first section of chapter four, *sūtra*s seven through eleven, reads as follows:

> [*sūtra* 4.1.7] Sitting, because of adequacy.
> [*sūtra* 4.1.8] And, because of absorption.
> [*sūtra* 4.1.9] And, in dependence on being motionless.
> [*sūtra* 4.1.10] And, *smṛti* says so.
> [*sūtra* 4.1.11] Where concentration, there, because of no distinction.[33]

The context of the section is the practice of the means to liberation, and despite the brevity, it is immediately obvious that this practice is meditative absorption of some kind, to be exercised in a sitting posture, wherever concentration is possible. No commentary is required to understand this much, and nowhere else in the book is there another section presenting some alternative means. Therefore, if a commentator advocates for another means to liberation or reinterprets meditation, as does Śaṅkara while commenting on these very *sūtra*s, they are introducing their own doctrine into Bādarāyaṇa's system. Methodologically this is important, as it allows us to disregard such interpretations.

At the opening of the third section in chapter three, in the first *sūtra* where the general principles of forming Upaniṣadic meditations are stated, there is an unmistakable reference to *Mīmāṁsā-sūtra* 2.4.9. From this, it is obvious that meditations on Brahman are formed after the model of sacrifices, by combining elements from their various iterations in Vedic literature. Consulting the *Mīmāṁsā-sūtra* on this point provides immense help in reading the *sūtra*, and since this is a crucial doctrine prominently placed in the text—an opening *sūtra* in the section—it is important for our understanding of the entire book.

Similarly, there are often in the *sūtra*s enough cues to point to the precise passage from the Upaniṣads that is under discussion. These also tend to be placed centrally, at the beginning of chapters or sections. Good examples are 3.4.1, which points very likely at *Taittirīya* 2.1.1; and 4.4.1, which is an easily recognizable reference to *Chāndogya* 8.12.3. Other well-known cases are two of the most famous *sūtra*s: 1.1.2, which defines Brahman as the origin etc. of the world, a direct reference to *Taittirīya* 3.1.1; and 1.1.13, which describes Brahman as bliss and points to the second chapter of *Taittirīya*. These are illustrations, and many more *sūtra*s can be tied to specific Upaniṣadic loci, the reading of which in their own context is crucial for understanding the *Brahma-sūtra* arguments. As a corollary to this, my own presentation here will constantly look toward the Upaniṣads, and often I will spare no words in presenting the Upaniṣadic contexts of specific *sūtra*s and explicating what is at stake in them.[34]

The second point is that Bādarāyaṇa for all his brevity has a predilection for repeating arguments, and a remarkable consistency in the use of terminology. To illustrate, first, Bādarāyaṇa repeats one statement in entirely identical form in three *sūtra*s—"Because of mention of difference"—and more generally he talks about "mention" of agency, kinds of verbal action, syntactic relations, and so on twenty-seven times in the text.[35] When such formulaic arguments are read in the context of their topical Upaniṣadic passages, it is quite straightforward to understand them without reliance on commentaries. Second, Bādarāyaṇa repeats important terms—for instance "residence" (*avasthiti*), "place" (*sthāna*), "manifestation" (*āvirbhāva, abhi-vyakti*), "intention" (*abhidhyāna*), "symbol" (*pratīka*)—in several distinct context, such that one can understand what he means in one place when the remaining several cases are clear, and by that much accept the interpretation of some commentators against others. I cannot present the details here, but I will illustrate it several times in the following chapters.[36]

The third point concerns the use of commentaries. I should like to make clear that, my first two points notwithstanding, I do not think it is entirely possible or even desirable to read the *Brahma-sūtra* independent of its commentarial tradition. As we have seen earlier, the *Brahma-sūtra* must have been intertwined with oral instruction from its very inception, and elements of its earliest interpretation certainly survive in the major commentaries. It is beneficial here to expand upon the observations of Daniel Ingalls, who noticed that Śaṅkara and Bhāskara are often unanimous in their interpretation of many *sūtra*s where they seem to follow an older commentator whose doctrine can be reconstructed by reading the two commentaries side by side.[37] This can be generalized further: whenever all commentators agree on the meaning of a *sūtra* or a heading, which is common in glosses and the explication of what is presupposed but unstated, before consequences are drawn out and disagreements emerge, they are likely following a tradition representing an early oral interpretation stratum. It is fair to assume in such cases that the meaning is unambiguous.[38]

In my reading of the *Brahma-sūtra*, then, I rely on five commentaries—of Śaṅkara, Bhāskara, Rāmānuja, Nimbārka, and Śrīnivāsa—for the entire text, and on a wider selection in Chapters 4 and 5. I introduce the commentators in Chapter 1, and here it is apposite simply to explain my selection of "the inner circle." The first four are all major commentaries that no serious reconstruction can afford to disregard. Śrīnivāsa's is a very lucid text that expands upon Nimbārka by drawing on Rāmānuja, without novel interpretations to worry about. As a practical choice, I decided not to rely on the post-fifteenth-century commentaries of Vallabha, Vijñānabhikṣu, and Baladeva—that would have prolonged the timeline of the book—nor that of Śrīkaṇṭha, whose work is a

Śaiva redressing of Rāmānuja's interpretation. The commentary of Madhva has generally been deemed unreliable; beyond that, Madhva's construal of the *sūtras* is so idiosyncratic that it entirely undermines the third pillar of my methodology, the seeking after commentarial accord.

Outline

In the chapters that follow I replicate the general structure of the *Brahma-sūtra*—ontology, practice, and the human good—with some degree of latitude. Chapter 1 is an extension of the Introduction and provides a brief account of *Brahma-sūtra*'s reception history in its classical commentaries. It may be desirable to read it both first, to become acquainted with the doctrines of the commentators that are occasionally mentioned in the text, and last, to see how they derive from and build on the *Brahma-sūtra*. The reader may also skip to the main body of the book, Chapters 2 through 7, and consult the first chapter whenever each commentator is mentioned first. Chapter 2 introduces Bādarāyaṇa's epistemology, succinctly stated in *sūtra* 1.1.3: Brahman is known from the Upaniṣads. This requires clarifying the nature of Bādarāyaṇa's reasoning as both theological and philosophical, and elucidating elements of epistemology that are explicit in the *Mīmāṁsā-sūtra* but presupposed in the *Brahma-sūtra*. Chapter 3 is about the *Brahma-sūtra* ontology, that is, about Brahman as the first principle and the theory of causality that accounts for the emergence of the world from it. While in most of the book I paint with a wide brush, Chapters 4 and 5 tackle the fine details of two interrelated problems that arise from Bādarāyaṇa's ontology: the purpose of creation, and the theistic problem of evil. In Chapter 6, we introduce the idea of Upaniṣadic meditations as the means to attaining the good promised in the Upaniṣads—liberation from embodiment and the end of transmigration—the nature of which forms the topic of Chapter 7. All chapters end with suggestions for further study, and all but the first include study questions that are conceived as essay or reading response prompts.

1

Reception History

Despite its esoteric intentions—if we agree with Hajime Nakamura that the hard-to-crack pithiness of our book is due to Brahmins not wanting to disclose their secret doctrine—few works in Indian intellectual history have been as influential and widely read as the *Brahma-sūtra*. Indeed, perhaps only the *Bhagavad-gītā* enjoys a comparable place of pride. Numerous commentaries, sub-commentaries, sub-sub-commentaries, and restatements have been written on Bādarāyaṇa's 550 or so brief *sūtras*, from various, often antagonistic, ontological and soteriological standpoints, eventually growing into philosophies described as "absolute monism," "identity and accidental difference," "identity and essential difference," "pure monism," "dualism," and so on.

In Indological scholarship from the nineteenth century onwards, one persistent manner of inquiry has marked the study of the *Brahma-sūtra*: namely, reading a number of prominent commentaries side by side so as to ascertain and adjudicate which one or more of them had captured Bādarāyaṇa's meaning most accurately and, conversely, which ones are to be treated as "unreliable."[1] In my own reading, I have found that one can be equally fascinated by the opposite question: How is it that such a relatively brief work could branch into such widely different readings and doctrines?

One avenue to pursue an answer to this question is the idea of *mahā-vākya*, which is both organic to the tradition and comparable to modern hermeneutic notions of text as a complex hierarchy of linguistic elements with a unitary meaning derived from its being a whole.[2] A text is not a series of disjoined sentences each expressing a meaning of its own: it is a whole with unitary meaning which subsumes the meanings of its constituents. The discovery of this unitary meaning must begin with a guess, that is, with a selection of certain of its sentences as likely candidates for expressing the unitary meaning more so than others—including their interpretation in a particular sense—and with a hierarchical structure of the entire text around them such that they do not make a discordant medley. While the guess may be determined by doctrinal presuppositions—and is often more of a choice than an open-minded quest for meaning—the point is that if we approach the *Brahma-sūtra* as such a *mahā-vākya*, we can imagine different readers making different initial guesses and producing different interpretations of the unitary meaning, leading them to construe individual statements of the entire text in various ways so as to make them cohere.

This approach to reading texts need not mean that any guess is as good as another—there are interpretations that make more sense in light of the unitary meaning—but it does mean that works come with some degree of "semantic potential," a capacity to produce varieties of understanding—we may call them "misreadings" that are yet "creative readings"—and lead to diverse interpretations. Writing the reception history of a text, then, becomes witnessing the actualization of semantic potentials. In this chapter, I want to introduce briefly the *Brahma-sūtra* reception history with some sensitivity to this notion. In the limited space available, I cannot adjudicate between various interpretations, and I will do that in the remainder of the book to the degree it seems required. Rather, I want to introduce the most prominent commentators on the *Brahma-sūtra*, whom we will rely on or engage with in the book, and see what they have brought to and adopted from Bādarāyaṇa's laconic treatise.

I have limited this survey to major commentaries written in Sanskrit no later than the eighteenth century—Sanskrit commentaries continue to be written to this day—and to a few specimens of the understudied genre of versified summaries and restatements. Much has been written on the *Brahma-sūtra* in European languages, in form of academic studies and translations. While I have benefited from many of them in the following pages, as well as in the Introduction, the limited length of a book such as this requires of the author to make difficult choices what not to include. I remain, therefore, proverbially hopeful to make up for this loss on some other occasion.[3]

The overview of the commentaries will focus on how the relationship between Brahman and the two other points of Bādarāyaṇa's ontology—the individual souls and the world—was conceived. This is the main bone of contention in the system, and the several traditions covered in this overview bear their characteristic names, "the doctrine" (*vāda*) of *x* where *x* stands for monism (*advaita*), dualism (*dvaita*), and so on, with respect to how they addressed this relationship. On the issue of practice the commentarial tradition is much more unified. An outlier in this is Śaṅkara's line of interpretation, for which reason I will briefly talk about his soteriology as well.

In the second millennium, which Sheldon Pollock aptly described as "the vernacular millennium,"[4] the reception history of the *Brahma-sūtra* became closely intertwined with that of the *Bhāgavata Purāṇa*, and through its medium the *Brahma-sūtra* often crossed into vernacular literature. Modern scholarship had started unraveling this close alliance between the two classics, and it is to be expected that much more will be written in this direction. I conclude the chapter, therefore, with a brief note on the *Bhāgavata Purāṇa* and some of the fruits of its cross-pollination with the *Brahma-sūtra*.

Before we begin, though, I wish to remind the reader that this chapter is best read *both* first *and* last: some understanding of the commentators is required to appreciate their role in the book, yet many elements presented here will make more sense "on hindsight" and should be revisited after the completion of Chapters 2 through 7.

Absolute Monism

From the commentaries of Śaṅkara, Bhāskara, and Rāmānuja, we gather there were several interpretations of the *Brahma-sūtra* that have not survived to our times. Some of them were not readily available even in Rāmānuja's days, but paraphrases and direct quotes are not uncommon in the three great *Bhāṣya*s. Prominent names include Upavarṣa, Bodhāyana, Vṛttikāra, Brahmānandin, Vākyakāra, Bhāṣyakāra, Dramiḍa, and so on. Several of these are generic titles meaning "a commentator," and scholars have debated precise identifications. It is, further, likely that the practice was to write a commentary on the *Mīmāṁsā-sūtra* and the *Brahma-sūtra* as a single work. In fact, the "commentator" on *Mīmāṁsā-sūtra* 1.1.5 whom we shall discuss in Chapter 2 probably did just that, and—depending on which scholar one chooses to agree with—he may have been identical with Bodhāyana, or with Upavarṣa, or bore both names.[5]

Be that as it may, the oldest fully preserved commentary on the *Brahma-sūtra* is the *Brahma-sūtra-bhāṣya* of Śaṅkara Bhagavatpāda (for all dates, see the Chronological Table), a work of an immensely rich—positive and negative—reception history. Śaṅkara's immediate student Padmapāda wrote a commentary on the first four *sūtra*s, called *Pañca-pādikā*, which was interpreted by Prakāśātman in his *Vivaraṇa*. The oldest full-length sub-commentary was the *Bhāmatī* by Prakāśātman's contemporary Vācaspati Miśra, and the two works morphed into two streams of Advaita Vedānta known as the *Vivaraṇa* and the *Bhāmatī* school.[6] Many more commentaries were written on the *Brahma-sūtra-bhāṣya* itself and on the *Bhāmatī*; and Śaṅkara's work also provided the basis for numerous restatements of Bādarāyaṇa's system.

On the negative side, everyone from without Śaṅkara's tradition wrote *against* the *Brahma-sūtra-bhāṣya*, and Indological scholarship had almost univocally found Śaṅkara's commentary unreliable. Truth be told, Śaṅkara is largely very reliable, if one can disregard the turns he takes after giving a straightforward reading of the *sūtra*s, if one can distinguish, as it were, between the trustworthy commentator and the brilliant philosopher and theologian.[7] We will have an occasion to illustrate Śaṅkara's habitual exegetic turns in Chapter 5.

One of Śaṅkara's major innovations concerned the interpretation of the very first word *atha*, "now," as the condition on which the study of Brahman was predicated. In pre-Śaṅkara Vedānta, "now" stood for the completion of the study of Pūrva-Mīmāṁsā and its rules of interpreting ritual texts, *in sequence* of which the study of Brahman would follow. Śaṅkara, however, argued that "now" had more of a proleptic orientation: rather than expressing a mere *sequence* of study, it looked *toward* the inquiry and the conditions of its possibility. The Sanskrit word for "inquiry," *jijñāsā*, is a desiderative noun that can be taken in a technical sense of "inquiry" pure and simple, *or* in an etymological sense of the "desire to know." Śaṅkara and his followers argued that "now" picks out precisely this desire, for if the desire to know had not arisen in the student of Brahman, the undertaking of study would be fruitless. "Now" answers to an existential condition of wishing to know Brahman, which can further be specified through four criteria: the ability to distinguish between permanent and transient things; the disgust with enjoyments of the here and the hereafter; the acquisition of virtues such as sense control and calm; and the pursuit of liberation. In effect, then, "now" is the desire to know, which in its turn is the desire to become liberated.

This emphasis on knowing had further ramifications on Śaṅkara's soteriology. We will see later in the book a distinction drawn between a "higher" and a "lower" Brahman. For Śaṅkara, this distinction was not only ontological, but it involved a difference in the *kind* of spiritual practice geared toward the attaining of the two respectively. Chapters 6 and 7 will reveal that in Bādarāyaṇa's system there was just one form of practice, meditative absorption on Brahman, but for Śaṅkara meditation was appropriate only with respect to the lower Brahman because it involved the complex of meditator, object, and process of meditation that was predicated on and reinforced duality. The higher Brahman was to be grasped by a wholly different kind of awareness, namely intellectual understanding that is facilitated by the Upaniṣads, knowledge *qua* knowledge rather than *qua* meditation. With that, Śaṅkara also rejected the other common elements of the meditation on Brahman, for instance, that it was supposed to be practiced in a sitting posture. Sitting was appropriate for *meditation*, but he who *understands* can do so sitting, standing, or hanging upside down from a tree.[8]

As for Śaṅkara's ontology, we will see in Chapter 3 that Brahman in Bādarāyaṇa's system has two sets of characteristics: positive and negative.

With Śaṅkara, this notion too came with a peculiar twist. The positive characteristics—Being, consciousness, bliss, infinite—were not really *distinguishing* features as characteristics tend to be. They were rather *defining* features constitutive of Brahman's nature, identical with it rather than properly descriptive. What does this mean? Brahman's Being, or its function of causality, is not like the being of any object, such as a clay pot, to which Being is predicated so long the object is existent: Brahman *is* Being that is predicated to everything, the Being that never ceases to be. Likewise, Brahman's consciousness is not any content of awareness that can be predicated of a subject, as when I say "I *see the pot*," but it is the light of consciousness that makes cognition possible yet does not admit of the subject-object distinction on which cognitive content depends. Brahman's being bliss likewise does not involve experiential bliss—it would be a misstatement to describe Brahman as bliss*ful*—and to Śaṅkara's mind this bliss was but synonymous with freedom from transmigration.

In fact, it is precisely the purpose of the negative characteristics—"unborn, deathless, beyond hunger and thirst etc.," all subsumable under "permanently changeless"—to deny any change in Brahman so as to arrive at the foregoing description. These characteristics are related to the positive as their determinants—their predication of Brahman means that the Being and consciousness that is Brahman cannot be liable to change—and through that, they have a massive hermeneutic significance. To begin with, since they make Brahman's Being permanently changeless, the Upaniṣadic descriptions of creation—of Brahman as the first principle from which real things proceed—cannot be read as statements with truth value, for then Brahman's transformation into the world could not square with Brahman's being permanently changeless. The Upaniṣadic descriptions of creation, then, must be read not as accounts of real creation, but as *illustrations of causality* that should intimate not that Brahman transforms into everything, but that everything just *is* Brahman. It is such kind of a cause that Brahman is, and the Upaniṣadic talk of transformation into beings is simply the closest approximation of causality that one could use for the sake of teaching.

The negative characteristics are also related to Brahman's characteristic of consciousness, but since for Śaṅkara consciousness is also permanently changeless, they do so through the Self (*ātman*) of every individual being. What does this mean? The Upaniṣadic accounts of creation say that Brahman, having created the world, entered into it as the cognitive agent: that is, as the individual soul. The negative characteristics of Brahman applied to consciousness, however, prevent cognitive agency from obtaining as an essential characteristic of the soul. To put it differently, Brahman through its characteristic of consciousness is each and every individual soul, not, however, as individual, nor as the soul that cognizes content of awareness, but as the pure awareness that makes cognition possible.

The two essential features of Brahman, however, Being and consciousness, carry some mutual uneasiness. As Being, Brahman is causal, in Śaṅkara's idiosyncratic sense of that plentitude that is coordinated with everything as the only real thing. That makes Brahman an external thing, as it were, the great reality "out there." As consciousness, Brahman is inner, to which the great external Brahman seems like a second entity. It is, therefore, in the identity statements of the Upaniṣads, such as *tat tvam asi*, "You are that,"[9] and *ahaṁ brahmāsmi*, "I am Brahman,"[10] that Brahman is most directly defined. Brahman's being the inner Self of the cognitive agent prevents Brahman from being causal, *external*, and Brahman's being great prevents there being a second entity to the inner Self. This is, then, the only absolutely true statement about Brahman, "I myself am Brahman," the light of consciousness, eternal, pure, bliss in the sense of being ever free. Brahman's being the cause, its entering the creation as the Self, and so on, is just a show, a way of facilitating the subject's understanding that the Being, consciousness, and bliss that is Brahman is nothing but myself, the ever-free great light of awareness.[11]

Unlike meditation on Brahman, this identity between Brahman and the soul is not of the qualitative assimilation kind, and Śaṅkara had evidently departed from the *Brahma-sūtra* doctrine in many crucial respects. Still, the semantic potential of the *Brahma-sūtra* is on full display here. Not only did Śaṅkara draw creatively on Bādarāyaṇa's system, and on such ambiguities as the meaning of *avasthiti* in *sūtra* 1.4.22—is the soul *just* a state of Brahman, ultimately one and only, or is it itself *ensouled by* but *different from* Brahman, discussed in Chapter 3—he was also an heir to views and strands of Vedānta expressed by Bādarāyaṇa's interlocutors, such as Bādari's principle that the course of the gods brings one to the lower Brahman, and Auḍulomi's claim that the liberated soul is just consciousness without cognitive content (discussed in Chapter 7).[12] Even if not faithful to Bādarāyaṇa's doctrine, Śaṅkara's absolute monism, Advaita Vedānta, was not outside of this doctrine.

Identity and Accidental Difference

Śaṅkara opened his commentary on the *Brahma-sūtra* with the notion of ignorance (*avidyā*), which for him and his followers had not only a psychological sense of mistaking one thing for another but also a cosmological sense of a grand yet creative power of illusion (*māyā*), neither identical with nor different from Brahman, that projects the world and binds the soul in it. In effect, though not in so many words, Śaṅkara replaced Brahman's creative role, its being the first principle, with this power of illusion.[13] The second major preserved commentary on the *Brahma-sūtra* was that of Bhāskara, who was likely a younger contemporary of Śaṅkara, and was indebted to him both positively and negatively. While Bhāskara generally follows Śaṅkara to the letter or with brief paraphrases, he was thoroughly repulsed by the illusionism of his older predecessor.

Although quite influential and often mentioned by later authors, Bhāskara did not have many followers, and no school of Vedānta in the institutional sense is associated with his name. His doctrine has become known as *aupādhika-bhedābheda-vāda*, a doctrine of "identity and accidental difference." Indeed, throughout his *Bhāṣya*, Bhāskara argues not only that identity-and-difference is Bādarāyaṇa's philosophy but also that all our reliable warrants or epistemic instruments (*pramāṇa*s) generally reveal reality as possessing these two aspects equally. How is that the case? A common illustration is that of the ocean and its waves, foam, and related phenomena, of which Bhāskara thinks as the ocean's products. These products are *mutually* different insofar as they are products, yet also identical insofar as they originate from the ocean, their shared cause.[14]

How does identity and accidental difference pertain to Brahman, and why call difference "accidental"? This brings us to the heart of Bhāskara's system. Brahman has two ontological powers or capacities (*śakti*s), called *bhoktṛ-śakti* and *bhogya-śakti* and roughly translatable to subjectivity and objectivity, or the faculty of sentience and the principle of materiality. The two are Brahman's projections or emanations, and through them Brahman transforms into the sentient individual souls on the one hand and the insentient elements of creation and the minutiae of the world on the other.[15]

Let us first describe the soul. In its essential nature, the soul just is Brahman, and after liberation, it does not maintain separate existence. In its *accidental* nature, however, the soul is related to Brahman both as distinct from and identical with it. The soul is individuated through the functioning of three principles, which are ontologically accidental determinants, *upādhi*s: therefore "accidental," *aupādhika*, difference. The three are ignorance (*avidyā*), which stands for the wrong identification of the soul with the body and matter and is equivalent to not understanding the soul's being Brahman; desire (*kāma*), which manifests in the form of habits (*vāsanā*) formed through many lives in transmigration; and karma the results of previous action. In this accidental state of individuation, equivalent to bondage, the soul is infinitesimal in size and is an agent of action and enjoyment, which is necessary for the functioning of the law of karma, and for which body and senses are required. In its *essential* state, however, the soul is *just* consciousness and limitless in size, being simply Brahman. Though this difference from Brahman is accidental, it is nevertheless real, not illusory as with Śaṅkara. However, even while different from Brahman *accidentally*, the soul is still *essentially* non-different: it is still Brahman itself.[16]

The world, on the other hand, is a transformation of Brahman's insentient capacity. Because the capacity itself is non-different from Brahman, the world *is* Brahman insofar as Brahman has assumed the state of an effect, yet it is different from Brahman insofar as Brahman is conceived as its cause. Through this distinction, Brahman becomes the cause of the insentient world while remaining itself sentient and unaffected by it, in yet another form of identity-and-difference.[17]

Forms of Non-absolute Monism

Second only to Śaṅkara in fame and influence, the Vaiṣṇava theologian Rāmānuja wrote three commentaries on the *Brahma-sūtra*: the *Śrībhāṣya*, his *magnum opus*, which was commented on by Sudarśana Sūri in the longer *Śruta-prakāśikā* and the shorter *Śruta-pradīpikā*; *Vedānta-dīpa*, a shorter and simpler work; and *Vedānta-sāra*, which provides the meaning of the *sūtra*s and their topical passages in as few words as possible. Rāmānuja was the fiercest and most original critic of Śaṅkara's absolute monism, and he directed some philosophical fury at all forms of *bhedābheda* as well, for the good reason that identity-and-difference makes it impossible to spare Brahman of the blemishes of the world and the individual souls insofar as they are identical with it. Rāmānuja also thought that *bhedābheda* was indefensible in the light of reason, and that brings us straight to the heart of his ontology.

Bhāskara and other proponents of identity-and-difference used the category of *śakti* to account for this relationship, but that was a double-edged sword. In Indian philosophical discourse, *śakti*s are generally *faculties* or *functions* or *capacities*: the faculty of vision is a *śakti*, and so is the power of words to convey meaning. They bear characteristics of their own—we describe vision as accurate—but are not different entities from the thing in which they are found: signification is not an entity over and above the word. This makes them ideally suited for the identity-and-difference relationship. But here is the deal: it is an abuse of the category to describe matter and souls as *śakti*s in this strict sense, because *they are not* that kind of things. *They are entities*, just like Brahman, and they cannot be identical with Brahman any more than a cow and a horse might be the same thing.

In terms of ontological reals, then, Rāmānuja was as dualist as they make them, and for him in the strict sense—although he did apply the term "*śakti*" to souls and matter, under a different relationship model—*śakti*s were faculties plain and simple, inherent to all ontological reals but not to their mutual relationship. Yet his philosophy eventually bore the descriptor of "monism." How can that be? To understand Rāmānuja's brand of monism, we may touch upon two of the several kinds of relationships that he talked about in preference to *śakti*s and their possessor. Imagine a person first without and then with a stick: surely, you would think that it is the same person, yet somehow distinguished in the two situations. Rāmānuja would say that the stick serves as a *mode* or a *distinguishing feature* of the man, the mode-possessor or the substance, who in the first case is a simple entity whereas in the second is the center of a man-with-a-stick unit. This is clearer in Sanskrit, where the man-with-a-stick would be called by the single word "*daṇḍin*."[18]

Likewise, think of the relationship between a soul and its body. Central to Rāmānuja's theology was Brahman's role as the *antaryāmin*, the inner dweller or the soul of everything, to whom the world and the individual souls are a body. By a "body," Rāmānuja meant any dependent reality that a conscious being can use for its own purpose, as its extension of a sort. The body and the embodied form a *unit of entities* that keep their separate being yet constitute an organic whole.[19]

Rāmānuja's monism, then, was not about bare unique Being or about identity-and-difference, but instead about an *organic whole with a center*, in which distinct ontological reals make for a complex being yet only one of them is ontologically independent, "for itself," whereas the rest are subservient to it, "for another." Rāmānuja's term for this relationship is *apṛthak-siddhi*, which literally translates to "not possible separately" but we may use instead "ontological dependence," a state of affairs in which prime matter and the souls exist as different, but would not exist at all were it not for Brahman. Unlike *bhedābheda*, *apṛthak-siddhi* does not admit of identity. Rāmānuja's doctrine later became known as *viśiṣṭādvaita*, "non-duality of the qualified whole."

Still, Rāmānuja's ontological integrity makes it more cumbersome to argue how Brahman is the material cause of creation—a key doctrine of the *Brahma-sūtra* as shall become apparent in Chapter 3—which now must depend mostly on philosophy of language. The soul-body ontological structure allows for a nested signification function of all words, including those that denote other ontological reals, such that Brahman always turns out to be their ultimate reference. We may think of our own names and the identities they pick out. "Aleksandar" denotes me, a Sanskritist of Slavic extraction, but if I believe that my true identity is that of a soul that sustains the body, then through the body the name further denotes the embodied self. My embodied soul, however, is the body of Brahman, and so the signification of "Aleksandar" continues to Brahman and terminates in him as its ultimate reference. Through this structure of ontological nesting, then, it is justified to call Brahman the material cause—indeed, it is justified and ultimately true to call him anything.

In addition, Brahman being the material cause refers to the state of affairs prior to creation, in which prime matter and the individual souls are in so subtle a condition that they do not merit a name of their own, one apart from that of Brahman: they are so indiscernible as distinct as to be unnamable, and thus Brahman alone musters to bear the appellation "cause." Even in that state, however, they are Brahman's body, and they—not Brahman—undergo transformation into the minutiae of the world and perpetual transmigration.[20]

While it is difficult to agree with Rāmānuja's interpretation of Bādarāyaṇa's account of Brahman's material causality, as we shall discuss in Chapter 3, his system is arguably closest to cracking the code. Rāmānuja's significance is most apparent in bringing out the feature of Brahman's residence in individual creations that so thoroughly permeates the *Brahma-sūtra* and on which its entire soteriology hinges. This too shall become apparent later in the text.

The Śaiva theologian Śrīkaṇṭha closely followed Rāmānuja, and his *Brahma-mīmāṁsā-bhāṣya* often simply reproduces Rāmānuja's *Vedānta-sāra*. To paraphrase Larry McCrea, Śrīkaṇṭha merely overlaid Rāmānuja's system with a mass of scriptural statements that present Śiva rather than Viṣṇu as the embodiment of Brahman, dubbing his system *Viśiṣṭa-śivādvaita* or the doctrine of "non-duality of Śiva the qualified whole."[21] In the *Śivārka-maṇi-dīpikā* commentary on the *Brahma-mīmāṁsā-bhāṣya*, Appayyadīkṣita brought Śrīkaṇṭha's doctrine closer to the absolute monism of Śaṅkara.

Under this heading, we may also include Vallabha, whose commentary on the *Brahma-sūtra*, completed from 3.2.34 to the end by his son Viṭṭhalanātha, is called *Aṇu-bhāṣya*. With Vallabha, we can illustrate another common trend among later commentators, to reverse—if so implicitly—the higher versus lower Brahman distinction. Vallabha, thus, talks about two forms of Brahman, the personal divinity Kṛṣṇa whom he calls *Puruṣottama*, "the highest person," and a form of his, which he calls *akṣara*, "the imperishable." It is this second form of Brahman that is properly causal, although creation happens by the will of and for the sportive pleasure of Kṛṣṇa. The *akṣara* Brahman is sort of *spiritual non-*

personal stuff of which the incorruptible body and abode of Puruṣottama are made. It non-temporally emanates the world and its individual souls by a dual process of "manifestation" (*āvirbhāva*) and "occlusion" (*tirobhāva*). Prime matter that becomes the world *is* the *akṣara* Brahman *in kind* but manifesting only its characteristic of Being. The individual souls are likewise *akṣara* Brahman in kind, manifesting not only Being but consciousness as well. What further constitutes them as prime matter and souls is that the characteristic of bliss is occluded in both of them, and prime matter also occludes consciousness.[22]

This doctrine has been called *avikṛta-pariṇāma-vāda*, which sounds almost as *contradictio in adiecto*, but may be translated as "causation without transformation." Now, since prime matter and the individual souls are Brahman in essence, such that some of Brahman's characteristics are manifested in them whereas others are concealed, Vallabha thinks this ontology is properly monistic, though obviously not so in the numeric sense. Since such monism does accommodate distinctions, it has been described as *bheda-sahiṣṇu advaita*, monism tolerant of difference.[23]

For Vallabha, the individual soul in liberation manifests bliss the third essential characteristic of Brahman, and acquires a form made of *akṣara* Brahman such as the one that Puruṣottama himself possesses. To avoid the contingency of numeric identity, Vallabha posits an ultimate distinction between the two: Brahman is bliss *substantively*, whereas the soul becomes bliss *attributively*. Aside from being a theological stratagem, this to me seems to have the benefit of explaining precisely the Brahman-liberated soul distinction intended by Bādarāyaṇa, on top of Brahman's function in creation that the soul also lacks (discussed in Chapter 7): an attribute, albeit innate, need not be manifest for a thing to remain what it is, whereas a cow cannot be a cow without cowness. In other words, Brahman cannot help being Brahman—it cannot conceal its bliss—whereas the soul obviously does.[24]

Dualism

Madhva was another famed commentator who wrote four compositions on the *Brahma-sūtra*: *Brahma-sūtra-bhāṣya*, a standard commentary; *Anu-vyākhyāna*, a polemical running commentary of 1,985 verses; *Aṇu-bhāṣya*, a summary in 32 verses; and *Nyāya-vivaraṇa*, a prose summary. The commentarial tradition on these works is immensely rich, and Jayatīrtha wrote on all of them except the *Aṇu-bhāṣya*, his most important work being the *Nyāya-sudhā* on the *Anu-vyākhyāna*.

Outside of his own school, the reception of Madhva as an interpreter has been harsh, both among traditional intellectuals and among modern scholars. Ghate's assessment is typical:

> [T]he commentary of Madhva is evidently inferior in character and is a performance of little or no merit. His interpretations differ from those of the rest very widely and in a very large number of cases. . . . [H]is explanations are far-fetched, fantastic and too sectarian in character; the scriptural passages he refers to for discussion more often belong to the Saṃhitās than the Upaniṣads, a procedure which can be easily explained by the fact that it is very difficult for him to find in the Upaniṣads a support for his own doctrine.[25]

Interpretation aside, however, Madhva was an original thinker, and such remarks cannot do justice to his philosophy in its own right.

An uncompromising pluralist and a realist—his doctrine would become known as *dvaita-vāda* or dualism—Madhva was the only founder of a school of Vedānta to argue that Brahman could not possibly be the material cause of the world: Brahman's essential nature is consciousness and bliss, and it is unthinkable that the insentient world as the locus of suffering could be a transformation of such a widely different cause. Brahman, then, is just the efficient cause of the world, and there obtains *absolute difference* between Brahman and the two other ontological reals. This doctrine is known as *prapañca-bheda*, a fivefold absolute difference between Brahman and the souls; Brahman and prime matter; the souls between themselves; prime matter and the souls; and the various material entities.[26]

What distinguishes Brahman as one of the several coeval reals is independence: Brahman is an independent principle, omniscient and omnipotent, whereas prime matter and the individual souls are dependent. Although prime matter is the stuff of creation coeval with Brahman, unlike Sāṅkhyan *prakṛti* it is not able to evolve the world alone, for which purpose it requires Brahman's guidance and control. Likewise, although the souls are essentially knowledge in nature and possess agency, they are obscured by ignorance, a feature of prime matter, such that without Brahman's intervention they would remain in bondage. Since matter is itself insentient, however, even this feature of obscuring the knowledge of the individual souls depends on the will of Brahman. Thus, both the souls and matter are dependent principles, incapable of independent action without Brahman's sanction. Brahman is, therefore, immanent to the world in a sense more direct than in any other brand of Vedānta.[27]

Identity and Essential Difference

A number of post-Rāmānuja commentators interpreted the ontology of the *Brahma-sūtra* as a form of *bhedābheda,* one, however, distinct from that of Bhāskara in that the difference part in the identity-and-difference relationship is not accidental but essential. Most prominent of these was the Vaiṣṇava theologian Nimbārka, whose doctrine became known as *svābhāvika-bhedābheda-vāda,* identity and essential difference between Brahman on the one hand and prime matter and the souls on the other. Nimbārka's *Vedānta-pārijāta-saurabha* is the shortest of all classical *Brahma-sūtra* commentaries, limited to making sense of the terse *sūtra*s in fewest words and to identifying their topical passages. Ghate's time-honored study had recognized Nimbārka's commentary as the most faithful to Bādarāyaṇa's system. Nimbārka's student Śrīnivāsa wrote the *Vedānta-kaustubha* commentary that is inspired by Nimbārka's, and Keśava Kaśmīrī expanded upon Śrīnivāsa in his *Vedānta-kaustubha-prabhā.*

In this system, the unity of the souls and prime matter with Brahman is in virtue of their having no existence and activity separate from that of Brahman. Each of the three ontological reals has their own peculiar attributes, but their relationship can be viewed from two aspects. The souls and prime matter can be seen through their individual attributes, *or* they can be seen through the fact that without Brahman they have neither existence nor activity. Thus, although Brahman and the soul are non-different insofar as the second is dependent for existence and activity on the first, they differ insofar as Brahman is eternally free, not liable to karma, and is the controller; whereas the souls can be bound to a body, experience the results of karma, and are controlled. Likewise, in relation to prime matter, Brahman has the characteristics of omniscience and omnipotence, whereas prime matter has the characteristics of materiality, mutability, and so on. The two categories are, thus, *essentially different* from Brahman, but are also *essentially related* to him through dependence.[28]

Nomenclature notwithstanding, this form of *bhedābheda* is Rāmānuja's system reupholstered with the *śakti*s-and-their-possessor relationship that Nimbārka and his followers reintroduce as the best language to talk about the creative Brahman. This is perhaps evident also in the use of terminology: Rāmānuja's preferred terms for the souls and matter were *cit* and *acit,* "the sentient" and "the insentient," instead of Bhāskara's *bhoktṛ-śakti* and *bhogya-śakti,* but especially Śrīnivāsa uses both pairs interchangeably. We find a more original statement of *bhedābheda* in the *Vijñānāmṛta* commentary, penned by one Vijñānabhikṣu, who was both a perceptive commentator and a brilliant philosopher at the absolute peak of Sanskrit learning and its conceptual sophistication toward the end of the sixteenth century. This sophistication had, in fact, allowed Vijñānabhikṣu to draw out quite accurately the intention of Bādarāyaṇa's ontology by specifying what kind of relationship the "identity-and-difference" must be.[29]

Regarding Brahman and the soul, Vijñānabhikṣu argued that the *bhedābheda* relationship cannot be understood in the sense of the principles of identity and contradiction that we are familiar with from Western philosophy and were also common in his context, discussed by the proponents of the new school of logic.[30] To use a favorite example, insofar as a cow is a cow, it is *not* anything else that is not a cow, such as a horse: there is mutual exclusion between these two things such that they cannot be *both* identical *and* different as substances. We should rather think in terms of "separation" (*vibhāga*) and "non-separation" (*avibhāga*) between them. The significance of these two terms can be approached from the creation standpoint. Before creation and upon liberation, the soul is not separate from Brahman in that their characteristics are completely identical—one would fail to perceive distinction between the two, to distinguish the one from the other—such that they are tokens of the same type. Identity, then, is not numerical, but qualitative and "essential" rather than "substantial." In creation, however, there obtains a difference of characteristics between Brahman and the soul—for instance, Brahman is omniscient whereas the soul is not—which is occasioned by the soul's embodiment, and thereby "accidental." Such divergence of characteristics is what constitutes separation between Brahman and the soul.

A similar relationship obtains between Brahman as the cause and the world as its product, but here like all other commentators Vijñānabhikṣu must also account for the causality of prime matter. He does so by diversifying the notion of material cause in two kinds. Brahman as the material cause is the "locus" or "substratum," a "non-transforming" cause *in* which or *supported by* which prime matter, the other material cause, transforms into the minutiae of the world. At first blush this may not be a terribly meaningful distinction from Rāmānuja's idea about an independent entity depending on which prime matter is the material cause proper, but Vijñānabhikṣu's conceptual apparatus draws from classical Sanskrit theory of language to see clearly a cause where others have struggled to do so.

Briefly, intellectuals in classical Sanskrit learning have understood world processes as actions accompanied by a set of six accessories that are represented in language by the verb and its syntactic relations. These six are: agent, patient, instrument, purpose, source, and location. There is no reason why all of these six cannot be understood as causes of a sort.

Theories of causality, however, particularly those of Sāṅkhya and Vedānta, have talked instead about three kinds of causes—efficient, material, and accessory—which correspond well to the agent, source, and instrument. Although Vijñānabhikṣu subsumes this locus-cause under the material, it seems to me that he reimagines the causality discourse by drawing from this wider set to pinpoint more usefully than his Vedāntin peers where one might place Brahman in the causal scheme of things. The benefit of understanding Brahman as the locus—and the locus as a kind of cause—facilitates rescuing the Upaniṣadic axiom that Brahman, although causal, is nevertheless changeless.

Unfortunately, Vijñānabhikṣu's commentary did not receive the reception it deserves, in the tradition of Vedānta or in Indological scholarship, and its significance had only recently begun to come to light thanks to the good work of Andrew Nicholson. An English translation of the *Vijñānāmṛta* remains a most important desideratum in the study of the *Brahma sūtra*.[31]

The last great classical commentary on the *Brahma-sūtra* was the *Govinda-bhāṣya* of Baladeva Vidyābhūṣaṇa, a native of Orissa and a follower of Madhva who later joined the tradition of Caitanya (1486–1533 CE), the great teacher of devotion to Kṛṣṇa and his divine female counterpart Rādhā.[32] Baladeva was active in peculiar religiopolitical circumstances, those of Sawai Jai Singh II (1688–1743 CE) the king of Jaipur. The king was a Vaiṣṇava who saw himself as the protector of Brahmanical orthodoxy, in the context of which he believed that there were only four legitimate Vaiṣṇava lineages to which every tradition had to be affiliated, and that each such tradition ought to have an authoritative commentary on the *Brahma-sūtra*. This was somewhat of a predicament for Caitanya's followers, since their affiliation was unclear, and they considered the *Bhāgavata Purāṇa* to be the natural *Brahma-sūtra* commentary. Additionally, in Caitanya theology the relationship between Kṛṣṇa and Rādhā was of the extramarital kind, which was not to the king's liking either. Baladeva wrote his commentary largely in response to these circumstances, to provide his tradition with a legitimation text in which he argued that Brahman and his "internal power," the Goddess Lakṣmī/Rādhā, were essentially and eternally non-different: their union was essential, the extramarital relationship incidental. Baladeva's former affiliation also proved handy: Madhva's lineage was considered one of the four original, and Caitanya's followers through Baladeva could claim proper religious extraction. This is a most interesting case of what may be called "the politics of theology."

In terms of contribution to the wider *Brahma-sūtra* discourse, Baladeva had provided an expanded set of ontological reals in Vedānta, adding time and karma to the common categories of Brahman/Īśvara, the individual soul, and prime matter. While the origin of this classification is not necessarily the *Brahma-sūtra* itself,[33] and time is not of Bādarāyaṇa's concern though certainly presupposed by him, we will see in Chapters 5 and 7 how central an idea karma was in the text. We should, therefore, credit Baladeva with bringing out the significance of karma to the fore of Bādarāyaṇa's system.

For Baladeva, four of the principles were ontologically Brahman's powers, *śakti*s, standing with respect to Brahman in a relationship of simultaneous identity and difference. This was part of the shared *Brahma-sūtra* legacy. Baladeva's specifically Caitanya background was reflected in an additional descriptor that was attached to Brahman's *śakti*s: they were "inconceivable," *acintya*. What does this mean? Two things. First, it means that from the evidential multiplicity of the world and the scriptural creation passages on the one hand, and the scriptural facticity of Brahman as a unitary first principle on the other, it must be postulated that the powers of Brahman described in scripture are simultaneously identical with and different from Brahman. This cannot be *inferred* from the world—it is *inconceivable* by mere reasoning—but must be *scripturally introduced* to reconcile the unitary Brahman with the variegated world and the multitude of individual souls. But Brahman's powers are not only inconceivable in their relationship to Brahman: they are so *unto themselves* as well, as they are capable of accomplishing what is otherwise humanly inconceivable. Thus, it is by the use of its inconceivable powers that Brahman creates the world from itself, without changing in the process. How can that be? Think of the idea of the "philosopher's stone" that transforms base metals into gold by its mere touch. How can one conceive of this unless it is postulated that the stone has awesome powers to do such things? Brahman is sort of an absolute "philosopher's stone," possessed of all kinds of magical powers to make the otherwise impossible: not only to *transform* things like the philosopher's stone, but to *project* the entire world out of itself without being changed in the slightest. For this reason, Brahman's powers must be inconceivable.[34]

Versified Summaries

Around the turn of the first, millennium, a new exegesis genre emerged in the form of versified restatements of the *Brahma-sūtra* and its traditions of interpretation, inspired partially by the need to keep the knowledge system compact against the constant proliferation of commentaries and sub-commentaries. Three works of this kind stand out in particular, and among them the most explicit about the need of conciseness and organization was the *Vaiyāsika-nyāya-mālā*, "Vyāsa's Garland of Headings," of the

Advaitin Bhāratītīrtha.[35] Written in 406 simple verses accompanied by an eminently readable auto-commentary, the work attempts to present all of the 192 *Brahma-sūtra adhikaraṇa*s, in Śaṅkara's counting, in two verses each: *nyāya* in the title stands for an *adhikaraṇa*, heading, in its underlying logic. The author is clear about his purpose in writing such a work: commentaries as that of Śaṅkara explain, yet also amplify, the meaning of the *sūtra*s, but they are suited for those of developed understanding. Bhāratītīrtha wishes to write for the slowwitted instead.[36] They would be particularly helped if they could easily appreciate the five constituents that organize the presentation of each *adhikaraṇa*, known to us from the Introduction: the topic, the doubt, the prima facie view, the conclusion, and the "coherence" or "propriety" (*saṅgati*).

Bhāratītīrtha's account of the last is particularly interesting. Any heading must be *appropriate* on the grand level to the subjects of the work, the particular chapter, and the section—*śāstra, adhyāya, pāda*—such that one should not discuss Āyurveda in a work on Brahman or epistemology in the section on the attainment. However, it should also form *coherence* or *internal propriety, avāntara-saṅgati*, with its preceding and following *adhikaraṇa*s and the work in general, making a *flow of topics* as it were. This second propriety must bear in mind many things, such as the "collision" of headings, that is, objections that arise from the contiguity of *adhikaraṇa*s; the appropriateness of illustrations and counter illustrations; potentially undesired consequences of a view that require immediate attention; and so on.[37] Thus, Bhāratītīrtha intends to present the topic, doubt, and prima facie view of a heading in one verse, the conclusion in another; and in doing so to make apparent the various proprieties that are pertinent or involved.[38]

The *Adhikaraṇa-sārāvalī*, "Continuum of the Essence of the Headings," is a work in 562 verses composed not in the short *anuṣṭubh* (four lines of eight syllables) as Bhāratītīrtha's book, but in *sragdharā* the longest commonly used meter in classical Sanskrit poetry (four lines of twenty-one syllables).[39] Written by Vedāntadeśika, a polymath and one of the most impressively learned and versatile figures in Indian intellectual history, it presents the essence of each of the 156 *adhikaraṇa*s as they were interpreted by Rāmānuja. Rather than the extensive dialectic that characterizes Rāmānuja's *Śrībhāṣya*, Vedāntadeśika's work tends to present in a nutshell the prima facie view that informs the heading and state the conclusion in concise terms: as its title suggests, it is about the "essentials" in a systematic manner. Still, in terms of philosophical significance it goes beyond Bhāratītīrtha, as it contains important clarifications, having had the benefit of acquaintance with critiques of Rāmānuja's views. Let us illustrate with verse 172, which tackles *sūtra*s 2.1.31–2 on the purpose of creation that we shall discuss in Chapter 4:

> [Objection:] In no way would he whose wishes are perpetually fulfilled create the world for his own sake. He would not create a world of suffering, either, if acting out of compassion, nor could such creation of suffering on the part of an omnipotent being be therapeutic. Therefore, the omniscient and self-content Brahman could not be the cause of the world. [Reply:] Such is the objection of the ignorant. Creation is play, like in the world. However, Brahman's desires are fulfilled because there is accomplishment right at the time of desiring.

To anticipate Chapter 4, we see in this short account that Deśika makes the important clarification that creation is *not* a desireless or non-intentional action, for in that case it would never take place. Rather, the Upaniṣadic doctrine of the desireless Brahman should be read in light of the ideas of *satya-kāma* and *satya-saṅkalpa*, having one's desires accomplished *immediately upon intention* rather than with delay. This brief remark at once condenses and clarifies the peculiarity of Rāmānuja's theology of play. The proper study of the *Brahma-sūtra* reception history must include Deśika's poem and its own commentarial tradition.

Somewhat different in kind and agenda, as well as enormously more influential, is the *Saṅkṣepa-śārīraka*, literally "*Brahma-sūtra* condensed."[40] Written by Sarvajñātman, the *Saṅkṣepa-śārīraka* is based on Śaṅkara's commentary, but condensation does not quite mean that it is a summary of Śaṅkara's work. Like the *Brahma-sūtra*, it consists of four chapters that bear titles identical to the prototype, but Sarvajñātman had trimmed all material pertaining to the so-called lower Brahman, meditations on it, and their results, leaving only that which was called *para-vidyā* or "higher knowledge" in Advaita Vedānta. Furthermore, he had presented the work as a paradigmatic dialogue between a student and a teacher, emulating thus the Advaita process of liberation—and Śaṅkara's treatise *Upadeśa-sāhasrī*—rather than doing a systematic investigation of the Upaniṣads as the *Brahma-sūtra* does. Consisting of some 1,240 verses in a number of highly aestheticized meters, the *Saṅkṣepa-śārīraka* became one of the famous Advaita Vedānta classics that would receive renewed attention in early modern India. Between 1500 and 1650 CE, six commentaries were written on it, including by the prominent Madhusūdana Sarasvatī and Nṛsiṁhāśrama.[41]

The Bhāgavata Purāṇa

We end this journey through the world of the *Brahma-sūtra* interpretation history with a brief mention of its relationship with another classic, the

Bhāgavata Purāṇa (ca. second half of the tenth century).[42] The *Bhāgavata* is one of the most important books in the religious history of the subcontinent in the second millennium, which was dominated by the ideal of *bhakti* or devotion to a personal divinity. It is the *locus classicus* on the story of Kṛṣṇa, reproduced often in vernacular literature and various forms of art, but it is also a work on Vedānta that uses a set of intertextuality strategies to present itself as a continuation of the *Brahma-sūtra*. To begin with, its first verse opens with the opening words of the *Brahma-sūtra* (1.1.2)—*janmādy asya yataḥ*:

> From him this (world) is born, etc. That cognizant and self-luminous one is (known) by meanings inferred from positive and negative reasoning. He is the one who revealed the Veda through the heart to the first seer, but the gods are confused about him. In him the threefold creation—such as the interplay of fire, water, and earth—is not false, for he has removed all deception by his own power. Upon that supreme truth let us meditate.[43]

Toward its conclusion, it repeats twice that it is "the essence of all Upaniṣads" (*vedānta*), which is how one might describe the *Brahma-sūtra* itself.[44] Most importantly, it is the first major Hindu scripture to identify Bādarāyaṇa the author of the *Brahma-sūtra* with Vyāsa the editor of the Vedas and author of the *Mahābhārata*.

The intention behind these strategies of self-representation seems to have been to overlay Vedānta, particularly its Advaita iteration of and for ascetics, with *bhakti* or the passionate devotion to Kṛṣṇa as its natural outgrowth and *telos*. In terms of formal arguments, it was the Gauḍīya Vaiṣṇava Jīva Gosvāmin (1517–1608 CE) who drew out the consequences of such self-representation. Jīva argued that the *Bhāgavata* was not only founded on the *Brahma-sūtra*, but was its "natural commentary," revealed to Vyāsa in meditative absorption in which the Vedāntic ontological vision was augmented with the soteriological vision of *bhakti* as the means of attaining the highest good.[45] "Natural" because the author himself had decided to emend his message.

In the twentieth century, the Bengali intellectual Rampada Chattopadhyay (1872–1956) took this thesis seriously—that the *Bhāgavata* was the best available commentary on the *Brahma-sūtra*—and attempted to demonstrate in his 2,200-page *Brahmasūtra o Śrīmad Bhāgavata* how verses from the *Bhāgavata* engaged with specific *sūtra*s. Particularly interesting and fruitful is Chattopadhyay's suggestion that the commentators on the *Brahma-sūtra* such as Śaṅkara and Rāmānuja have emphasized the feature of consciousness from the canonical definition of Brahman as *sat-cit-ānanda*, Being, consciousness, bliss, but that only the *Bhāgavata* made a full portray of Brahman's characteristic of bliss.[46] The Gauḍīya intellectual Haridāsa Śāstri (1918–2013) went even further in his *Vedānta-darśanam* by illustrating *every sūtra* with at least one verse from the *Bhāgavata*.[47]

The *Bhāgavata* was important in almost every brand of Vedānta, including the Advaita of Śaṅkara's followers.[48] We will end this brief survey with a note on its prominent place in Vallabha's *Aṇu-bhāṣya*. Vallabha changed the idea of *prasthāna-traya* that we saw in the Introduction, the three departure points of Vedānta—the Upaniṣads, *Bhagavad-gītā*, and the *Brahma-sūtra*—into *prasthāna-catuṣṭaya*, adding the *Bhāgavata* as the fourth and ultimate departure point. The relationship between these was one of progressively higher importance, since any succeeding point was supposed to remove the doubts of its predecessor.[49]

In short, from Madhva's commentary onwards, the *Bhāgavata* became a major locus of Vedānta exegesis and interaction between the discourses of Vedānta and *bhakti*.

Suggestions for Further Study

A selection of reliable translations of commentaries is provided in the Bibliography. On Śaṅkara's philosophical system, a good reading is Suthren Hirst (2005). The details of Śaṅkara's soteriology are worked out in Uskokov (2018c), particularly chapters 6 through 9. Bhāskara's commentary has not been translated to English, but Khanna (1998) provides a reliable synopsis of the entire work (pp.143–430) and a comparison of its differences from Śaṅkara. A very brief and readable account of Bhāskara's philosophy and soteriology is available in Ingalls (1967). The best account of Rāmānuja's theology is still Carman (1974). Rāmānuja's *Vedārtha-saṅgraha*, which is a conspectus of his system and a critique of other forms of Vedānta, has been translated by van Buitenen (1956). Chaudhuri (1962) is a detailed study of Śrīkaṇṭha's Vedānta. McCrea (2014) is an excellent reading on the significance of Appayyadīkṣita's engagement with Śrīkaṇṭha's commentary. Duquette (2014) is a study of Appayya's *Śivādvaita-nirṇaya*, an attempt to reinterpret Śrīkaṇṭha's doctrine along the lines of Advaita Vedānta. Unfortunately, the *Aṇu-bhaṣya* of Vallabha and Viṭṭhalanātha hasn't been translated into English, but Vrajlal (1964) provides a detailed study following its entire content (pp.62–435) and a very useful overview of Vallabha's system (pp.435–567). Madhva's philosophy may be approached through the works of B. N. K Sharma: 1962 is long and detailed, 1997 is short and very readable. Bose (2004), volume 3, provides a detailed account of the history and doctrine of Nimbārka's tradition. Chapters 2 and 3 of Nicholson (2010) make an excellent study of Vijñānabhikṣu's Vedānta. Okita (2014a) is a very reliable and historically nuanced study of Baladeva Vidyābhūṣaṇa, with chapter 4 plumbing the depths of his *Govinda-bhāṣya*.

2

Philosophy, Theology, and the Idea of Scripture

The third *sūtra* says, "[Brahman is the cause of the world] because scripture is its womb."[1] The commentators interpret "womb" as the "reliable warrant" or "epistemic instrument" (*pramāṇa*, simply: *how* we know things) by which Brahman is known, and most of them identify the prima facie view overturned by the *sūtra* with the Nyāya-Vaiśeṣika doctrine that God as the cause of the world is known not from scripture but from analogical inference. Although it is unlikely that Nyāya-Vaiśeṣika is its background, the *sūtra* introduces us directly to a cardinal doctrine of Vedānta, that the Upaniṣads are the only means of knowing Brahman. As it is said in a *Bṛhad-āraṇyaka* passage that Vedāntins often quote under *Brahma-sūtra* 1.1.3: "I ask you about the *upaniṣadic* person," *aupaniṣadam puruṣam*.[2] For the commentators: I ask you about Brahman who is taught in and known from the Upaniṣads.

This statement, incidentally, is the reply of the famous sage-philosopher Yājñavalkya to the persistent questioning of one Vidagdha Śākalya about the foundation of everything. Yājñavalkya concludes his reply to Śākalya with a characteristic negative theology. It is the Self which is the foundation of everything, ungraspable, undecaying, stainless, and unbound, describable only as "not thus, not thus," *neti neti*. If Śākalya does not know about this Self, the "*upaniṣadic* person," his head will shatter. We learn from an earlier exchange of Yājñavalkya with a female theologian by the name of Gārgī Vācaknavī that one's head would shatter because of "asking too many questions about a deity about whom one should not ask too many questions."[3] Poor Śākalya does not know the "*upaniṣadic* person" and his head does shatter rather spectacularly: robbers steal his bones, mistaking them for something else. Yājñavalkya dares the remaining Brahmins to ask him further, one by one or all together, but they prefer to keep their heads and bones.

So do Bādarāyaṇa and later Vedāntins interpreting his work. We will see how exactly one comes to know the "*upaniṣadic* person" such that one's head does not shatter in Chapters 6 and 7, but for now we may join hands with the commentators in taking the statement to stand for Brahman who is taught or revealed in the Upaniṣads, in affirmation of *sūtra* 1.1.3 that we quoted above and may now paraphrase: Brahman is known only from scripture, *not* from inference. We should be careful, however, not to draw the simplistic revelation versus reasoning distinction, for if Bādarāyaṇa thought that reasoning had no value in knowing Brahman he would not have written the *Brahma-sūtra*, which is, as we saw in the Introduction, the *nyāya-prasthāna* or the "reasoning departure point" of Vedānta.

In this chapter, therefore, I will focus on the *Brahma-sūtra* epistemology and begin by distinguishing two kinds of reasoning that Bādarāyaṇa engages in, which I will describe as theological and philosophical, by looking briefly over how he argues against the two intellectual traditions that were most pertinent for his conceptual universe, Mīmāṁsā and Sāṅkhya. I will then move to the idea of "scripture" that was, as we saw, central to Bādarāyaṇa's way of knowing Brahman, pursuing primarily the significance of a statement that he is credited with in the *Mīmāṁsā-sūtra* (1.1.5) rather than the *Brahma-sūtra*. What *is* scripture, that "womb" of Brahman? We will discover that scripture for Bādarāyaṇa was something epistemically as primitive as perception, providing the "raw data" for theological reasoning just as perception provides the data for inference and other derivative means of knowing. Since Mīmāṁsā will loom large throughout the chapter, in the conclusion I will briefly touch upon the relationship between the *Brahma-sūtra* and the *Mīmāṁsā-sūtra* in an *ideological* sense rather than the *historical* that we mentioned in the Introduction. We will see that the two works and traditions share a sphere of certain commitments such that the *Brahma-sūtra* presupposes the *Mīmāṁsā-sūtra* whatever their historical relationship may have been.

Brahma-sūtra as Theology

There has been a growing trend in Hindu studies in recent years to make theology a legitimate field of inquiry.[4] While this occasionally comes in the form of a plea for Hindu theology as a way of *doing* theology today, more pertinent is the claim that *understanding* certain traditions and individuals in the Hindu context is facilitated by treating them as theological. A corollary to this claim is that theology in such cases fits the bill better than philosophy. The justification for the claim is simple: philosophy is an inquiry that does not assume the authority of religious texts, whereas theology, although itself a reasoned inquiry, accepts the epistemic validity of texts and tradition. Theology is scriptural interpretation; philosophy is not. Vedāntins mostly argue about the correct meaning of texts, and use texts as arguments; *ergo*, they are not philosophers in the present sense of the term.

This is a welcome intervention insofar as it recognizes that many Indian intellectuals whom we generally call "philosophers" engage in theological reasoning, but the binaries theology *or* philosophy and theologian *or* philosopher are less helpful. Focusing on the *Brahma-sūtra*, I suggest that it is more useful to consider carefully *modes of discourse* and *kinds of arguments* that an individual or a tradition may put forward, and to be mindful of *shared spheres of commitment*, constituted by the context or scope in which arguments are made. Resisting essential definitions, there are several senses in which one may talk about Brahmanical theology, concerning questions of subject and method, but most relevant for illustrating the kinds of arguments used in the *Brahma-sūtra* is that of exegesis or scriptural interpretation.

Now, it is said that "theology" is obliquely applicable even to religions or systems that are not focused on God (*theos*), but have a "transcendent point of reference," such as Buddhism.[5] I take such "transcendent point of reference" in the Indian context to stand for ontological reals (including causal relations) that are supersensible, that is, not knowable through perception. Aside from the materialists who have always been the minority in denying the knowability of the non-perceptual, the two dominant approaches to knowing supersensible reals in India have been those of inferential reasoning and scripture (or more generally knowledge from linguistic utterances). We may illustrate the two by comparing the traditions of Mīmāṁsā and Sāṅkhya. Both delineated their unique scope as that which is supersensible. The Mīmāṁsaka Śabara (ca. 500–550 CE) famously said in his commentary on the *Mīmāṁsā-sūtra* that *dharma*, the topic of the *Mīmāṁsā-sūtra*, refers to things—specifically, causal relations—that are minute, hidden, or remote, that is, supersensible. They are causal relations between common, perceptible things, namely ritual and things offered in it, and a future imperceptible state of affairs, such as heaven, for which reason they are knowable only from Vedic injunctions. That is, they are not traceable inferentially, but must be discerned from scripture.[6] Sāṅkhya, on the other hand, while accepting that there are things which are knowable only from scripture, claimed that its characteristic objects of inquiry, prime matter and the soul, are both knowable from inference that proceeds through analogical reasoning, and did not concern itself with scriptural objects.[7]

Thus, while both Mīmāṁsā and Sāṅkhya posit a thing with a "transcendent point of reference," the scope of the first is theological because of being knowable from scripture, whereas the scope of the second is philosophical, or properly metaphysical. This distinction obtains not necessarily through the content or the subject of the inquiry—in both cases it is a supersensible reality—but through the method. The first proceeds through interpretation of texts, concerning supersensible reals: it takes scriptural statements as its data, whose understanding requires interpretation, and for the sake of which it uses characteristically theological arguments. The second proceeds through analogical reasoning that pursues inferred, supersensible reals, from data that is empirically or perceptually knowable.

Let us now turn to Bādarāyaṇa to illustrate what I call "characteristically theological arguments," drawn from a dispute between him the champion of Vedānta and Jaimini the paradigmatic Mīmāṁsaka. In *Brahma-sūtra* 3.4.1–20, there is a long discussion where Bādarāyaṇa puts forward the claim that the Upaniṣadic meditations are the means to human good independent of Vedic sacrifices and goes on to consider several Mīmāṁsā objections. He gives the knockdown argument in *sūtra* 15: there is a Vedic text where it is evident that some Vedic men do not marry and cannot perform ritual because they have not lit the sacrificial fire that is presupposed on marrying, yet do pursue the Self, that is, perform Upaniṣadic meditations.[8] Such could not be the case if meditation was supererogatory to ritual, which is what Mīmāṁsakas claim. Further, the practice of lifelong celibacy is justified in the *Chāndogya*.[9] Jaimini then retorts: the *Chāndogya* mention of lifelong ascetics is just that, a mere mention that recognizes the fact of there being such poor fellas, but not an injunction that justifies what they are doing. There is another text, in fact, which condemns such lifelong celibacy.[10] Bādarāyaṇa finally concludes, it is not just a mention, because there is "a direct statement of sameness," that is, the lifelong celibate is listed in the *Chāndogya* passage under consideration along with the householder, such that nothing really separates the two as good and bad; and he provides a case of precedent from Vedic interpretation in the light of which the *Chāndogya* statement should be read as an injunction for renunciation.[11]

We need not understand all the technical details to appreciate the theological mode of discourse that involves a shared sphere of commitment constituted by the acceptance of Vedic statements as reliable epistemic warrants and of recognized canons of interpretation such as "injunction," "mention," "direct statement," "Vedic precedent," etc. Such arguments were possible and made sense because of this sphere of commitment that Mīmāṁsakas and Vedāntins shared, and would have had little force against Sāṅkhya, which had a technical term for the Vedic variety of bondage, *dākṣiṇaka* or the bondage respective to honoraria that one pays to priests,[12] and would have been useless against the Buddhists and Jains, who did not accept the Vedas at all.

Theological and Philosophical Arguments

If we, next, restrict supersensible reals to first principles—those which may be said to be the origin of things—theology need not be confined to scriptural exegesis. In the West, insofar as God was understood as such first principle, theology was part of the discipline of metaphysics and, in aspiration at least, independent of religious commitments. Such is the case, for instance, in Aristotle's definition of metaphysics as the inquiry into the first principles of reality, most specifically God the first mover and pure actuality that keeps the world rolling as its final cause but is itself not liable to change.[13] In the Catholic tradition, the inquiry into God as the subject of philosophy came to be called "natural theology," a properly philosophical discipline that takes its data from the world and pursues factual and possible causal relations through the light of reason, in the hope of arriving at the first principle. To quote Frederic Copleston on St. Thomas's understanding of the domain of the two disciplines, "the fundamental difference between theology and philosophy does not lie in the difference of objects concretely considered."[14] The prominent German philosopher of Enlightenment Christian Wolff characterized this natural theology as special metaphysics, that is, the terminus of the metaphysical inquiry into Being in the most general sense of any possible thing.

How may one go about distinguishing scriptural from philosophical theology and from philosophy more generally in the Brahmanical context? I suggest that we need to look again at modes of discourse and shared spheres of commitment. A line is drawn sometimes between Nyāya-Vaiśeṣika as rational theology, thus, proper philosophy, and Vedānta as "revealed" theology: indeed, the Naiyāyikas (i.e., proponents of Nyāya-Vaiśeṣika) developed inferential proofs for the existence of God, whereas Vedāntins generally stuck to their guns and claimed that Brahman was knowable only from the Upaniṣads. It is more instructive, however, to look at Vedānta and Sāṅkhya, since the second was not theological either through the subject or through the method. Both traditions were *primarily* and *originally* concerned with first principles, the proper domain of metaphysics, whereas the philosophical theology of Nyāya-Vaiśeṣika did not really develop before the Buddhist challenge, and was, thus, more of an afterthought.

We turn to Bādarāyaṇa again. Along with the concern with first principles, Sāṅkhya and Vedānta also shared the general theory of causality, *sat-kārya-vāda*, the doctrine that the effect was not essentially a new thing, but a transformation of the cause. They parted ways on two questions. First, in Sāṅkhya the material cause was prime matter, and the efficient cause was the proximity between prime matter and the soul; in Vedānta Brahman was both the material and the efficient cause.[15] Second, the first principles of Sāṅkhya were knowable through inference, as we saw earlier, whereas Brahman was knowable from the Upaniṣads. Thus, Sāṅkhya and Vedānta were at odds in terms of the appropriate means of knowing the first principles, as well as the specifics of such first principles. Finally, Sāṅkhya was historically Vedānta's main rival at the time of its codification in the *Brahma-sūtra*, and the bulk of the first two chapters of the *Brahma-sūtra* consists of clarification of Vedāntic doctrines primarily in view of a Sāṅkhya challenge. Let us now pay some attention to the anti-Sāṅkhya arguments in the *Brahma-sūtra* and see what kinds of reasoning they involve.

The *Brahma-sūtra* opens with the definition of Brahman, "It is that from which come origination, etc. of the world," and immediately proceeds to affirm Brahman's essential characteristics—consciousness and bliss—not directly, but through distinguishing Brahman from the first principles of Sāṅkhya. Brahman is known from scripture, and a proposed first principle will not fit the bill if it does not have the characteristics of Brahman that are known from the Upaniṣads. Prime matter cannot be the first principle, because it does not satisfy the scriptural criteria. That is, in the Upaniṣads, specifically the sixth chapter of the *Chāndogya*, it is said that the first principle which is Being, *sat,* "reflected" or "visualized" (*aikṣaka*) before creating the world: "And it thought to itself: 'Let me become many. Let me propagate myself.'"[16] Prime matter is an insentient principle—it cannot reflect—and so it fails the scriptural test: it is *aśabdam*, "non-scriptural," and throughout the *Brahma-sūtra* Bādarāyaṇa calls it "the inferential."[17] But imagine, the Sāṅkhya opponent may retort, that "reflection" is used in a figurative sense: doesn't the Upaniṣad say further that heat and water likewise "reflected"? No, replies Bādarāyaṇa, because the first principle is afterwards explicitly called "the Self," which implies sentience in the literal sense. Furthermore, liberation in the Upaniṣad follows for him who *identifies* with this Self as the first principle, whereas liberation in Sāṅkhya is a result of *dis-identification* from prime matter the first principle. And, if the intended meaning is figurative, one would expect this particular statement to be an exception, but in fact *all* Upaniṣadic creation passages present the first principle as the Self or otherwise sentient.[18]

Similar is the case with Brahman as bliss in *sūtra* 1.1.13, "That which is bliss abundant is Brahman, because of repetition."[19] This is a denial that the Sāṅkhyan individual soul is the ultimate reference of a *Taittirīya* text that describes five successively higher layers of Selfhood, culminating with the Self of bliss, because the Upaniṣad makes a gradation of "bliss" in a series of repetitive statements such that nothing compares with the bliss of Brahman. The *Taittirīya* also says that Brahman "gladdens" the individual soul, which obtains bliss in association with Brahman upon liberation.[20] The arguments, thus, are not that the first principle must be conscious and blissful because causality demands such a first principle, but that Brahman is presented as consciousness and bliss in the Upaniṣads, for which reason prime matter and the Self of Sāṅkhya cannot be the references of "Brahman."

This, I believe, is the context of *sūtra* 1.1.3 with which we opened the chapter: it is not about Nyāya-Vaiśeṣika inferential arguments of God, but about the inferential categories of Sāṅkhya, which are not the scripturally known Brahman. The whole first book of the *Brahma-sūtra* has Sāṅkhya in large perspective, and Bādarāyaṇa painstakingly goes through sections of the Upaniṣads to show that Brahman, not prime matter or the soul or some other suchlike principle, are their topic, pursuing what he programmatically says in 1.1.4: "That [Brahman is the subject of inquiry], on the account of full [Upaniṣadic] concordance."[21]

Such arguments are what I call characteristically theological arguments, driving home a point by an appeal to scripture in its correct interpretation, although the subject in this case—first principles—is a proper subject of philosophy or metaphysics. They were possible arguments because the older variety of Sāṅkhya was the philosophy of the *Bhagavad-gītā* and other books of the second layer of the Brahmanical canon, where prime matter and the soul stand in some ontological relationship to Brahman. Sāṅkhya had, in other words, a stake in the Brahman-talk, and it shared with Vedānta a sphere of commitment in the "Vedic community." As Śaṅkara says, the good Vedic folks accept many Sāṅkhyan principles, and therefore it becomes imperative to state, for the sake of this community which obeys the force of scripture as arguments, just what in Sāṅkhya is not acceptable, and if found in scripture, requires interpretation.[22]

But Sāṅkhya was also an independent, non-scriptural tradition, with which Vedānta shared, as we just stated, the *sat-kārya-vāda*. It is in this context that we see characteristically philosophical reasoning on the part of Bādarāyaṇa. This reasoning is still somewhat scripturally constrained, and expressly so: inferential reasoning is inconclusive, and one never gets to avoid all undesirable consequences of a causal theory solely through reasoning.[23] Yet, Bādarāyaṇa goes on to engage precisely in such reasoning, with the general claims that Brahman fits best the requirements of a first principle in virtue of its characteristics; that the competing first principles make little sense under our common understanding of causality; and that, when no satisfying arguments from reason are forthcoming, the Sāṅkhya notion of causality faces the same objections as Brahman does.[24]

To illustrate, Bādarāyaṇa takes exception to the Sāṅkhya *sat-kārya-vāda* claim that the effect must share the characteristics of the cause. The Sāṅkhya opponent of the *Brahma-sūtra* claims that it is not possible for Brahman to be the material cause of the world, because the world the effect is radically different from Brahman the cause.[25] The world is evidently insentient, impure, and full of suffering, whereas Brahman is defined as essentially sentient, pure, and blissful: it cannot be that the first is an effect of the second. Bādarāyaṇa's reply is that precisely such cases of causal relations where the effect was radically different from the cause are in evidence.[26] The commentators give several instances of such cases, most of which fail to impress—worms produced from honey, dung-beetle from dung, and so on—but two have intuitive appeal: the insentient hair that grows from a sentient body, and the insentient cobweb that a sentient spider produces. Such cases of empirically knowable causal relations, then, are proof that it isn't necessary for the effect be of the same nature as the cause. It must be real, *sat* or Being, and to that degree, Vedānta endorses *sat-kārya-vāda* equally with Sāṅkhya, but the effect has a surplus of characteristics beyond Being that are not shared with the cause.

Whether one finds the arguments compelling or not, they are characteristically philosophical insofar as they endorse Sāṅkhya's own game, analogical reasoning from known to unknown causal relations and entities in the light not of scripture but of inference. Such arguments were possible, again, because of a shared sphere of commitment, the doctrine of *sat-kārya-vāda*. Bādarāyaṇa was explicit about it: charged by the Sāṅkhya opponent that his account of causality amounts to *asat-kārya-vāda*, a doctrine that the effect is constitutively a new thing, he replies that his contention is not against *sat-kārya-vāda,* just against the claim that the effect must be like the cause.[27] Bādarāyaṇa was also willing to engage metaphysics outside *sat-kārya-vāda*, such as Nyāya-Vaiśeṣika and Buddhism, because he had a larger shared sphere of commitment to the general discourse of causality. This is the part of the *Brahma-sūtra* where there are no topical passages referenced by the individual *sūtras* because the context is such that arguments from scripture don't fly. It is strictly a philosophical mode of discourse.

While its purpose was obviously not to advance original *proofs* about Brahman or ascertain Brahman's peculiar characteristics—the Upaniṣads are the sole *pramāṇa* in that regard—insofar as Brahman was *sat,* Being, early Vedāntins had a keen interest in engaging philosophically with other traditions. Śaṅkara, for one, bears witness to this: whenever the question of Being and non-Being presents itself in a text he is commenting on, he finds the occasion to advance his peculiar understanding of Being and argue against the several doctrines of *asat-kārya-vāda*, specifically Nyāya-Vaiśeṣika and the Buddhist philosophies, solely on the grounds of reason, and he expressly claims that it follows not only from scripture but from inference as well that the world was Being in the beginning. To illustrate, in the *Brahma-sūtra* section against Buddhist ontology, Śaṅkara says that the reality of space or ether is established from scriptural statements, "but for those who are opposed to the authority of scripture, it must be presented as inferable from the quality of sound."[28] This is a typical case of the Sāṅkhyan inference of unknown causal relations and ontological reals from what is empirically known.

Thus, although first principles are established from scriptural statements, Bādarāyaṇa endorsed philosophical reasoning and made characteristically philosophical arguments because he had a shared sphere of commitment to the discourse of causality through non-sectarian forms of argument. In adjudicating whether something is theology or philosophy, then, one should look at the kinds of arguments that are made, and they will depend on the shared sphere of commitment. No matter one's religious tradition, when it comes to defending one's position in a context of diverging presuppositions, specifically regarding doctrinal authority—when it comes to arguing how one's understanding of the first principles makes more sense than competing doctrines—there is no avenue for arguing, so long as argument is wanted, but for non-sectarian, nontheological forms of reasoning.

One final point. Both theological and philosophical arguments are forms of reasoning. In many cases, however, the two are so intimately intertwined that sifting the one from the other would be at the cost of understanding. While identifying the various modes of discourse helps us appreciate arguments in their intended context, Bādarāyaṇa in his theology tells us how he reads specific Upaniṣadic passages such that his particular metaphysical outlook emerges. We will, therefore, approach the study of the *Brahma-sūtra* holistically. Larry McCrea is fully justified in claiming that, at least in Mīmāṁsā and Vedānta, philosophical issues and matters of scriptural interpretation are "inextricably bound up together in manifold and complex ways."[29] Although this is a book about Bādarāyaṇa the philosopher, we will let him wear his theological mantle at his own pleasure, particularly as we move from ontology to soteriology in the later parts of the book, and we will not refrain from calling him and his fellow Vedāntins "theologians."

The Idea of Scripture

Scripture, then, is the means to know Brahman. But, what does Bādarāyaṇa mean by "scripture," *śāstra*? We know the short answer to this question from the Introduction, where we discussed topical passages in the *Brahma-sūtra*: scriptures for Bādarāyaṇa are primarily the Upaniṣads and the rest of the Vedic canon, what is commonly called *śruti,* "hearing," or *śabda,* "speech;" and secondarily, works of the wider Brahmanical canon, such as the *Mahābhārata*, commonly called *smṛti* or "memory." Bādarāyaṇa also comes in a tradition of theologians who have a refined understanding of the significance of *śāstra/śruti/śabda* (henceforth I use *śruti* metonymically for all three) and the paired term "*smṛti*," one that he presupposes but does not explicate in the *Brahma-sūtra*, and to which he himself is credited with an important contribution in the *Mīmāṁsā-sūtra*. Of central importance in this understanding is the association of "hearing" and "memory" with another pair, "perception" and "inference" (*pratyakṣa* and *anumāna*). We will unpack some of that importance in this and the following sections.

The pair "perception" and "inference," which are otherwise the terms used for the two common reliable warrants in general epistemology, is how *śruti* and *smṛti* are called in early Brahmanical theological works. "Perception" and "inference" with respect to scripture are first used in the *Dharma-sūtra*s, the earliest books of Brahmanical law, which talk about express Vedic rules, called "perceptual" or "immediate" injunctions, that govern social practices and trump in validity customs which are only inferably Vedic. The express rules stand for injunctions that are found in the Vedas, which an orthoprax member of Vedic society recited daily, and they are "perceptual" because they are directly attested in the Vedas, known "from hearing," *śruti*. On the other hand, customary practices are *not* attested in the Vedas: one does not know about them "from hearing," but may *infer* that they originate in lost Vedic texts because good men follow such practices. The problem with inferable rules is the intervening human factor: the justification for the practices is not found in the Vedas as they are heard, but only in the conduct of Vedic men, and men—as *Mīmāṁsā-sūtra* 4.1.2 claims—have pleasure as motive inherently and universally. Since there are no direct legitimizing statements for such practices, they may turn out to be unjustified.[30] A similar doctrine is found at the beginning of *Mīmāṁsā-sūtra* 1.3, and we may conclude that an understanding must have been common in the intellectual space of early Brahmanical theology that there are direct Vedic injunctions, and there are customs whose origin cannot be related to express Vedic statements; since both are practiced by Vedic men, the customs which are not supported by Vedic texts must have origin in textual rules and injunctions which are not known anymore; such customs are good, as long as they do not contradict something in the express statements.

The *Dharma-sūtra*s and *Mīmāṁsā-sūtra* do not talk about "memory," but about inferable rules and lost Vedic texts.[31] By the time of Śabara, the celebrated commentator on the *Mīmāṁsā-sūtra*, "memory" has become the term of art. Śabara describes the inferential rules as based on the memory of something previously experienced or seen, a prior cognition of a Vedic text that is no longer evident.[32] David Brick had argued that originally the term *smṛti* or "memory" did not refer to textual rules, but to traditional time-honored norms, comparable, for instance, to the modern rule that the father of the bride should pay for her wedding. When they became canonized in a distinct textual corpus, *smṛti* initially meant works that document such traditional rules of conduct, such as the Brahmanical lawbook the *Manu-smṛti*, but their scope was eventually extended to include the *Mahābhārata* and the *Purāṇas*.[33] These *smṛti* works contain material from the Vedas: they explicitly evoke known Vedic texts and preserve the memory of Vedic texts that are no longer known, but in their present state they are human compositions, their authors being sages such as Manu and Vyāsa. *Śruti*, then, are the Vedas, including the Upaniṣads, and *smṛti* are texts of the wider Brahmanical canon.

All throughout, however, the two terms, *śruti* and *smṛti*, stand for the respective textual corpora—the Vedas and other canonical texts—*secondarily* or *by association:* the primary meaning remains that of individual rules or of unique scriptural passages more generally. The two terms mean more something like individual *scriptural facts* than *scripture* as a book. Bādarāyaṇa very much inherits this discourse. Whenever he talks about "perception" in the *Brahma-sūtra*, it is individual statements from the Vedas that he has in mind, not what we commonly think of as perceptual experience. Likewise, "inference" are statements from the *smṛti* literature.[34]

But, the perception-inference distinction for our theologians was not restricted to the mere fact that some rules and statements are found in the Vedas, and some are not: it was not *just* a distinction of presence in one set or texts rather than another. They further argued that *śruti* was like perceptual knowledge in terms of its *epistemic validity and immediacy*. Interpreting the terms "perception" and "inference" in their comments on *Brahma-sūtra* 1.3.28, standing for *śruti* and *smṛti*, Śaṅkara and Bhāskara distinguish them with respect to epistemic validity and independence:

> "Perception" is "hearing" (*śruti*), because it is independent with respect to epistemic validity. "Inference" is "memory" (*smṛti*), because it is dependent with respect to epistemic validity.[35]
>
> "Perception" is "hearing," because it is independent. "Inference" is "memory," because it depends on an inferred *śruti* statement.[36]

There is, in fact, a common practice across Mīmāṁsā and Vedānta of identifying scripture in the restricted sense of *śruti* with perception in general, not just with the presence of certain statements in the audible Veda.

One passage from Śabara's comment on the *Mīmāṁsā-sūtra*, echoed by Bhāskara, is particularly striking:

> Scripture should not be much doubted, being more reliable than the words of one's mother and father, for one cognizes through scripture directly. It occupies the same rank as the senses.[37]
>
> Scripture tells how things really are. It is more reliable than the words of one's father and mother.[38]

Much more than mere aural availability is involved in claiming that the epistemic validity of scriptural statements is like that of perceptual awareness episodes, and that one knows from scripture directly. Scripture is a form of knowledge from linguistic utterances, verbal knowledge, and we generally take such knowledge to be testimonial, a report of events or states that were witnessed perceptually or, perhaps, in some form of mystical experience. We take such reports to be valid because we trust the reliability of the witness: their validity is mediated by witness reliability, and so is our knowledge of the events or states mediated by the very fact of their being reports. In any case, our knowledge doesn't seem to be either direct or independently valid. What is at stake in positing validity and independence of scripture that are equal with the realm of the senses? What more is involved in this claim? It is to this "more" that we turn now.

Knowing Supersensible Things

This "more," in fact, relates to a statement with which Bādarāyaṇa is credited in the *Mīmāṁsā-sūtra*, rather than the *Brahma-sūtra*, and to an early commentary on the *Mīmāṁsā-sūtra* by someone called "Vṛttikāra," a common noun meaning "commentator." Vṛttikāra's commentary has been lost except for a long passage that interprets *sūtra*s 1.1.3–5 and is quoted, or perhaps paraphrased, by Śabara. The statement is *Mīmāṁsā-sūtra* 1.1.5, and it is commonly called the *autpattika-sūtra* after its first word, *autpattika*, "innate." The *sūtra* as interpreted by the Vṛttikāra says:

> The word-meaning relationship is *innate*. It is known through instruction, and it is inerrant with respect to supersensible things. It is a reliable warrant, according to Bādarāyaṇa, because it is independent.[39]

This statement is part of the first chapter of the *Mīmāṁsā-sūtra* where Mīmāṁsā epistemology is discussed. The key word here is *pramāṇa*, which

I translate as "reliable warrant" because *pramāṇa* covers both evidence or ground for a belief or an argument, and the epistemic means by which a veridical awareness episode is produced.[40] The chapter makes the distinction between perceptible and imperceptible things, "imperceptible" meaning those that cannot be seen *in principle,* that is, supersensible. The second in the context stands for things that the *Mīmāṁsā-sūtra* defines as *dharma*, namely ritual and its characteristic to bring about a future state of felicity, heaven, but the Vṛttikāra clearly has a broader scope in view, his illustration being the divinities of the Vedic pantheon. Such imperceptible things can be known only from "instruction." Perception cannot be the means of knowing imperceptible things precisely because they are supersensible, whereas perceptual awareness is produced by the senses.

There are, of course, facts that are not perceptible at any given moment yet are known to us by some other means. We know, for instance, from analogical reasoning that the sun moves, although we do not see its motion because of distance. Sāṅkhyas, as we saw earlier, adopted such analogical reasoning as the means of knowing not only imperceptible characteristics of visible things, such as the motion of the sun, but of first principles as well, prime matter and the souls. In all such cases of knowing imperceptible things, our knowledge of them is not primitive, insofar as we need some prior cognitions to work with: we need to see the sun in various places—we need perceptual data—and a notion of causality. What Bādarāyaṇa and his commentator claim, however, is that knowledge from "instruction" or scripture is just as primitive as perception. Let us see how this is the case.

The Vṛttikāra goes through six reliable warrants and draws a distinction between those whose scope are objects that are "near" (*sannikṛṣṭa*) on the one hand and those whose scope are objects that are "remote" (*asannikṛṣṭa*) on the other, that is, directly perceptible or otherwise, and we take note that scripture is classed in the second group, with the other four that are not perception.[41] Normally that the object is not immediately given to perception yet is otherwise knowable would mean that there had to have been a perceptual knowledge at some earlier point on which this new, non-perceptual cognition is based. Resemblance, for instance, tells us something not about what is presently seen, but about what is otherwise known but not immediately present. "Resemblance or similarity produces a cognition about a thing which is not present, like in the case of remembering a cow upon seeing a wild buffalo."[42] Seeing a wild buffalo in the forest is not knowing something about the buffalo, insofar as resemblance is concerned, but about the domestic cow, because it is the cow which is not perceptually present. Resemblance, then, proceeds by way of remembrance of prior perceptions of the cow and a present perception of the wild buffalo, giving rise to a new cognition about the non-present cow. The object is already perceptually known, but the specific *new* information about it, which a reliable warrant must provide, is not knowable through perception.

Scriptural knowledge, however, is odd because its object is perceptually inaccessible—it is "remote"—but it does not share with the other four the fact of having a prior cognition as the *sine qua non* through which it proceeds. Scriptural knowledge is derived *just* from a verbal cognition, one which does not presuppose some other perceptual cognition for its very possibility:

> Scriptural knowledge is a cognition about a thing which is not present, from cognition of a linguistic utterance.[43]

The Vṛttikāra insisted that this feature is essential to scriptural knowledge, which is had when "the word itself talks" and which, for this reason, cannot possibly be wrong.

What does it mean, however, for "the word itself to talk?" Let us work through Prabhākara's (ca. 620–670 CE) example, "There are hundreds of herds of elephants on the fingertip." This statement, of course, is not true, but the reason is not that it fails to communicate meaning. We do understand what "hundreds of herds of elephants" means and insofar we do understand it, we have a verbal cognition.[44] Such knowledge from verbal cognition cannot be wrong as long as we grasp the meaning. If one is a competent user of a language, one will have verbal cognitions, and if an utterance proves to convey an error, as in the case of elephants on fingers, we should look for the source of this error elsewhere. Mīmāṁsakas advanced various theories on the sources of verbal errors. It is not necessary to follow such developments, however. In the "elephants on the fingertip" situation, the error stems from the compositeness of two verbal facts—herds of elephants *on* the fingertip—which compositeness is properly in the domain of perception, not linguistic knowledge. An error may happen because the speaker is a fraud "who knows one thing but says another,"[45] or is trustworthy and yet still mistaken about what she is reporting, and so on. In any such case, no error would come from the verbal cognition itself, for such cognition, like perception, is presentational, "perceptual," and a meaning would be immediately given to it.

The "Non-personal" Character of Language

Why is such verbal knowledge inerrant, that is, informative and meaningful? Why does one have veridical verbal cognitions to begin with? This brings us to considering what our theologians, primarily the Vṛttikāra, mean under "word" and "meaning." Let us begin with the second. In classical Indian philosophy of language, there was a lively debate on whether the terms of language stand for individual substances, what we otherwise call "particulars," or for generic or class unique properties, "universals." When I say "cow," what is it that the word denotes? Milka the cow, or "cowness" that is present in any individual object that can be described as a cow? The Naiyāyikas had a third possibility, the "form" or "configuration" that is an external or visible property by which one recognizes the thing as a cow. In Mīmāṁsā, as well as the tradition of the grammarians, the second and the third were essentially collapsed into one: the meaning of words are universals or class properties, which generally but not necessarily include the form of a thing: not all class properties have a form. In the case of "cow," then, the meaning of the word is "cowness," which includes the form of having a dewlap, tail, hump, hoofs, and horns. It is the idea that comes to mind when we hear "cow" such that any member of the species can be intended.

A "word," on the other hand, says the Vṛttikāra, is a combination of phonemes—individual and irreducible sounds—that are pronounced in a particular sequence such that the last of them expresses the meaning, but enriched with the impressions of the preceding phonemes. In the Sanskrit word for a cow, *gauḥ*, the word is the sounds *g, au,* and *ḥ*, in that sequence.[46] There is an ontological reason for breaking down words to phonemes, but it will have to wait a little.

So far so good. The crucial question, however, is: How does an individual word express particular meaning? How is it that a word has the "standing-for" relationship to whatever it denotes? We tend to think that such relationship is conventional. When we think of "cow," we tend to take it as a conventional sign, and we do so because words in various languages differ. A speaker of English will use "cow," of French "vache," and of Serbian "krava," and in doing so they will rely on semantic conventions that inform a particular language. Bādarāyaṇa as interpreted by the Vṛttikāra, however, makes a startling claim: this spoken term that stands for the natural term, the universal "cow," is *not* conventional, and its "standing-for" relationship to the natural term has *no origin in time or agent*. This is why the name-named relationship is innate, *autpattika*.

To be specific, that "cow" or rather *gauḥ* should bring about the mental image of a something with a dewlap, tail, hump, hoofs, and horns is not predicated on a prior performative speech act of naming, a point in time when someone said, "let us call this thing 'cow'" and people agreed to do so. An act of naming that our philosophers have in mind is well illustrated with the name-giving ceremony that a father performs for his son, such that from that point onwards the boy is known by the given name. Such naming has origin in time, the name-giving ceremony, and in agent—the father. The words in our natural language, on the other hand, do not and *could not* involve naming events. The Vrttikāra in his comment glosses *autpattika* with *apauruṣeya*, "non-human" or "non-personal." The word-meaning relationship is non-personal, not based on the semantic conventions of a language community.[47]

The Vṛttikāra proposes several arguments to support this claim. Philosophically the most interesting is the argument from the impossibility of the opposite case, namely that all naming is conventional. Imagine that a human agent had established the word-meaning relationship, between "cow" the word and the idea of "something with a dewlap, tail, hump, hoofs, and horns," like a father names a son. How would such an agent perform the act of naming except through an already existent language practice that involves the use of referring words? If there are no words that are directly related to their meaning, the performative act of naming would just not be possible because it would involve infinite regress, no firm or final ground.

Doctrinally most significant, however, is the argument from the absence of memory of an agent establishing the word-meaning relationship, because this argument speaks to the perceptual or direct character of language. The argument is intertwined with the Vṛttikāra's understanding of the process of language learning or acquisition, with which he proposes to explain Bādarāyaṇa's claim that knowledge of the word-meaning relationship is had from "instruction," *upadeśa*. When children learn language, they learn, in a sense, "on their own," simply by observing the practice of adult competent language users. A child hears an elder telling someone, "bring the horse," and sees how that someone brings a horse. S/he then hears the elder saying, "bring the cow," and sees a cow being brought. The action of bringing remains identical, but the object changes. The child, thus, understands that "bring" stands for the action, the word being identical in both cases, whereas "horse" and "cow" stand for the two different objects. The important point is that nobody establishes the word-meaning relationship for the child's sake, telling her "this is a cow" or "this is a horse." In that sense, the meaning of words for the child is direct, "perceptual," related solely to her own cognition of language practice, not reflecting the cognition of an agent who might name things for her. The word "*upadeśa*" which I translated with "instruction" is used throughout the *Brahma-sūtra* synonymously with *śruti/śāstra/śabda*, "hearing" that is a "scriptural fact."[48]

The Vṛttikāra argues further that such absence of the notion of an agent just means that there is no first agent to be discovered either, because the invention of language would have been such an event of a tremendous magnitude, the *memory* of which could not ever be lost. To illustrate this as well as to contrast natural language acquisition with learning grammar, he compares the sense of the word-meaning relationship in natural language to that in the highly technical and formal grammar discourse that is associated with the famous grammarian Pāṇini. When one learns the meaning of the technical terms of grammar, there is a persistent awareness that someone invented the "standing-for" relationship between the word and the meaning. To illustrate, Pāṇini's term "*LyuṬ*" stands for the suffix "*āna*" that is added to a verbal root to produce a noun of a certain kind, for a phonetic change that happens to the verbal root when the suffix is added, and for the placement of the accent in the final word. Unless one is aware that Pāṇini had established this word-meaning relationship in the case of *LyuṬ*, one simply would not be able to learn grammar.

Curiously, the technical terms of Pāṇini's grammar are also called *upadeśa*, which is generally interpreted as "an original utterance," pointing to the event of Pāṇini's introducing them with a meaning which that they have *in his system* but not in natural language.[49] In classical Indian culture so dominated by Pāṇinian learning, this is the paradigmatic instance of an event of naming, and it is little wonder that Pāṇini's work in Mīmāṁsā is treated as *smṛti* or memory: it is the memory of Pāṇini establishing the relationship of his technical terms with whatever they stand for.[50] For the Vṛttikāra, writing as he does eight centuries after Pāṇini, it is an enduring memory of an event of a tremendous magnitude, as it still is for Sanskrit students today. In *śruti*, "hearing" the words of natural language, on the other hand, there is no such memory, the meaning is "perceptual," not mediated by another person or her cognition of the idea associated with the word.

To answer our question, then, why is verbal knowledge inerrant, that is, informative and meaningful? It is because words *naturally evoke* the meaning to which they are *innately* related.

The "Non-personal" Character of the Vedas

Why do our philosophers need such a counterintuitive theory, that words are eternal and their "standing-for" relationship to meaning is innate? They need it for the second—and more important—part of the argument, which is that not only is the word-meaning relationship authorless but so are the Vedas. The Vedas are not compositions of human or even divine agents. Like the word-meaning relationship, they do not have an origin in time or agent: they too are *apauruṣeya*, "non-personal." It is this second argument that is epistemologically the more significant, yet it absolutely requires the first. We saw earlier that sentences such as "there are hundreds of herds of elephants on the fingertip" were false, but not because of not being informative. Insofar as the distinct linguistic elements bring about the ideas of elephants, fingertips and the like, there was nothing wrong with the sentence, although the composite is obviously false. The error was human- or agent-contingent: agents can be frauds, or they can simply be mistaken no matter how honest they otherwise are. They possess what Mīmāṁsakas call *vivakṣā*, which we may, in the context of texts, translate as "authorial intention." But imagine texts or textual rules and statements that do not have an authorial intention! They would be like natural and infallible laws, free from the frailties that beset human agents.

We can see, now, why scriptural knowledge is like perception and contraposed to inference and the other reliable warrants. Perceptual knowledge does not require data from another reliable warrant, and neither does the non-personal Veda. There is a difference between the two insofar as their spheres are proximate and distant objects respectively, perceptible and supersensible, but there is no difference in immediacy. Sure, the non-personal character of language and the Veda does require a learning process, but so does perception require light and other things; in either case, these are accessory factors that facilitate the manifestation of the respective objects, but are not directly instrumental. "When the word itself speaks," it does not rely on authorial intention, and it does not report a previously experienced state of affairs through the lens of an agent. Being like that, scriptural knowledge is "perceptual." The Vedas are, as it were, the "senses" for knowing that which is beyond the senses, the third eye of the theologian. Human speech, on the other hand, insofar as after "the word had spoken" there is the concern about the validity of the source or the veracity of the report, is "inferential," or, as Śaṅkara says with respect to *smṛti* statements, dependent on something else for its validity.

"Perception" and "Inference"

It is useful at this point to refer to a familiar distinction in Mīmāṁsā and Vedānta between two discrete domains, called *loka* and *veda*. The first stands for the world as we know it, with natural objects and laws knowable directly through perception and the other reliable warrants that harness perceptual data. The second refers to the scriptural domain, which has its own "verbal" laws and scriptural objects which are knowable directly from Vedic statements (and smaller units of language), *śruti/śāstra/śabda/upadeśa,* and different sets of reliable canons of interpretation that employ *śruti*-data. Each realm has a basic reliable warrant providing a direct access to the realm;

because scripture shares such directness with perception, it *is* perception in its own domain. This does not mean that everything in scripture will turn out to be true for our theologians in the literal sense, for if it did, they would be left without employment. They would, nevertheless, argue that interpretation through recognized canons is not radically different from deciding whether the object in the distance is a man or a post in cases of perceptual doubts. The only substantial difference is where you get your data from.

Little wonder that Mīmāṁsakas have classed all canons of interpretation other than direct Vedic statements as "inference," *anumāna*. These include, as we saw, not only the statements from *smṛti* literature, because of the concern about their validity and the inference from memory of texts that are no longer available, but also all cases where something is accepted as veridical without "the word itself speaking." These include figurative meaning when the literal is not possible, and various sets of interpretation tools in which direct Vedic statements are supplemented by other "reliable warrants," *pramāṇa*s. We need not go into their details, but the most important among them, for the sake of illustration, include things such as implied meaning, syntactic relations within a text, context, textual proximity of various passages, and significant technical terms. In Vedānta, philosophical reasoning that is in conformity to scripture is also such an interpretation tool, to be used when various—conflicting—meanings of scriptural statements are possible. The point, however, is this: direct statements from the Vedas and the Upaniṣads in all such cases are "perception," whereas everything else is "inference."

The two realms, then, have not only a single primitive reliable warrant or *pramāṇa* respectively, perception and scripture, but sets of derivative *pramāṇa*s as well, all of which are metonymically called "inference." In the sphere of *loka*, the world, these are inference proper, resemblance, postulation, and so on. In the sphere of *veda,* these are *smṛti*, the canons of interpretation, and philosophical reasoning. Since perception and scripture are equally primitive, inferential arguments cannot defeat them *no matter which realm they belong to*. Witness Śabara's and Vṛttikāra's reply to the charge that the words of the Vedas could be mistaken because they are words, like common language that has elephants on fingertips:

> This [charge] is inference; the cognition in regard to Vedic speech, however, is perception. Inference which is against perceptual evidence is not a reliable warrant.[51]
>
> The notion, "since there is fault in the case of another cognition, this one will be false as well," is inferential; being contradicted by this perceptual cognition, it is defeated.[52]

Conclusion

The doctrine of the non-personal nature of language and the Veda involved some important presuppositions and doctrinal commitments, and it gave rise to various problems. If the word-meaning relationship was innate, it would have to follow that words are not only non-conventional, but eternal as well: it cannot be that they originate if their "standing-for" relationship to meaning is "original." When they are uttered, they merely "manifest" in articulated sounds, but do not originate. Their being eternal was why the Vṛttikāra argued that the last phoneme, along with the impressions of the preceding phonemes, was the meaning-evoking sound: composite objects are liable to decomposition, which prima facie speaks against their eternity. A fix to this problem is to take the irreducible phonemes as permanent, not liable to decomposition, and then posit constant and uniform series in which these phonemes participate.

And, how could Bādarāyaṇa and the Vṛttikāra claim that language is not conventional in light of the existence of various languages? What would they say about "cow," "vache," and "krava?" They would likely have some difficulties with the French and the Serbian, but not so much with the English. Śabara, in fact, had anticipated a variation of this problem. There were in his time speakers of Middle Indic languages who did not say *gauḥ* for "cow" but *gāvī*. Their intention, claimed Śabara, was to say *gauḥ*, not *gāvī*, and one who knows the proper form of the word would understand from *gāvī* that they just did not have the requisite ability to say the correct word.[53] As a Balkan joke from the nineties had it, they were like Macedonians who are, in fact, speakers of Serbian, with a severe speech impairment (and the other way around). And "cow," mind you, is phonetically closer to *gauḥ* than *gāvī* is.

The most important consequence of the doctrine was that the Vedas did not report on *historical* events—that would have made them testimonial in kind—but presented *paradigmatic* events and norms of behavior that humans should emulate. Related to this was the consequence that the characters in the Vedic corpus, the various gods and sages, were not individuals in historical time: they too were paradigmatic. So, when the Veda says that "one should sacrifice a goat for Soma and Agni," all the words stand for general terms which could potentially be instantiated by any individual that could be subsumed under them, in an actual ritual in historical time as an actualization of the textual ideality. And, when the Veda narrates stories, such as Yājñavalkya discoursing with Gārgī Vācaknavī and Vidagdha Śākalya, neither could the stories be historical nor the characters properly individual.

There were many more points to clarify and objections to answer, and Buddhists kept piling even more. Mīmāṁsakas in reply developed important epistemological arguments and theories. They also drew further radical consequences, such that the world today is as it has always been, that there is no omniscient creator of the world, that the Vedas today are recited just as they were recited from the (non)-beginning of time, that the sages—including, alas, Yājñavalkya and Śākalya of head-shattering fame—are not real, that the gods do not come to the rituals in their honor, and that the validity of the Veda was restricted to presenting paradigmatic obligations to paradigmatic agents and did not include supersensible reals of the Brahman kind. Vedāntins parted their ways with the Mīmāṁsakas on all of these counts, but we will pick up this thread in the next chapter because it penetrates deeply into the *Brahma-sūtra* ontology and cosmology. As far as Bādarāyaṇa's *sūtra* and the Vṛttikāra's comment, however, Mīmāṁsakas and Vedāntins were in agreement, and the Vṛttikāra's comment was more amenable to Vedānta than Mīmāṁsā ontology.

This brings me to the final point I wish to make in this chapter. We saw in the Introduction that scholars have pondered over the relationship of the two Mīmāṁsās and their respective canonical texts: In which sense is the Pūrva-Mīmāṁsā prior to the Uttara-Mīmāṁsā, and the *Mīmāṁsā-sūtra* to the *Brahma-sūtra*? Historical considerations aside, there are several *ideological* commitments that provide for a continuum. Let me begin with the remarks of Śaṅkara's student Padmapāda.[54] The commentators on the *Brahma-sūtra* spill a lot of ink on the meaning of the first word of *sūtra* 1.1.1: "Next, therefore, the inquiry into Brahman," *athāto brahma-jijñāsā*. The word is *atha*, which can also be translated as "now." When is "now," and what does "next" follow after? Advaitins have been the most radical interpreters of this word, claiming that the inquiry into Brahman does not presuppose nor require prior acquaintance with the *Mīmāṁsā-sūtra*, as most other commentators claim: knowing the *Mīmāṁsā-sūtra* is not the meaning of "next," and the "one thousand rules of interpretation" of Mīmāṁsā are immaterial for knowing Brahman. Except, comes in Padmapāda, the inquiry into Brahman *does* depend on *two* of these rules.

First, the inquiry into Brahman depends on the candidate knowing the Vedas, in their full extent, because the Upaniṣads are learned as part of the wider Vedic corpus after one had become initiated as a Vedic student. The rule that an eight-year-old boy should approach a teacher for investiture with the sacred thread, which, Advaitins think, is referenced by the first *sūtra* of the *Mīmāṁsā-sūtra*, is operative in the inquiry into Brahman as well, because the Upaniṣads are the means of knowing Brahman. In other words, knowledge of ritual and of Brahman is equally available *just* to members of the three higher classes of idealized Vedic society: Brahmins, royalty (*kṣatriya*s), and rich landlords and merchants (*vaiśya*s).

The Vedic student invested with the sacred thread, however, learns the Vedas by reciting and memorizing them first, in a manner, our philosophers argue, that is identical with natural language acquisition. The meaning of the Vedas gradually becomes manifest *to* him, without anyone establishing the word-meaning relationship *for* him. The Mīmāṁsaka Kumārila (ca. 600–650 CE), whom Padmapāda follows, says that the student who recites the Vedas gradually recognizes individual words, then their individual meanings, and then the meaning of larger language units.[55] Vedic recitation, in fact, is another meaning of that all-important term *upadeśa*. The *autpattika-sūtra*, then, is the second Mīmāṁsā rule which is operative in the inquiry into Brahman just as it is operative in the inquiry into *dharma*.

But, Padmapāda did not mean that the *Brahma-sūtra as a book* was independent from the *Mīmāṁsā-sūtra*. Advaitins have divided the scope of the *Brahma-sūtra* into higher and lower knowledge, or knowledge proper and meditation, and many of the "one thousand rules of interpretation" of Mīmāṁsā were absolutely required for the various meditations on Brahman which were formed on the blueprint of ritual. Many meditations, further, combined with various rituals. Bhāskara, therefore, charged against Advaitins that if "next" did not mean "after the study of the *Mīmāṁsā-sūtra*," Advaitins would not even be able to figure out which Upaniṣadic texts combine with rituals, and which are "just about" Brahman.[56] For all their arguments against Mīmāṁsā and in favor of there being no need to study the *Mīmāṁsā-sūtra*, the most prominent Advaitins such as Śaṅkara, Sureśvara, Padmapāda, and Sarvajñātman were all superb Mīmāṁsakas.

To conclude, then, the *Brahma-sūtra* just as the *Mīmāṁsā-sūtra* presupposes immersion in a world of *plentitude of scriptural data* from which the theologian constructs his experience through the application of canons of interpretation. This scriptural data is what perception is to ordinary men and to philosophers, "it occupies the same rank as the senses and should not be much doubted, being more trustworthy than mother and father," as Śabara said. It is the commitment to such an understanding of scripture as the sole reliable warrant for all things supersensible, to scriptural data as one's source, and to the canons of the theological mode of discourse that are elaborated in the *Mīmāṁsā-sūtra* and assumed in the *Brahma-sūtra* that makes the second hardly intelligible without, and posterior to, the first. We will take this as a given and pursue further links in Chapters 6 and 7.

Study Questions

1. Why is it that philosophy and theology have a shared sphere of study?
2. In what circumstances are theological arguments acceptable?
3. Is the claim "Brahman is known only from the Upaniṣads" in the domain of theological or philosophical reasoning, or both? In either case, why?
4. Why did Mīmāṁsakas and Vedāntins think that knowledge from scripture is perceptual in kind? Do you find their argument convincing? Argue either way.
5. What did Mīmāṁsakas mean by saying that the "word-meaning" relationship is "non-personal"? How might one challenge their central argument, that the act of naming presupposes the use of language?
6. What is, for the Mīmāṁsakas, the problem with "authorial intention," *vivakṣā*? In this regard, think about the issue of personal agency more broadly in contexts such as the judicial system: Is it desirable for some processes to be "non-personal," free from human contingency? Is something like that reasonable or achievable?

Suggestions for Further Study

Clooney (2003) provides a justification for "Hindu Theology" as a mode of discourse in Hindu studies. Dasti (2013) is an excellent overview of forms of theism in Indian philosophy, and a contextualization of Nyāya-Vaiśeṣika as "rational" theology and of Vedānta as "revealed theology." Edelmann (2013) is a plea for conceptual distinction between philosophy and theology in the Hindu traditions. Okita (2014b) considers the challenges faced those who want to *do* theology within contemporary Hinduism. Pollock (1997) is the first study to recognize clearly the association of *śruti* and *smṛti* with perception and inference. Holdrege (1994) tackles the issue of formation of the Vedic canon under the notion of *śruti*. Brick (2006) is a very useful account of the early history of *smṛti*. McCrea (2000) is an eminently readable account of the presuppositions of Mīmāṁsā philosophy of language. Taber (1992) and Arnold (2005: 57–114) are both excellent readings on the Mīmāṁsā ideas about the epistemic validity of the Vedas.

3

Ontology and the Problems of Causality

"Now, therefore, an inquiry into Brahman," opens the *Brahma-sūtra*, and goes on to define Brahman in 1.1.2 as that thing "from which proceed birth etc. of this."[1] The "this" in the *sūtra* is the world as we know it, and it is customary for the Upaniṣads to use the proximate pronoun to refer to what we would call "the here" as opposed to the "hereafter." "Birth etc." has almost uniformly been interpreted as the triplet of creation, sustenance, and dissolution of the world. Indeed, the topical passage in which this *sūtra* takes its bearings is the *Taittirīya* 3.1.1:

> That from which these beings are born; on which, once born, they live; and into which they return upon death—strive to know that distinctly! It is Brahman.

The *Bhāgavata Purāṇa* (1.1.1) will repeat this definition and add an important descriptor of the thing defined: it is *satyaṁ param*, "highest Being," or what we call in ontology following Aristotle the "first principle" or "first cause," the ultimate origin and nature of reality.

The history of the idea of Brahman, however, is not as straightforward as it might appear at first blush. In the early Vedic corpus, *bráhman* (with the acute accent on the first syllable) was exclusively associated with a hymn that an inspired poet would fashion, or with a charm or a sacrificial formula that a priest would use in ritual, through which the gods would be strengthened or otherwise help would be derived for achieving a purpose, such as getting rid of one's enemies, of evil spirits, or of danger in general. *Bráhman* was, further, commonly and explicitly identified with speech (*vāc*), as a consequence of which the poet or priest who utters such speech was called *brahmán* (with the acute accent on the last syllable) through association. Brahman, then, involved a complex of related ideas focused on inspired speech with creative power and the prerogative of men who utter it.[2]

The early scholarship on Brahman recognized this complex and focused on what *bráhman* meant in the various early Vedic texts and how it developed to stand for the great ground of Being and origin of everything:

the investigation of Brahman the origin commonly proceeded through searching after the origin of Brahman, and through negotiating the space between *bráhman* the holy speech and Brahman the universal principle. In many cases, the arena of such polemics was comparative Indo-European linguistics. Without going into the details, we may point out two views that were at the extreme not only conceptually but methodologically as well. Paul Thieme claimed that the original import of *bráhman* was a "formulation" that was created specifically for ritual use. In other words, *bráhman* was a poetic creation. By implication, *brahmán* was a "formulator" in the sense of Brahman that creates.[3] Jan Gonda, on the other hand, was much more willing to side with the native tradition that always interpreted Brahman as the power that makes things grow: "To my mind, brahman is a more or less definite power . . . which often, and especially in the more ancient texts, manifests itself as word, as ritual . . . sacred or magical word."[4]

As hinted earlier, the native tradition had consistently related Brahman to a principle that is itself great and makes other things grow, and its etymology was associated with the verbal root √*bṛṁh*. This etymology is found, for instance, in the *Viṣṇu Purāṇa*: "It is called Brahman because it is great and because it makes things grow."[5] Likewise Śaṅkara: "It is Brahman because it is the greatest."[6]

The association of Brahman with speech as a creative principle, however, was not at all lost on the native tradition, and Brahman is occasionally identified with the Vedas, with the performance of ritual, and through that with growth. In such contexts, it is explicitly called *śabda-brahma* or the verbal Brahman. One such case is in the third chapter of the *Bhagavad-gītā*, which delineates a primordial social contract between the gods and the humans, forged by the highest Vedic divinity Prajāpati, in which men are obliged to offer sacrifices for the gods and the gods to reward men by pouring rain. Verses 14 and 15 say that beings grow from grain, grain grows from rain, rain is produced through sacrifice, sacrifice is rooted in action, and action is rooted in "Brahman." Brahman itself is rooted in the "imperishable," *akṣara*. Śaṅkara and most other commentators identify "Brahman" with the Veda, and the "imperishable," with Brahman itself.[7] The speech that is Brahman, thus, makes things grow though laying out ritual performances that cause rain, and through that food, but is itself grounded in Brahman the first principle.

In the philosophy of the grammarians and of the Vedāntin Maṇḍana Miśra, further, Brahman the first principle itself was speech in nature. Bhartṛhari's *Vākyapadīya* famously opens with the statement that Brahman which has no origin and death but is itself the origin of the world is *substantively* verbal (*śabda-tattvam*), whereas external things are its apparent transformations.

This *śabda-brahma* as the first principle is, further, commonly identified with the Vedic *praṇava*, the holy sound Oṁ, which too like Brahman is called the "imperishable," or more precisely—the syllable, *akṣara*.[8]

In this chapter, then, I will reconstruct the ontology of the *Brahma-sūtra* revolving around the notion of Brahman the first principle, with a special nod to the creative role of speech or language. We will begin by exploring Bādarāyaṇa's ideas about Brahman *in itself*, that is, the characteristics of Brahman that are not relative to creation even if indefinable without reference to it. Cosmology or the manner in which Brahman creates the minutiae of the world will keep us busy next, before we delve into Bādarāyaṇa's theory of causality and its distinctions from competing systems, primarily that of Sāṅkhya. Along the way we will introduce the other two ontological principles of the *Brahma-sūtra*, matter and the individual souls, not avoiding the question of Brahman's relationship with them, specifically in light of Bādarāyaṇa's doctrine that Brahman is both the material and the efficient cause of the world, and—in some sense—the only existent thing.

The Being That Is Brahman: Positive and Negative Theology

Although much of Bādarāyaṇa's efforts in the *Brahma-sūtra* are spent on proving that the Upaniṣads in their entirety are about Brahman, not all Upaniṣadic passages are made equal and only some of them describe Brahman's essential nature. Most important among them is the opening of the second chapter of the *Taittirīya*:

> Brahman is Being (*satya*) and consciousness (*jñāna*), infinite (*ananta*). He who knows it hidden in the heart, in the highest heaven, attains all desires together with the wise Brahman.[9]

This is the origin of the popular characterization of Brahman as *sac-cid-ānanda*. The *Taittirīya* verse explicitly says that Brahman is absolute Being and consciousness, and the part about attaining all desires with that Brahman has been clearly associated with bliss (*ānanda*). In fact, bliss looms large in the entire *Taittirīya* chapter. Toward its end, there is an interesting approximative simile about this bliss of Brahman, arranged by what pleasure various classes of beings, from humans to Prajāpati, enjoy. Ten classes are listed, and the bliss of each subsequent is one hundred times greater than the bliss of the preceding group. Finally, the bliss of Brahman is a hundred times greater than the bliss of Prajāpati, but even that is a mere indication, for the passage is followed by another Upaniṣadic verse of high celebrity:

> Words with the mind turn back from there even before they arrive: it is the bliss of Brahman. He who knows it is not afraid of anything.[10]

The entire *Brahma-sūtra* is predicated on this definition of Brahman. As I have showed in the previous chapter, Bādarāyaṇa's first hands-on arguments are that prime matter and the individual soul cannot be the reference of "Brahman" because the definition of Being, consciousness, bliss is not fully applicable to them.

An important *adhikaraṇa* where Bādarāyaṇa presents these as the essential characteristics of Brahman is 3.3.11–17.[11] Why they should be "essential" is eloquently stated by Rāmānuja.[12] An essential characteristic is one that is directly related to the apprehension of the object, explicative of its nature, and as such equivalent to it. In practice this means that other positive characteristics of Brahman in the Upaniṣads, for instance that he is of the size of the thumb or is the abode of heaven and earth, can be reduced to a function of his, such as residence, or a primary characteristic of his, such as Being, but these *Taittirīya* characteristics are constitutive of Brahman's nature.

That Brahman is Being means that Brahman is the cause of everything. That this Being should be a conscious principle is clearly what Bādarāyaṇa argues in 1.1.5–12. Brahman's being limitless may be read as a qualifier to the three other characteristics, as indeed the *Taittirīya* account of bliss might suggest, but Śaṅkara and Bhāskara on *Brahma-sūtra* 3.1.11 associate "limitless" with characteristics that are common descriptors of Brahman in Vedānta and belong to what we may call "the omni-" kind: that is, omniscience, omnipresence, omnipotence, and so on. We will return to these, in light of the essential characteristics, later in the chapter.

A second complex of Upaniṣadic texts, about the so-called *akṣara*, "the imperishable," is of central importance for the *Brahma-sūtra* notion of Brahman. The most significant of these is Yājñavalkya's dialogue with Gārgī Vācaknavī in *Bṛhad-āraṇyaka* 3.8. There, Gārgī challenges Yājñavalkya to tell her about that on which all things above the sky, below the earth, and in between are woven warp and woof. Yājñavalkya says that it is the imperishable, *akṣara*, and proceeds to describe it in thoroughly negative terms:

> That, Gārgī, is the Imperishable, and Brahmins refer to it like this—it is neither coarse nor fine; it is neither short nor long; it has neither blood

> nor fat; it is without shadow or darkness; it is without air or space; it is without contact; it has no taste or smell; it is without sight or hearing; it is without speech or mind; it is without energy, breath, or mouth; it is beyond measure; it has nothing within it or outside of it; it does not eat anything; and no one eats it.[13]

The second important locus is the *Muṇḍaka* 1.1.5–7, where this imperishable is presented as the object of "higher knowledge," which in the context must be something other than scriptural learning and likely denotes Upaniṣadic meditation. Here too the imperishable is portrayed in thoroughly negative terms, as what cannot be seen or grasped and is generally devoid of characteristics. Crucially, however, the *Muṇḍaka* explicitly describes the imperishable as the origin from which beings are born, and that fits perfectly Bādarāyaṇa's notion of Brahman:

> As a spider spins out threads, then draws them into itself; As plants sprout out from the earth; As head and body hair grows from a living man; So from the Imperishable all things here spring.[14]

The identification of Brahman with the imperishable, then, is commonplace to the Upaniṣadic worldview, and the *Bhagavad-gītā* (8.3) makes their identity explicit: "The imperishable is the highest Brahman," *akṣaraṁ brahma paramam.*

In Bādarāyaṇa's system, the negative characteristics of the imperishable are innate to Brahman. This comes out clearly from *Brahma-sūtra* 3.3.33, which we may paraphrase as follows: notions of the imperishable should be included in all meditations on Brahman, "because of generality" and "because of its being that."[15] We will worry about meditations on Brahman and the "generality" stated of the *sūtra* in Chapter 6, but what does Bādarāyaṇa mean by "because of its being that," *tad-bhāva*? Surely that the imperishable just *is* Brahman. Yet, his wording immediately points us to a prior passage in the first chapter, where Bādarāyaṇa's objective was to clarify all the Upaniṣadic texts that are about Brahman. There he says that the imperishable is Brahman "because of excluding other beings," *anya-bhāva-vyāvṛteḥ.*[16] This clarifies the manner in which the imperishable is Brahman: its negative characteristics specify Brahman's nature such that it is clearly distinct from other ontological entities.

Rāmānuja's is a particularly insightful comment on *Brahma-sūtra* 3.3.33.[17] To know a thing is to know it in its unique nature. The positive characteristics of Brahman are *shared* characteristics. Prime matter is Being, and the individual souls are sentient principles. Brahman's being bliss is also shared with the individual souls—although that does not become apparent in the *Brahma-sūtra* until its fourth chapter and Chapter 7 of this book, and is truly manifest only in their liberated state—but what is not shared is that the soul is liable to, as Rāmānuja puts it, "connection with what should be rejected." "What should be rejected" are the characteristics the absence of which texts about the imperishable predicate of Brahman. Put differently, Brahman's Being, sentience, and bliss are incorruptible, and that is what distinguishes Brahman from prime matter and the souls.

I have named this heading "Positive and Negative Theology," and the reader will have recognized in this a nod to modes of theology, also called *kataphatic* or affirmative and *apophatic* or negatory, shared in the Abrahamic religious traditions. I want to conclude with a note that in doing so I have not imposed a foreign nomenclature over the *Brahma-sūtra* worldview. "Affirmation" (*vidhi*) and "negation" (*niṣedha, pratiṣedha*) are terms of art in the *Brahma-sūtra* commentaries, and the two represent common ways of doing not only theology but all kinds of reasoning, philosophical or otherwise, in the intellectual universe of South Asia.[18]

World Creation

How does, then, this Being that is Brahman create the world? Several Upaniṣadic passages again inform Bādarāyaṇa's reasoning, and lurking in the background is the old idea of Brahman as creative speech, growing now into the first discord with Mīmāṁsā.

The sixth chapter of the *Chāndogya* is where Bādarāyaṇa begins.[19] There Brahman, called Being (*sat*), is said to create in the beginning "three divinities" which are evidently secondary creative principles. They are heat, water, and food. This *Chāndogya* account is modified based on the second chapter of the *Taittirīya*. There, after stating the full definition of Brahman, the Upaniṣad says that from this Brahman, which is the Self, space originates; from space, air; from air, fire; from fire, water; and from water, earth.[20] These are the five great material elements common in Indian philosophy, particularly in the tradition of Sāṅkhya.

Several points are important for Bādarāyaṇa to make with respect to this account of creation of the five elements. First, some traditions such as Nyāya-Vaiśeṣika do not include space among the elements, and the commentators rehearse their reasons, the most important of which is that space *accommodates* origination—things originate *in* space—such that it makes no sense for space itself to originate. Bādarāyaṇa rejects their arguments on theological grounds, which we need not rehearse.[21] It is important, though, to mention that elsewhere he identifies Brahman itself with space, different from the "elemental space" that is originated.[22] The consequences of this are twofold. Brahman itself is the "location of origination," and insofar as such is the case, Brahman itself *is* space. The originated space, then, should be taken in the restricted sense of being the medium for the propagation of sound.

This brings us to the next point. In the cosmology of Sāṅkhya, the five elements are gross manifestations of corresponding subtle or fine elements that are simultaneously sense objects, *tan-mātra*s or *viṣaya*s. Thus, space is a gross form of sound, air of touch, fire of form, water of taste, and earth of smell. They are gross forms because they are directly evolved from the fine elements.[23] Bādarāyaṇa, however, does not have a separate rubric for such fine elements—they do not appear in his tally of primary items of creation—and he certainly does not think in terms of the five elements being a solidification of prior, separate principles. Bhāskara interprets one *sūtra* to this effect. Scripture does not delineate the origin of qualities in general, and those that appear as sense objects in particular, such as sound and touch, because they are not different from their substance and do not originate separately.[24] While it is uncertain if Bhāskara's interpretation of the *sūtra* is right—he stands alone in his reading—he is certainly not wrong in bringing out what may be an implicit assumption for Bādarāyaṇa: the qualities of things form a continuum with their elements and with substances more generally; they are *continuous* with rather than *prior* to them.

The remaining items of what may be termed Brahman's primary creation are the faculties, generally called *indriya*s in Indian philosophy but known as *prāṇa*s in the Upaniṣads.[25] These include five cognitive faculties—of hearing, touch, vision, taste, and smell; five active faculties—of speech, action (associated with the hands), motion (associated with the feet), evacuation, and procreation; the mind, *manas,* which is the seat of all kinds of specific mental functions and inner states;[26] and life-breath in all its modes involving respiration and other metabolic functions, called *mukhya-prāṇa* and *śreṣṭha*, "the chief," by Bādarāyaṇa.[27] These are not quite "elements" as the initial five: Bādarāyaṇa describes them as *aṇu*, which means they are infinitesimal or intangible, too fine to have a perceptible form.[28]

A third text informs this final intervention in which the faculties are said to originate alongside the five elements. It is *Muṇḍaka* 2.1.3 where the full tally is stated:

> From this are produced life-breath, the mind, all the faculties, space, air, fire, water and earth the support of all.

Rāmānuja aptly calls this "the creation of aggregates," *samaṣṭi-sṛṣṭi*.[29]

Conspicuously absent in this list of primary creations are the two most prominent Sāṅkhya principles. One is the so-called *mahat* or *buddhi*, which is the first transformation of Sāṅkhya's prime matter as sort of "cognitive stuff" that accommodates transitive consciousness—awareness of objects—of which the Sāṅkhyan soul is incapable. While Bādarāyaṇa elsewhere uses the term "*vijñāna*," which is commonly synonymous with *buddhi* in Advaita Vedānta, the sense is that of totality of the five cognitive faculties that pair up with the mind as the sixth, and there just isn't a separate category in his system for *buddhi*.[30] The absence has significance for *Brahma-sūtra*'s psychology, which we will discuss later in the chapter. Likewise absent is the first product of *mahat*, the so-called ego or *ahaṅkāra*, from which all the remaining elements of Sāṅkhya are produced.[31] This too has consequences for Bādarāyaṇa's soteriology, which we will tackle in due course.

Bādarāyaṇa calls the subsequent creation of individual beings "triplication," following the *Chāndogya*, although with the updated account it should properly be called "quintuplication," as noted by Śrīnivāsa.[32] Whatever the term, we may disregard the Upaniṣadic nuances and understand "triplication" simply to mean the creation of individuals through combination of the five elements.

To describe this process, I want to draw your attention back to Chapter 2 and the doctrine of the eternity of the Vedas and the non-personal relationship between words and their meaning. Mīmāṁsakas drew out as a consequence of this doctrine that the world itself was never created—otherwise someone would have assigned meanings to words at the time of creation or sometime thereafter—and that personal names in the Vedas could not signify beings in historical time. As a consequence of the second, some Mīmāṁsakas even argued that the Vedic gods were only nominal recipients of ritual offerings rather than real beings who come to sacrifices when they are invited.[33] Bādarāyaṇa as the theologian of creation rejected this consequence by relying on the long-standing association of Brahman with speech that we opened the chapter with. To paraphrase his short *sūtra:*

> If it be said that a contradiction would follow with respect to the Vedic word, that is, that gods are beings in historical time, then we say no, because they *originate from the word.* The proof of this are perception and inference.[34]

As we have seen, "perception and inference" for Bādarāyaṇa are statements from the Vedas and from *smṛti*.

What does he mean by this? The sixth chapter of the *Chāndogya* goes on to say that Brahman upon the creation of the three elements entered into them with the "living soul" (*jīvenātmanā*, 6.3.2) so as to "diversify" what is called "name-and-form," *nāma-rūpe*, a term used by Bādarāyaṇa himself along with its synonym *sañjñā-mūrtī*.[35] This specific living soul here is the so-called Hiraṇyagarbha, "the golden embryo," identified with Prajāpati the highest Vedic divinity. In later Hinduism he is the four-headed Brahmā the creator god, but in Bādarāyaṇa's context he is called "Brahman the effect," *kārya-brahma*, as opposed to Brahman the cause.[36] The commentators call him "the collective individual," that is, the soul ensouling the world as a whole, which world on its part is represented as a macrocosmic person and typically called *virāj*.[37] By means of this Hiraṇyagarbha, Brahman diversifies name-and-form, the details of which process are derived from the *smṛti* literature. The crucial point is that Hiraṇyagarbha creates all beings in the world by understanding or recollecting the original, Vedic names of things, and fashioning everything in the image of their meaning out of the elements of creation.

The crucial term in this account is *nāma-rūpe*, "name-and-form," and it is Bhāskara who gives its clearest gloss, though the other commentators share his idea: "name-and-form" are the words, *nāman*, of the Vedas, and the universals denoted by them, called *ākṛti* by Bhāskara, Śaṅkara, and Śrīnivāsa, and *ākāra* by Rāmānuja.[38] Both terms are, in fact, synonyms with *rūpa*, form, but have been used as terms of art for universals or generic properties that are denoted by words. Especially *ākṛti* eventually came to mean genus or *jāti*—the *-ness* of a thing such as cow-ness, to keep with the example from the previous chapter—although obviously the original idea must have been that things form a class in virtue of their common shape. We should understand *nāma-rūpe*, then, as a continuum of words and shapes that are constitutive of the essential nature of a thing.

In this light, then, one can say that there is a seed form of the Vedas that is equivalent to the creative Brahman. Indeed, some of the *smṛti* references, reminiscent of Bhartṛhari's verse from the beginning of the chapter, talk about the divine Vedic word without a beginning or end, from which all things proceed.[39] This seed form of the Vedas is the repository of all words that are simultaneously universals and the blueprint of all created things, but it also contains the Vedas as texts in their potential form. When Brahman as Hiraṇyagarbha creates the beings of the world, he diversifies this name-and-form; or, we could say that he "triplicates" or "quintuplicates" the elements of creation to produce the minutiae of the world in the image of the Vedic words and the universals that they denote.

We will tackle the issue of the relationship between these universals and their individual instantiations later in the chapter. Hiraṇyagarbha's creation pertains to classes of beings—gods, humans, animals, rivers, mountains, and so on—but for the sake of Bādarāyaṇa's immediate argument, the "things" created from "the word" are the sages who intuit the Vedic hymns from the same repository of "name-and-form" and begin their transmission, as well as the Vedic gods, both of which seem to bear *personal names*. Bādarāyaṇa's argument, then, is that they become beings in history as embodiments of non-temporal blueprints. Further, their names are "offices" (*ādhikārika*) rather than personal appellations.[40] The principal Vedic divinities are the superintendents of the various faculties, *prāṇa*s, which we described earlier: in the macrocosmic person, *virāj*, they represent Hiraṇyagarbha's own faculties, and in the microcosmic individual, they govern their operation.[41] The point, however, is that as superintendents they are functionaries. They can be replaced—and as we shall see in the next chapter, there is a point when they are *all* replaced—such that, at the end of the day, there are no personal names in the Vedas, only classes.[42]

Efficient Causality and the Function of Residence

Bādarāyaṇa's final intervention concerning the five elements is about their successive origination from one another. Such origination is not a naturalistic, unguided, or spontaneous process. It is a result of Brahman's intention or will, reaffirmed at every stage of creation. This picks out Upaniṣadic passages such as the opening of the sixth chapter of the *Chāndogya*, where Being reflects, "How about I become many, propagate myself." Heat and water in their turn have the same reflection, so one may be provoked to read this somewhat deistically, as a creation of God the first principle who starts things off but then lets them take their own course, remaining—as Rāmānuja's prima facie opponent says—the efficient cause *remotely*.[43] Bādarāyaṇa argues instead that Brahman's will remains the efficient cause throughout creation. That is, when Brahman creates things, he always enters into them to guide their functioning, and so when heat and water are said to reflect, the reflection is properly Brahman's.[44]

Bādarāyaṇa likewise emphasizes that the function of diversifying name-and-form belongs not to Hiraṇyagarbha but to Brahman personally; or, as he puts it, it belongs to the agent of triplication, the one who reflects in the *Chāndogya* statement "let me triplicate each of them."[45] This is a continuation of the same argument about Brahman's being the efficient cause throughout creation, predicated on the function of residence. We may, then, vocalize one of the critical arguments of the *Brahma-sūtra*: Brahman is the efficient cause of creation, *nimitta-kāraṇa*. The lexeme "efficient cause" in philosophy comes from Aristotle's theory of causality, where it stands for that cause by which change is produced in a substance, for instance the artisan who casts bronze into a statue, or, in the Indian context, the potter who shapes clay into a pot. That Brahman is the efficient cause of the world means that Brahman guides creation, and the functioning of the world generally, from beginning to end, by entering each created principle and effecting the origination of the next product.

The notion of Brahman's residence in the things of the world informs every bit of Bādarāyaṇa's system,[46] and it is ultimately drawn from another important Upaniṣadic text, the *antaryāmi-brāhmaṇa* of the *Bṛhad-āraṇyaka* (3.7), where Uddālaka Āruṇi queries Yājñavalkya about the inner controller of the world. Yājñavalkya replies that it is the Self, *ātman*, the inner ruler who controls all things from within unbeknown to them. "All things" here includes three levels of creation: first, what Yājñavalkya calls *adhidaiva*, "pertaining to the divine sphere," that is, the elements of creation and phenomena such as the sun and moon, the quarters, and so on, which in the *Brahma-sūtra* system represent the macrocosmic faculties; second, *adhibhūta*, "pertaining to beings," and arguably referring to the *classes of things*; and third, *adhyātma*, "pertaining to oneself" and referring to the faculties on the level of an individual. Yājñavalkya concludes his teaching with a bang:

> He sees, but he can't be seen; he hears, but he can't be heard; he thinks, but he can't be thought of; he perceives, but he can't be perceived. Besides him, there is no one who sees, no one who hears, no one who thinks, and no one who perceives. It is this self of yours who is the inner controller, the immortal. All besides this is grief.[47]

Brahman is the efficient cause because it is the conscious principle.

The function of Brahman's residence is significant not only for efficient causality but also for the attaining of the highest good, and there is more to the story of Brahman's being "*the* Self." To piggyback on the *Chāndogya* again, Brahman was there said to have entered the three divinities, the elements, "with the living soul," *jīvātman*. In fact, as Bādarāyaṇa notes, the Upaniṣads talk about *two* Selves or souls which have entered "the cave," a common trope for the heart where the Self is said to reside, and there are also verses which talk about these two Selves as two friendly birds residing on the same tree.[48] The tree is the body, and while one of the birds is engrossed in enjoying its fruits, a trope for karma on which we will focus in Chapter 5, the second merely observes.[49] I will call the "living soul" the "individual soul" to distinguish it from Brahman. So, the first entry with the living soul is recreated with respect to every being.

In addition to the explicit statement about the two Selves, Bādarāyaṇa presupposes the same throughout his work, and in *sūtra* upon *sūtra*, he affirms that the two Selves are different. Their difference is mentioned, for instance, in his comment on the *Muṇḍaka* section where the "two friendly birds" verses appear,[50] but most importantly in the aforementioned comment on the *antaryāmi-brāhmaṇa*, where he argues that the inner ruler is *not* the individual soul, "for in both it is taught as different."[51] "Both" here refers to two lines of transmission of the *Bṛhad-āraṇyaka*, the so-called "Kāṇva" which is the more common and generally considered *the Bṛhad-āraṇyaka*, and the so-called Mādhyandina in which the *Bṛhad-āraṇyaka* is the concluding part of the *Śatapatha Brāhmaṇa*. The reading in the second is particularly important, as it explicitly says that the inner ruler resides "in the Self," *ātmani*, unbeknown to it, replacing the more ambiguous *vijñāna* of the Kāṇva, a term that not only becomes a common appellation for the individual soul in Vedānta but also refers to its cognitive faculties. The upshot of this is that Brahman as the inner Self resides not only in all products of creation, but in the individual soul as well, the one which enters with it in the elements and the "cave," and occupies the same "tree."

That Brahman is the Self of the self by residing in the self is Bādarāyaṇa's most important soteriological doctrine, and we will plumb its depths in chapters Six and Seven. We introduce the individual soul properly later in this chapter.

Material Causality

Brahman, however, is not only the efficient cause of the world; it is its "material cause" as well. By material cause, the stuff of which something is made is intended, the bronze that the artisan casts into a statue, or the clay that the potter shapes into a pot. The term of art for this in Indian philosophy is *upādāna-kāraṇa*, that cause which is "appropriated" or "seized" by an agent, but Bādarāyaṇa uses instead *prakṛti*, which translates to an "original" of which "derivatives" or *vikṛti* are made. "*Prakṛti*" specifically is the term used in Sāṅkhya, both in the epic literature and in the *Sāṅkhya-kārikā* where it is called *mūla-prakṛti* or "prime matter"; it is also used by the grammarian Pāṇini to label that syntactic relation to the verb which denotes both the point of origin or birth of something and the stuff of which a thing is made. To illustrate with two common examples from Pāṇini's commentators: "An arrow is born—comes into being—from horn; a scorpion is born from cow-dung."[52] We should note that these are not comparable examples, though, and do not involve the same model of causality: although both are predicated on some continuity of the cause and its effect, in the first we can envision a necessary external efficient cause of the turning of the horn into an arrow, whereas in the second no such external cause is apparent. The two examples, in fact, illustrate the line of demarcation between two variants of a shared frame of causality, those of Sāṅkhya and Vedānta, as we will see shortly.

Bādarāyaṇa's argument that Brahman is the material cause is theological, derived from the same all-important chapter six of the *Chāndogya* buttressed by the *Taittirīya* and the *Muṇḍaka*.[53] The sixth chapter of the *Chāndogya* opens with a thesis about knowing that one thing by means of which everything else would be known, and an illustration is provided: by knowing a lump of clay one could know all things made of clay, the specific variations being names that are based on speech. The chapter goes on to present Being, *sat*, as that thing from which everything else originates, so if Being is not the material cause then both the thesis and the illustration of the Upaniṣad would be defeated. Further, Being reflects at the beginning of creation, "How about I become many, procreate myself," thus also presenting itself as the material cause, but not necessarily in the clay-and-pot sense. Whereas the onus in the *Chāndogya* account is on reflection, in the *Taittirīya* it is on the reflectivity of creation: "It itself created itself."[54] Finally, in the *Muṇḍaka*, Brahman is directly called *yoni*, the "source" or "womb" where and whence things are born.[55]

Particularly significant of the five *sūtra*s where Bādarāyaṇa makes this argument is 1.4.26, in which a reference is made to the reflectivity of creation: "[Brahman is the material cause] because of self-creation, through transformation."[56] That is, Brahman is the material cause because it transforms itself into the world. We should note here that the commentators generally do not take Brahman to be the material cause *directly*, but through the medium of another ontological principle. That is, it would be more accurate to say not that Brahman *is* the material cause, but that Brahman is *that thing which is* the material cause.[57] In other words, Brahman is the totality of primary creation, which is the material cause, and is so by way of self-transformation into it.

Needless to say, there is significant disagreement as to which ontological model best expresses Brahman's being the material cause. A radical approach is that of Rāmānuja, in whose doctrine prime matter stands in relation to Brahman as a body to a soul, through means of which body Brahman changes itself without changing in essence. That is, Brahman is the material cause through *residence* in the material cause, which material cause transforms into the world as its product. It is difficult to see that Bādarāyaṇa would have meant something like this, since he adduces the principle of residence as an argument for the individual soul's being Brahman—which we will see later in the chapter—but not the material cause. In any case, such an interpretation seems to forgo entirely Bādarāyaṇa's claim that Brahman is the material cause because it transforms itself into it. Bhāskara, Nimbārka, and Śrīnivāsa seem to be closer to the mark in this case. They describe Brahman's transformation as a case of "projection of capacity" or "power," *śakti-vikṣepa*, which they elsewhere call the "capacity of being an object of experience," *bhogya-śakti*.[58] Whereas the world is a transformation of this capacity, the capacity itself is a projection or emanation of Brahman.

The idea of "capacity," *śakti*, then, becomes the predominant model of talking about this ontological principle, and it is a convenient model because *śakti* is definitionally something neither identical with nor independent from the thing to which it is related, an ontological no-man's-land. A commonplace *śakti* in Indian philosophy is the power of vision: vision is dependent on the eyes, yet not identical with them insofar as we predicate characteristics of it, for instance when we speak about good or poor vision. The positing of *śakti*, then, is meant to spare Brahman of some of the objections that follow from its being the material cause.

While it makes sense that Bādarāyaṇa would have thought of the material cause as a *śakti*—it is how the *Śvetāśvatara* describes—its ontological significance is not limited to its being something neither identical with nor distinct from Brahman.[59] If the material cause is a capacity in Brahman, it possesses other capacities that are *potentials* or *seeds* that become *actualities* or *sprouts* in the world, and Bādarāyaṇa never intends to break the causal continuum from Brahman, through the elements of creation, to the world. That is, Bādarāyaṇa's theory of causality is uniform throughout, and the potentials in the material cause are ultimately potentials in Brahman.

But, let us go through his philosophical reasons in support of the theological argument to get to the bottom of this. In their background is the model of causality known as *sat-kārya-vāda*, the doctrine of continuation of the cause in its effect, and its Sāṅkhya variety that Bādarāyaṇa rejects to promote his own iteration. The Sāṅkhya *sat-kārya-vāda* is succinctly stated in the *Sāṅkhya-kārikā:*

> The effect is existent in the cause for the following reasons: (1) that which is not already existent cannot be produced; (2) the material for the effect is selected; (3) it is impossible that anything may be produced from anything else; (4) someone competent can produce only what is possible; and (5) the effect is of the same nature as the cause.[60]

It is the first of these five reasons that anchors the doctrine, and the fifth that restricts it. For an effect to be produced from a material cause, it must already be present in it. The classical example in the *Sāṅkhya-kārikā* commentaries is the production of oil from sesame seeds rather than sand, the consequence of which is that oil as the effect is present in the first but absent in the second. The fifth reason requires that the effect must share the nature of the cause. Now, this certainly cannot mean that the effect must be identical with the cause in all its characteristics, for in that case the very notion of causality would be pointless. In fact, the *Sāṅkhya-kārikā* immediately launches an inventory of all the characteristics in virtue of which its ontological principles are identical or different. The point seems to be, rather, that certain characteristics are so definitional of a thing that its product could not possibly lack them. Thus, for instance, prime matter is insentient, productive, intersubjective, and extramental, whereas the individual sentient soul is none of that.[61] Therefore, Sāṅkhya wants the product to be not only present in its cause but also exhibit a continuity of certain definitional characteristics, while at the same time possessing a degree of ontological surplus.

The thesis that Brahman is the material cause in this light is problematic, and the gist of objections Bādarāyaṇa must tackle is well vocalized by Śaṅkara: "The world is seen to be a product, possessed of parts, insentient, and impure. Its cause must be of the same kind, because uniformity between the cause and its effect is a matter of observation."[62]

It is with the objection of uniformity that Bādarāyaṇa deals first: "Brahman cannot be the cause of the world, because the world has different characteristics."[63] His reply is pithy yet very clear: "But, it is seen."[64] That is, there are obvious cases of discontinuity of characteristics between the cause and the effect, an "ontological surplus" as I have called it. The commentators supply the example that we encountered at the opening of this heading—scorpions are born from cow-dung—that is meant to illustrate how a sentient being is born of insentient material. This is an unfortunate illustration for Vedāntins, however, as it leads directly to the doctrine of ancient Indian materialism that consciousness arises as an epiphenomenon of mixing of the four elements; defeats Bādarāyaṇa's own thesis that prime matter cannot be the first principle because it is insentient; and does not illustrate the reverse relation which is required in the context.[65] Their other examples are preferable—insentient nails, hair, and teeth originate from a sentient man; and the spider spins out its cobweb out of itself—and are derived from the time-honored Upaniṣadic background of *Muṇḍaka* 1.1.7 that we cited on Brahman as the "imperishable."

In the defense of the Vedāntic iteration of *sat-kārya-vāda* on the part of the commentators, it becomes clear that the disagreement with Sāṅkhya is about the *extent* to which there must be a continuity of definitional characteristics. "In all cases of causality, there is partial homogeneity and partial heterogeneity between the cause and the effect."[66] "A causal relationship between dissimilar things is also seen."[67] The fundamental characteristic that a thing must have is Being, and consciousness is not necessarily part of the causal continuum. The Vedāntic *sat-kārya-vāda*, then, is the original statement of this doctrine presented in the *Chāndogya*, from where arguably the name itself derives: all things that are products emerge from Being, *sat*, as their cause, and remain Being throughout.

Another objection helps us pinpoint exactly what kind of material cause Brahman is, and it seems to be coming from the Nyāya-Vaiśeṣika side.[68] Causality always involves a *causal complex*—an agent, stuff, instrument, and much more—whereas Vedāntins argue for Brahman as a *unique* cause. In reply, Bādarāyaṇa offers the illustration of milk as the kind of cause that Brahman is. Milk *itself* and *left to its own devices* transforms into curd; it does not require a causal complex. One may object to this that what makes milk turn into curd are proteins, but Bādarāyaṇa's point is that these would still be inherent to milk—milk *naturally* possesses them—and Brahman is precisely that kind of thing that is naturally possessed of "all," *sarva*.[69] This statement clearly references Upaniṣadic texts of what we may describe as the "all-" or "omni-" kind. Particularly prominent among these is Śāṇḍilya's teaching in the *Chāndogya*, opening with the statement "Brahman is surely all of this," *sarvaṁ khalv idam brahma*:

> This self (*ātman*) of mine that lies deep within my heart—it contains all actions, all desires, all smells, and all tastes; it has captured this whole world; it neither speaks nor pays any heed. It is *brahman*. On departing from here after death, I will become that.[70]

"All" in the *sūtra* is interpreted by the commentators as "all capacities," *śakti*, that we introduced earlier. Brahman inherently possesses all capacities to transform itself into the minutiae of the world. These capacities must be interpreted in the sense of undeveloped seeds that become manifest in creation.

This brings us to another term that has been used for the postulated intermediary ontological principle that constitutes Brahman's material causality, favored by Śaṅkara but used by Bhāskara as well. We have already encountered it, it is name-and-form, *nāma-rūpe*. Śaṅkara describes this intermediary principle as "the undeveloped, subtle state of things, consisting of the *capacities* of name-and-form," and he too says it is a "divine capacity," *daivī śakti*.[71] A capacity in Brahman that, further, has the capacities for everything. In this light, name-and-form is more than a term for blueprints that Hiraṇyagarbha intuits to make things in their likeness, like the demiurge in Plato's *Timaeus*. It is a descriptor for the totality not only of the principles of creation before they are emanated—the elements and *prāṇas*—but also of the *potential state of particular things* which consists of linguistic seeds that are fleshed out in creation. And let us not forget the Vedas too.

At this point, we should make the final note in the story of eternal words that we have been following since the previous chapter. If words denote universals rather than individual things, and universals are some sort of real entities, there appears the question of how such universals are instantiated in particular objects. To pick up on our example, if "cow" is an eternal word—in the Sanskrit language—and stands for universal "cowness," what is the ground of applying it to Milka the cow? The predominant Indian realist account—realism is the ontological worldview in which universals are real entities, rather than mental abstracts—is that of Nyāya-Vaiśeṣika, in which universals are omnipresent real properties that become localized in things by means of the relation of "inherence." When Milka is born, this inherence, which is sort of an ontological glue, localizes cowness in her, making Milka *a* cow. Now, Bādarāyaṇa rejects the category of inherence as ontologically unsound: since in the Nyāya-Vaiśeṣika classification of entities inherence is a real thing, it too would require further inherence by means of which it itself would be related to its relata—for instance, Milka and cowness—leading to infinite regress of further and further necessary inherences.[72] This rejection implies that in Bādarāyaṇa's system universals are *potentials,* linguistic and conceptual *seeds*—name-and-form the stuff of the world—that become fleshed out in the process of triplication, a DNA as it were that *innately* contains all the capacity required for the thing to be what it is.

Here, then, we fully cross the ontological bridge from the opening of the chapter, between Brahman as the first principle and Brahman as creative speech. If this interpretation is right, the ontological surplus of the effect with respect to the cause must be taken in the sense of actualization of potentials present in the cause, not in the sense of their total absence. Bādarāyaṇa's point, then, seems to be that the presence of potentials does not affect the cause, such that the cause in some important sense always remains prior to and distinct from the effect, which will, in fact, become apparent at the end of this chapter. And yet, in terms of the effect having the characteristic of Being required by Bādarāyaṇa's iteration of *sat-kārya-vāda*, Being must be interpreted precisely in the sense of the potential to be what the effect becomes upon its transition into existence, or its actuality.

Let me end this heading with two points. First, the classical example of clay and its products, although ultimately derived from the *Chāndogya*, is not the ideal model to think about material causality in Vedānta. It is like the illustration of arrow made from horn where one must envision an external efficient cause. Although it has the benefit of illustrating *varieties* of things that are made of *single* material, it is the transformation of milk through inherent faculties that must be the preferred Vedāntic model of material causality. Analogies are illustrations, not equivalences.

Second, there is a theological point to be made, piggybacking on Brahman's essential characteristics: Being, consciousness, and bliss. Vedāntins describe Brahman as "omnipotent," *sarva-śakti*, and this doctrine is stated in the context of Bādarāyaṇa's *sūtra*s where he references the "all" kind of Upaniṣadic texts. This is a form of *ontological omnipotence*, the inherent possession of capacities to become everything, and is what constitutes Brahman's essential characteristic of Being. That Brahman is consciousness in terms of Upaniṣadic theology refers to Brahman's reflection at the beginning of creation, what the Upaniṣads call *satya-saṅkalpa*, "true resolve," and what Bādarāyaṇa calls *abhidhyāna*, the ability to create the elements out of itself and evolve name-and-form by the mere intention.

By means of this doctrine Bādarāyaṇa also tackles the problem of Brahman's being partless—non-composite—yet transforming into composite products. Has Brahman changed in its entirety, like milk into curd, and how precisely should one conceive of the relationship between Brahman the cause and the world—its effect?[73] Bādarāyaṇa rejects two possibilities. The world is not just another state of Brahman in the manner of a straight and coiled serpent. That would involve Brahman changing in its entirety, which is not desirable. Brahman is also not the origin of the world in the manner of light that emanates from a source, as one may be led to think by reading the *Chāndogya* account in which heat/light (*tejas*) is the first product, and presumably that is so because such an understanding would involve some sort of partitive relationship.[74] So, what is Bādarāyaṇa's solution? While ultimately this must be accepted on scriptural ground—the Upaniṣads describe Brahman as the cause yet a non-composite thing—it may be, nevertheless, conceptualized "as in the case of the gods," that is, of beings in the Vedic pantheon that create by mere wish: they think of things and they simply appear, à la sage Vasiṣṭha's fabled cow of plenty. Brahman has "true resolves"—whatever it intends comes about—and that constitutes Brahman's feature of Being pure and simple that is a conscious principle. Little wonder that the most prominent Vedāntic tradition reinterpreted Brahman's transformation, *pariṇāma*, into "apparent modification," *vivarta*, and that Vedāntins would generally describe the capacities of Brahman, its *śakti*s, as "inconceivable," that is, capable of accomplishing what is otherwise impossible.[75]

A corollary of this—Brahman transforms itself without change—is that Brahman is not limited by its being the first principle: in some sense, Brahman remains transcendent to creation.[76]

We will pick up Brahman's bliss in Chapter 7.

The Individual Soul

The individual soul (most commonly called *jīvātman*, "the living self," after *Chāndogya* 6.3.2) in Bādarāyaṇa's system is essentially Brahman, yet it is also embodied in a sense in which Brahman is not. As we have seen, both Brahman and the soul enter the numerous creations, but when they do so, the essential nature of the soul "is not fully manifest." The soul assumes a "dual character," whereas Brahman does not. This dual character is that the essential nature of the soul becomes concealed, and the soul undergoes transmigration that constitutes its "bondage," yet upon the full manifestation of this essential nature the soul is liberated and becomes Brahman. Bādarāyaṇa states two reasons for this concealment, one instrumental and one constitutive. The essential nature of the soul is concealed by its contact with a body, whereupon consciousness becomes associated with and restricted by the cognitive faculties and the mind, collectively called *vijñāna-manasī*. Indeed, another common name for the soul in Vedānta is *vijñānātman*, the self of cognition. The constitutive reason is simply the will of Brahman, which in the *Brahma-sūtra* always refers to Brahman's reflection at the beginning of creation and throughout its stages. Remember that Being in the *Chāndogya* reflects, "How about I enter these three divinities *with the living soul*." The entrance in a body for the soul is a concealment of its essential nature, but it happens by Brahman's will.[77]

This is a good occasion to illustrate parenthetically Bādarāyaṇa's consistent use of terminology that facilitates our interpretation. The pertinent *sūtra* says *parābhidhyānāt tirohitam*, where the operative term is *abhidhyāna*. Śaṅkara and Bhāskara interpret this to say that the concealed nature of the soul becomes manifest by meditation, *abhidhyāna*, on Brahman, in effect making the statement not about the cause of concealment at all but about its removal. Elsewhere and to commentarial agreement, Bādarāyaṇa uses "*abhidhyāna*" and its equivalent "*abhidhyā*" to denote Brahman's intention in the process of creation, so Śaṅkara and Bhāskara are on their own here.[78] That embodiment is a result of Brahman's will, however, does not work in Śaṅkara's system—to take him for illustration—where it is predicated on ignorance or cognitive superimposition of characteristics of what is not the self over the self. Such ignorance and the Sāṅkhyan elements of the intellect—*buddhi* or *mahat*—in which the self reflects to originate a false sense of self, *ahaṅkāra*, are simply not parts of Bādarāyaṇa's ontology, as we have seen, whereas for Śaṅkara they are essential. We conclude that Nimbārka and Rāmānuja interpret this *sūtra* reliably, and thereby reject Śaṅkara and Bhāskara. The philosophical problems raised by this will of Brahman to conceal the nature of the soul will reappear in Chapter 5.

Two important issues to clarify are the ontological status of the soul and its relationship with Brahman. The second is particularly important because throughout the *Brahma-sūtra*, Bādarāyaṇa affirms that the soul is different from Brahman and that Brahman is "more" than the soul—superior to it—yet the soteriological potential of the soul is predicated on its being Brahman.[79] Bādarāyaṇa's term for the ontological status of the soul is "part," *aṁśa*, which for him seems to best satisfy the requirement of being both different from and identical with Brahman.[80] Unfortunately it is not clear what "part" means in the context. The closest illustration is that of a stone which is in a sense non-distinct from earth yet maintains a degree of distinction.[81] This would prima facie suggest a partitive relationship, and a verse from the *Muṇḍaka* is customarily quoted to illustrate this:

> As from a well-stoked fire sparks fly by the thousands, all looking just like it, so from the imperishable issue diverse things, and into it, my friend, they return.[82]

Sparks of fire and rays of the sun become the common illustrations for the soul's relationship with Brahman.

A notion of this kind, that the soul is a transformation of Brahman, its splinter as it were, a product in some sort of partitive relationship, seems to have been advocated by one Āśmarathya: "There is an indication of the soul's being Brahman, for the sake of establishing the thesis."[83] The thesis is the one from the sixth chapter of the *Chāndogya* that we encountered in discussing material causality: Brahman is that one thing by knowing which everything else is known. "Everything" includes the soul, such that the soul must also be a product of Brahman, that is, identical with it. So, although the soul is not *said* to originate from Brahman as the elements of creation are, the thesis is an *indication* of its origination.

Two issues cripple this interpretation, though. First, Brahman is not a complex entity to allow for a partitive relationship; and, second, Bādarāyaṇa claims that the soul, unlike the elements of creation, does not originate but is eternal.[84] Although Bhāskara and Śrīnivāsa apply the same category of "projection of capacity," *śakti*, on the ontology of the soul, just as they did with respect to material causality, there is no hint in the *Brahma-sūtra* that

Bādarāyaṇa envisioned the status of the soul on the model of the world, and there is every indication that he thought of the soul as a distinct ontological entity, albeit in some sense identical with Brahman. Such being the case, we may be better served by remembering the *concealment* as the cause of the soul's dual character and think of the soul as a part in the sense of being a "partial manifestation" of Brahman's essential nature. In this light, the soul's being a part of Brahman would mean that the soul is Brahman *in part*.

The second reason why it is justified to speak about the individual soul as Brahman, attributed to one Auḍulomi, may be adduced in support of this interpretation. Auḍolomi says that the soul upon liberation will become identical to Brahman, such that it may be described as Brahman prospectively.[85] The soul is Brahman *in part,* but it can be Brahman *in full.* We will tackle the details of this in Chapter 7, but a consideration of the third reason for the soul's being Brahman—expressed in a *sūtra* that is, to the mind of all commentators, Bādarāyaṇa's own final standpoint may help us appreciate why the soul in liberation does not become *numerically* identical with Brahman. One Kāśakṛtsna says that the soul may be said to be Brahman "because of residence," that is, because Brahman resides in the soul as it does in everything else, a point which we have discussed, such that terms denoting the "resided" may be applied to the "residing one."[86]

Now, this is a controversial *sūtra* that I have read in the sense of Rāmānuja and Nimbārka to the exception of Śaṅkara and Bhāskara, and would like now to use it as another prop for illustrating Bādarāyaṇa's consistency in terminology. Kāśakṛtsna says that the reason for talking about the soul as Brahman is *avasthiti*, which is an action noun that generally means "residing" or "abiding." Śaṅkara and Bhāskara gloss this with the etymologically related *avasthā*, which however tends to mean a "state." Their interpretation, then, becomes that the soul is a state of Brahman, and it turns on the same *Chāndogya* statement in which Being reflects, "how about I enter these three divinities *with* the living soul and diversify name-and-form." Śaṅkara and Bhāskara, however, read "*as* the living soul" or "*through the means* of the living soul" that is a state of Brahman, rather than *with*, such that the individual soul *just is* Brahman, the one and only, who happens to reside in the three elements and further along the chain of creation, and upon liberation will be the one and only Brahman.[87] How is the soul a "part" in this reading that makes it a "state"? It is by way of accidental delimitations or contingent conditions, *upādhi*s—including the aforementioned ignorance, *buddhi, ahaṅkāra*, and so on—that make the soul separate from Brahman in a manner of speaking, just as clay delimits space in a non-partitive way.[88]

Bādarāyaṇa, however, to commentarial accord, elsewhere uses *avasthiti* in the sense of "residence" in a body, and where ontological relations are involved—of internal guidance.[89] The central text behind the idea of residence is the *Bṛhad-āraṇyaka* section about the inner ruler that proved crucial for efficient causality, and *avasthiti* is not used in arguments about identity between two entities that are, even prima facie, distinct. The individual soul is said to be Brahman, then, to paraphrase Nimbārka, because it is resided by Brahman the supreme Self as its guiding agent.[90] This doctrine has massive significance for the practice of the process of liberation, as we shall see in Chapter 6.

With this, we can circle back one more time on the meaning of "part." The idea that the soul is a part, *aṁśa*, of Brahman comes from the *Bhagavad-gītā* 15.7, to which Bādarāyaṇa makes direct reference.[91] There Kṛṣṇa tells the following to Arjuna:

> A particle of myself, as the eternal individual soul in the order of souls, pulls on the senses and the mind that are part of Prakṛti.[92]

The operative idea here is that the soul is *eternal*, which Bādarāyaṇa surely presupposes when he says that the soul does not originate. This had provoked the great Mīmāṁsaka Pārtasārathi Miśra (ca. eleventh century CE) to argue that an eternal entity cannot have a partitive relationship to a source, as composition and division are incommensurable with eternity. Rather, the soul is a part in the sense of a servant who may be said to be a part of his master, or of ministers who are parts of a king.[93] Clearly, Pārthasārathi intends a relationship of ontological distinction that involves dependence, which is very much amenable to how Rāmānuja and Nimbārka would interpret *aṁśa*. If this is the right interpretation, it makes sense why Bādarāyaṇa would think that *avasthiti*, guidance through residence, is the most accurate way to talk about the soul as identical with Brahman, since *aṁśa* and *avasthiti* would involve the same idea.

Bādarāyaṇa spills most of his ink in the section on the soul on two of its characteristics by which it is different from the soul of Sāṅkhya. The soul is a "knower," a conscious principle,[94] but unlike Sāṅkhya where it is said to be omnipresent in dimension, for Bādarāyaṇa it is infinitesimal, *aṇu*.[95] This is important for soteriological purposes, as we shall see in Chapter 7, for the soul attains liberation not only by rising to the world of Brahman but also because the soul is spatially located in the heart—as we saw in the section of residence—moves along with the body, and motion of an omnipresent principle is generally impossible. Still, it is important for the soul to extend beyond its minuteness, to be aware of the entire body in which it is present, and it does so by means of its quality or attribute of sentience that is channeled through the cognitive and active faculties. Bādarāyaṇa illustrates such extension through quality with the examples of illumination that spreads from a localized source, and smell, the characteristic quality of earth, which extends beyond the substance that it qualifies. So, the soul is substantively minute but attributively extended—indeed, in liberation it is attributively omnipresent—which is why Rāmānuja is right to describe it as both substantive and attributive consciousness, *dharmi-jñāna* and *dharma-bhūta-jñāna*. This makes it possible to argue that the soul is both changeless as substance, eternal, and changing in attribute, and thus capable of transitive awareness—awareness of objects, cognitive content—unlike its Sāṅkhya counterpart.

The second feature through which the soul is different from that of Sāṅkhya is agency: whereas the Sāṅkhya soul is merely a knower, for Bādarāyaṇa it is also an agent. We will return to this in Chapter 5, and we will finish the story of the soul in embodiment and liberation in Chapters 6 and 7.

Brahman's Purity

Bādarāyaṇa's account of Brahman through the function of residence associated with efficient causality raises several problems that need tackling, and they are tackled in section two of chapter three. This is the most obscure part of the *Brahma-sūtra*, and my short presentation here requires more than the proverbial single grain of salt.

We saw that the dual character of the individual soul was consequent on its embodiment. However, Brahman is also embodied in some sense: through the function of residence, it enters all created beings just as does the soul. Does Brahman acquire a similar dual character? Bādarāyaṇa rejects this—not even through residence in places does Brahman have two sets of characteristics, as does the soul—with a medley of philosophical and theological arguments.[96] First, Brahman is omnipresent, and as such, it cannot be embodied in the sense in which the soul is. Second, when the Upaniṣad adduces the principle of residence, after each locus in which Brahman is said to reside in the *antaryāmi-brāhmaṇa*, it is denied that Brahman is affected by such residence: "This is your Self, the inner dweller, *the immortal*," in other words, not liable to transmigration that constitutes the soul's dual character. And then, Brahman is the one who diversifies name-and-form: *it is prior to form*, for which reason it could not possibly be embodied.[97]

How does Brahman reside—how does an omnipresent thing become localized—and how does it not become affected by the changes that embodied beings undergo, such as increase and diminution of form? Additionally, *seeing* Brahman and the meditation on Brahman *as residing in* embodied beings are necessary soteriological conditions. But then, how is a formless thing seen? These are evidently most difficult problems, and Bādarāyaṇa explicitly acknowledges that here only forms of analogical reasoning may be helpful.[98] Brahman resides in created beings in the manner of the sun that is reflected in limited water containers. The sun "resides" from a distance, in a manner of speaking, and without being affected by the vagaries of form, and so does Brahman. And, Brahman's essential nature of consciousness is like that of light, a formless substance which is, nevertheless, intimately associated with vision as its *sine qua non*.

These considerations are decisively important in the *Brahma-sūtra* soteriological doctrine, and they too will reemerge in Chapters 6 and 7.

Study Questions

1. Think about the ideas of "material cause" and "efficient cause." Can you find cases where the two are identical and cases where they are different?
2. Relate the discussion on theological and philosophical reasoning from the previous chapter to the section "Material Causality" in this chapter. Can you reconstruct Bādarāyaṇa's characteristically philosophical arguments and argue whether they make sense on their own, without being buttressed by scriptural doctrine?
3. The problem of universals is one of the defining issues of ontology. Research it (a good place to start is the entry in the "Internet Encyclopedia of Philosophy" by MacLeod and Rubenstein, see Bibliography) and compare the Nyāya-Vaiśeṣika account of universals with that of Bādarāyaṇa. What challenges each of them faces? Is either of them satisfactory?
4. Summarize the two versions of *sat-kārya-vāda*, of Vedānta and Sāṅkhya, and argue in favor of one or the other.
5. Related to the previous question, think about the two illustrations of causality: clay that is transformed into pots, and milk that is transformed into curd. Add to this the argument that Brahman creates by mere intention—it thinks of things and they just "pop up." Are the three models mutually compatible if understood literally? Alternatively, if they are read analogically, what does each of them illustrate?
6. What is, in brief, the nature of the individual soul? Why is it important that Brahman's residence in created things be different from that of the individual soul?

Suggestions for Further Study

Griswold (1900) is a very good study on the notion of Brahman, particularly pages 1–42 on the pre-Upaniṣadic sources. The early disputes on the interpretation of Brahman in Indo-European linguistics are succinctly stated in Brereton (2004). Gonda (1950) may also be consulted, but it is typically dense. On Brahman as the "imperishable," the most informative reading is van Buitenen (1988: 157–97). Clooney (1988) is an excellent account on the Mīmāṁsā-Vedānta disagreement over the existence of divinities. Larson (1979) remains the model study on the history and philosophy of classical Sāṅkhya. Halbfass (1992) is a classic on ontology in Indian philosophy, particularly chapters one through three. Kumar (1983, Chapter IV) provides a very reliable account on how Sāṅkhya is treated in the *Brahma-sūtra*, including the commentaries of Śaṅkara, Rāmānuja, Nimbārka, Madhva, and Vallabha.

4

The Purpose of Creation

"I would only believe in a god who knew how to dance," wrote Friedrich Nietzsche, adding, "And when I saw my devil, there I found him earnest, thorough, deep, somber: it was the spirit of gravity—through him all things fall."[1] Whatever the great philosopher of affirmation might have intended to say in his collection of odd musings, for Hindus God always knew how to dance and, more generally, *play* and *have fun*. Indeed, Kṛṣṇa danced with the *gopīs* in the dead of night, and subdued the great menace of Vṛndāvana, the serpent Kāliya, by dancing on his hoods. He tended the village cows and played with his cowherd friends daily, a *deus ludens* if there ever was one. In the theology of the *Bhāgavata Purāṇa* (1.8.19), this *deus ludens* was, properly, *deus dramaticus*: "Covered by the veil of your magical power, you are inexhaustible, beyond the perceptual faculties of the ignorant. The foolish spectator cannot recognize you, just as he wouldn't recognize an actor (*naṭa*) in his costume."

Or should we rather say a dancer, *naṭa*? Theatrical playing and dancing are never quite distinct in South Asia, just as Kṛṣṇa's dancing with the *gopīs* and playing with the cowherds in Vṛndāvana were not quite distinct from his acting. In Kṛṣṇa, the doctrine of divine play is intertwined with the notion of *avatāra*, God's descent in the world of men, a notion modeled on the descent of an actor from the stage wings onto the stage itself.[2] This intertwining of the theologies of play and incarnation have produced the category of *līlā-avatāra*, Kṛṣṇa's descent to earth—again, analogous to the descent of the actor onto the stage—specifically for the sake of play.

Play, however, is God's general mode of functioning and it includes the godliest of all roles, that of world creation. Such cosmological play or dance—I fancy calling it the "ontological dance of becoming"—is more characteristically associated with Śiva than Kṛṣṇa. In the theology of Śiva as the Lord of dancers, Naṭarāja, the five essential divine activities are represented through the symbolism of dance. When the four-armed Śiva Naṭarāja dances, and he does so perpetually, from the beating of his drum all beings are created; his hand set in the gesture of protection maintains the world; another hand holds fire, and not just any fire, but that of universal destruction: indeed, perhaps Śiva's most famous dance is his *pralaya-tāṇḍava*, the dance of dissolution. His two feet symbolize the remaining two divine functions: with one, he provides divine grace, and with the other, he conceals himself.[3]

Whatever the origin, a God who dances and plays, often doing so in the manner of an actor, a *naṭa*, on the world as his stage, has become one of the most peculiar features of Hinduism: *whatever* God does, he does it in the manner of *līlā* or play. In Vedānta, this particularly concerns God's being the first principle. In fact, the *locus classicus* on the doctrine of divine play is the *Brahma-sūtra* and the context of creation, rather than the more obviously fun activities of embodied divinities. In the *Brahma-sūtra*, the doctrine of divine play is introduced to answer the question of why the world creation is necessary: What purpose would the perfectly content Brahman achieve by creating the world, and might Brahman's having a desire that is presupposed by the action of creation be a blemish to divine purity and excellence?

In both positing this question and providing the answer, Bādarāyaṇa is characteristically laconic: Brahman has no purpose, and creation is but a play. Or, perhaps he does have a purpose: that of play itself? Although the commentators discuss the issues of purpose and play at length, in contemporary scholarship this specific Vedāntic doctrine—that creation is Brahman's play—has been rather poorly represented. What does it mean for Brahman to create the world in the manner of play? To illustrate, Arthur Herman in his extensive monograph on the problem of evil in Indian philosophy writes the following: "Sport (*līlā*) is understood here to be a third sort of activity; it is therefore neither purposive nor purposeless. . . . Thus *līlā* prompts creation out of sheer joy, and overflowing from God's great and wonderful sportive nature."[4] As we shall see in this chapter, Herman collapses several very distinct responses to the question of purpose and divine play into one that reminds us more of Neoplatonism than of any proper form of Vedānta. Julius Lipner in his *The Face of Truth* likewise attributes to Rāmānuja claims about Brahman's "totally spontaneous nature" instantiated in "non-competitive undertakings," failing thereby to appreciate what Rāmānuja's account of play is about.[5]

In this chapter, then, we take up the question of the purpose of creation. Our focus changes significantly from the rest of the book, where we primarily attempt to reconstruct Bādarāyaṇa's own doctrine and take the broad strokes approach. The *sūtra*s pertinent for this chapter are only two in number, and so we not only engage the commentaries in more depth but also probe a much wider selection of them. Context guides us throughout: we try to recover the background of Bādarāyaṇa's thinking, and also leave no historical stone unturned insofar is required for understanding the commentaries. This will often bring us outside of the *Brahma-sūtra* confines.

I will argue here that creation as Brahman's play has been interpreted in three distinct ways. In the first, in order of presentation, the activity of creation has been compared to something like organizing a game or staging a play—we may call it "The Game of Creation"—a self-teleological activity which nevertheless needs all kinds of requisites if it is to take place. This account is most directly associated with Rāmānuja. The second account, in the *Brahma-sūtra* context that of Śaṅkara and Bhāskara but looking back to Śaṅkara's predecessor Gauḍapāda (ca. 600 CE), the Naiyāyika Uddyotakara (ca. 560–610 CE), and ultimately Yājñavalkya of Upaniṣadic fame, interprets creation as a manifestation of Brahman's essential nature. It is an account of deep discontent with play, to which it pays lip service or which it rejects outright. The third account, stated by Madhva and refined by Baladeva, explicitly draws on the motif of dancing as a kind of action that is not *for* pleasure as purpose but rather originates *from* pleasure, refashioning thus Śaṅkara's account to turn Brahman's essential nature into proper playfulness.

The two *sūtra*s discussed here are a part of a longer heading that goes on to tackle the consequence of Bādarāyaṇa's reply and of his general claim that Brahman is the first principle: If Brahman had created the world, isn't he responsible for all the suffering in it? This is the problem of evil and the project of defending God in the face of evil, theodicy. We will seamlessly glide into it in the next chapter, without breaking the flow with a separate introduction, and that chapter will follow a similar methodology: interpreting a few *sūtra*s through a multitude of commentaries. Chapters 4 and 5, thus, should be approached as a unit, and also as sort of a "case study" of the depths in which Bādarāyaṇa's breviloquent work has been interpreted in its reception history, to complement the "broad strokes" reading of the rest of the book.

The Context

The pertinent *Brahma-sūtra* passage is the final heading of the first section of Chapter 2, which is concerned with defending Brahman as the first principle against the ontology of Sāṅkhya. As we discussed in the previous chapter, the bulk of the argument defends Brahman as the material cause of the world against prime matter of Sāṅkhya but within the common frame of the doctrine of causal continuity: the world in all its variety is a continuation of its material cause—Brahman for Vedānta, prime matter for Sāṅkhya—and not a constitutively new thing as in the other prominent Brahmanical theory of causality, that of Nyāya-Vaiśeṣika. The concluding several *sūtra*s, however, move from the problem of Brahman being the material cause to his being the efficient cause of the world. This becomes patent when we recognize that Naiyāyikas who accept God just as the efficient but not the material cause of the world had to answer the same objections as those posed by Bādarāyaṇa's opponent in *Brahma-sūtra* 2.1.31–35.[6] The shift also brings us to a domain that we can more directly recognize as theological and not merely ontological: if the first principle is God as a world creator, then we may ask questions about the purpose of creation and the facticity of suffering.

The objection to Brahman creating the world is, curiously, shared with the classical teleological argument for the existence of God turned on its head. To paraphrase the commentators, Brahman could not have possibly created the world because creation, specifically the creation of such a variegated product as the world, is a form of action, and action is bound to a purpose. Purpose on its part is predicated on desire, which is a psychological torment associated with bondage, and this vitiates the Upaniṣadic doctrine that Brahman is self-content. This contains an implicit reference to Yājñavalkya's teaching to king Janaka: "Clearly, this is the aspect of his where all desires are fulfilled, where the self is the only desire, and which is free from desires and far from sorrows."[7] If Brahman creates the world in all its variety, we must ascribe intentionality to his creation, but that would make it seem that Brahman lacks something for the sake of which he creates, whereas the Upaniṣads teach that Brahman lacks nothing and wishes for nothing.[8]

Several commentators, following Vācaspati's lead, anticipate the possibility that the purpose behind creation need not be personal: Brahman may have created the world for the sake of others, us, to do us a favor. This, however, invites the common argument against God in the face of evil: creating a world of suffering is a favor to no one.[9] Such being the case, one must concede that, there being no purpose on the part of Brahman, creation could not have taken place from Brahman as the first principle. The *sūtra*, then, gives voice to the following prima facie view that Bādarāyaṇa will seek to overturn: "It is not [that Brahman is the creator of the world,] because [creation] is purposeful."[10] Contrary to the teleological argument, where the evidence of purpose in the world is an inferential mark for intelligence behind it, for our Vedāntins purpose proves to be a rather stubborn stain on God's nature that they will struggle to explain, accommodate, or eliminate.

It is unclear which precise direction this prima facie view is coming from in Bādarāyaṇa's context. We may, still, hazard the guess that it is coming from a Sāṅkhya corner, as that would fit the general polemic course of the chapter. If so, the prima facie view expresses the Sāṅkhya doctrine that the creation of the world is occasioned by the union or proximity between prime matter and the individual soul, a union, however, of a specific kind: one with a "sake" (*artha*) or a "purpose" (*prayojana*). This purposeful union between prime matter and the soul is that the soul may experience the objects of the world and through such experience understand itself as different from them and from prime matter, their source. Such purposeful union pulls prime matter, as it were, to create the world, insentient though she is, just as insentient milk spontaneously flows from a cow for the sake of nourishing the calf. It is, really, the purpose that prime matter obtains in the union with individual souls that serves as the efficient cause of creation, such that we can describe this efficient cause as also a final cause in the Aristotelian sense, a *telos*: creation happens so that liberation would be possible. The soul of Sāṅkhya is not an agent, and *eo ipso* it cannot have a purpose that would prompt it to create. Prime matter *is* an agent: its purpose is to show itself to souls and facilitate their liberation. When the purpose is no longer present because the soul has become liberated—or, rather, has realized that it has never been really bound, never in real contact with prime matter—creation no longer obtains, although prime matter and the souls remain in proximity.[11]

The objection on this reading, then, is just another way to say that the first principle of the Upaniṣads is simply prime matter, whatever name it may otherwise bear.

This I believe is the background behind the *sūtra:* Brahman cannot be the creator, because Brahman as depicted in the Upaniṣads is not—could not be—for the sake of anything, as it is just the soul in its natural liberated state, whereas creation is, as Sāṅkhyas say, *puruṣārtha*, for the sake of the soul. Vedāntins and Naiyāyikas have generally rejected this Sāṅkhya doctrine, that liberation is the purpose of creation, as circular. Uddyotakara had argued, for instance, that the individual souls couldn't experience the objects of the world unless prime matter is already transformed into them, at which point *only* could liberation become a purpose. It is circular to claim that liberation is the cause of creation when liberation *presupposes* creation.[12]

Rāmānuja had teased out the circularity further. The key element in this account is the Sāṅkhya principle of *mahat* or *buddhi*, the "intellect" in which the soul reflects itself and becomes transitively conscious, that is, both conscious of objects external to itself and self-conscious as distinct from prime matter. The soul could never be in contact with prime matter—it could never be bound—were it not for the intellect. The very sensible question, therefore, poses itself: how can the soul identify with the products of prime matter and become bound—that is, think "I am the intellect, the body, this is my wife," and so on, a thought that must happen in the intellect—when creation is posterior to such identification, whereas the intellect is posterior to creation. This is patently circular: presupposing the union of souls and prime matter is the condition for creation, yet their union depends on there already being creation. The mere proximity of prime matter and the soul, which is what Sāṅkhyas really want, will not do either, because then bondage would become utterly capricious and could befallen even those who are already liberated.[13]

It may also be the case that Bādarāyaṇa at this point needs to consider those Upaniṣadic statements that do talk about creation as an intentional act of the first principle, in which desire is involved. We have seen these throughout the previous chapter, and they were instrumental for establishing Brahman's being the efficient cause, for instance *Taittirīya* 2.6, which talks about the first principle desiring (*akāmayata*), "How about I become many and procreate," or the *Chāndogya* counterpart where Being reflects (*aikṣata*) rather than desires. Desire is a pointer to sentience but also a psychological torment in that it presupposes a lack of something and an urge to get it. I have associated these passages with Brahman that has "true desires and resolves," *satya-kāma, satya-saṅkalpa*. This would prima facie suggest that Brahman's creation is an intentional act, and it would also bring to mind the role of desire in Vedic rituals where it serves as the impetus for the creation of future desirable results such as heaven and well-being, which keep one in the cycle of transmigration. How does this square with Yājñavalkya's teachings about that Brahman which has no desires? Is Brahman's creation an intentional act, predicated on desire? If so, what does it intend, and how does such intention reflect on the nature of Brahman if desires are psychological torments?

For most of the commentators, however, the context of purpose behind the *sūtra* is clearly—though ahistorically or perhaps meta-historically—that of Kumārila Bhaṭṭa's famous argument against God as a world creator, expressed in the *Sambandhākṣepa-parihāra* chapter of his *Śloka-vārttika*.[14] In the course of this argument, Kumārila makes the following statement: "What desirable thing would God fail to accomplish without creating the world? Not even a fool would act without a reference to some purpose. And if he did act in just that way (without purpose), what good would there be of his intelligence?"[15] Śaṅkara's presentation of the prima facie view clearly takes its bearings from Kumārila:

> For, in the world, men act with circumspection, and are not seen to engage in actions that are unrelated to some personal purpose, however easy the undertaking may be. . . . If you say that conscious men are, in fact, seen engaging without a personal purpose—mad men with deranged intelligence—and, therefore, the Supreme Self may act in a similar manner, that will compromise the omniscience of the Supreme Self known from the Upaniṣads.[16]

Bhāskara who habitually follows Śaṅkara's interpretation, often to the letter, directly quotes Kumārila's statement, and Rāmānuja leaves no doubt that the same doctrine is at the back of his mind too: "The undertakings of those who act based on reason are purposeful."[17] Although it could not have been Bādarāyaṇa's context, Kumārila's hallmark doctrine about the association of intelligence and reason with purpose and desire as the firm ground of action will permeate positively and negatively most future Vedāntic accounts of Brahman's *modus operandi*. We will return to it shortly.

Creation as Play

Bādarāyaṇa's reply to the objection that Brahman would lack purpose in creating the world is a bit ambiguous: "Rather, there is only play, like in the world."[18] While it is clear that the action of creation is compared to "play," "game," or "sport," all of which are possible translations of *līlā* used by Bādarāyaṇa and its synonym *krīḍā* common in the commentaries, it is unclear if the intention is to say that creation is only *for the sake* of play but without an extraneous purpose—a form of self-teleological action—or that creation is not a purposeful activity at all, but *is* a mere play. Rāmānuja and Vallabha offer the first reading, while Bhāskara and Keśava Kāśmīrī give the clearest expression of the second:

> Rāmānuja: There is mere-ness of play as the purpose. Pure play is the purpose of creation.[19]
>
> Vallabha: For, there is no purpose whatsoever in play, since play itself is the purpose.[20]
>
> Bhāskara: Brahman does not have purpose in creation, but only the mere-ness of play.[21]
>
> Keśava Kāśmīrī: The supreme Brahman all of whose desires are fulfilled engages in the creation of the variegated world in the manner of pure play, in which there is no reference to purpose.[22]

It is also unclear if the distinction is significant at all, since the intention in any case is that Brahman's creation is not the kind of action prompted by a lack or a need, such that it would compromise Brahman's perfect self-content.

What does Bādarāyaṇa mean when he says that creation is a play "like in the world?" An example runs through most of the commentaries. Imagine a king who has accomplished all his desires and discharged all public obligations, who is brave and powerful, and who rules the entire world. Even such a king goes out to play ball with his ministers, or rolls the dice, not in order to gain anything—indeed, there is nothing left for him to gain—but only for the sake of play or in the manner of a game. Even if he does have subsequent obligations or motives, Vācaspati reminds us, his playing ball is not with respect to them. Brahman creates the world in this manner: not for any personal gain, but for the sake of play.[23]

Commenting on Rāmānuja's engagement with the theology of play, Julius Lipner has made the point that we need to distinguish here competitive from non-competitive sport, since the first kind "by its non-spontaneous and calculating nature, through its inherent motive to worst others, is self-centered and grasping," emphasizing further the "totally 'spontaneous' nature" of the non-competitive undertaking.[24] This is a useful conceptual clarification, although the claim for spontaneity is overblown. The important distinction that Rāmānuja is referencing at this point is that self-content and enjoyment of external objects are not of the same kind, and therefore do not stem from identical motives. However, that does not make non-competitive sport "totally spontaneous." Something else, rather, is "at play."

It is prudent at this point to remember the Vedic context of the notion of "desire" that the Upaniṣads are addressing and must be on Bādarāyaṇa's mind. "Desires" in one sense are "desirable objects," those which the agent hopes to attain (and in a way create, insofar as they are *kārya*, products) by performing ritual—well-being, heaven, wealth, sons, and so on. In another sense, they become the motivating factor for the ritual undertaking by lodging in the agent's psyche. To quote from Śaṅkara:

> Under "desire" (*kāma*) sons and the like are intended. That is, they are desired.—But, the word *kāma* stands for a type of desire, does it not?—No, because it is clear from the context that the word *kāma* is used in the sense of sons, etc.[25]

Now, Buddhists have very usefully drawn the distinction between *vatthu-kāma* and *kilesa-kāma*, desires as objects and desires as psychological torments, for instance a woman and the sexual appetite that has women as objects and is the motivating factor for their pursuit, much as desires are the impetus for those objects attained by ritual.[26] Brahman cannot have such psychological torments, so why would he create objects in the manner of the ritualist who creates future enjoyments?

Imagine, however, Brahman staging a play called "The Game of Creation." The objects of creation are required *for the play*, but their origin is neither "totally spontaneous" nor motivated by the desire to enjoy them. It is the performance that is a purpose unto itself: the objects are not the "prize money" created for the sake of enjoyment; they are rather, to use Rāmānuja's turn of phrase, the required accessories:

> When play is the motive although all Brahman's desires are fulfilled, it is justified to say that there is no expectation [of gain], for it is seen that balls and similar things are used in ordinary life for the sake of mere play. In the case of the self-contented, fulfilment of all desires means the presence of all required accessories for enjoyment at all times. Enjoyment of objects is of a different kind from self-content. For the relish of game, which is different from the enjoyment of external objects, the prime matter of three modes, the individual souls etc. are just the required accessories.[27]

The point is not about the non-competitive character of play, even though this is a valid point. It is, rather, about the status of the ball, used here as the standard of comparison against which the being of prime matter, the individual souls, and the particular creation products is measured. Play is a self-referential and self-teleological action: unlike ritual and similar productive undertakings, it does not terminate in the creation of extraneous desirable objects. Still, play necessitates the presence of accessories such as a ball, a field, etc., and being perfectly self-content just means having such accessories always at hand, not depending on a productive undertaking for them. Likewise, if creation is conducted in the manner of a game, prime matter and the individual souls are its prerequisites or required accessories, and for Brahman they are *always* right at hand, ready for him "to play ball." They belong to play as part of its organic whole, not as its outcome.

The manner in which Brahman creates is that of *satya-saṅkalpa*, "true intentions," which does not stand for total spontaneity but for creation through mere will or intention, and, as we have seen, is coextensive with Brahman's omnipotence. It means that Brahman unlike created beings does not depend on effort or accessories in the action of creation: indeed, everything is "right at hand for him," such that Brahman's mere will is sufficient for the game of creation to take place.

It is notable that most of the commentators do not supply a topical scriptural passage for the *sūtra* nor cite from the Upaniṣads to support this doctrine, and that must be because Upaniṣadic cosmologies do not use the concept of play. Vijñānabhikṣu, nevertheless, usefully quotes a verse from the *Viṣṇu Purāṇa*, which is a sufficiently early source that Bādarāyaṇa might have drawn from. The verse compares creation with a child's play or the actions of a frolicsome boy, and Śrīdhara Svāmin in his comment references the purpose of creation and the *sūtra* under discussion.[28] The image of a child playing ball may fit this idea better than that of a sovereign king, who surely keeps the competitive spirit even without the desire for gain.[29] Still, we will see in Chapter 7 that liberation is a state where the soul can create objects of enjoyment by its one's will, "in the manner of play," *and* a state of freedom like that of a sovereign king.

Creation as Brahman's Essential Nature

Be that as it may, the doctrine that creation is play or for the sake of play has had a bit of an underwhelming reception among the *Brahma-sūtra* commentators. The problem with play is that, granted it may not be for any palpable gain, it is still for the sake of inner pleasure. While the accessories serve the purpose of the play, play itself is for diversion, happiness. That seems to indicate a prior state of lack of happiness and speaks against the Upaniṣadic doctrine of Brahman's full contentment.

It does not matter prima facie whether Bādarāyaṇa affirms play as the purpose of creation or rejects purpose by describing creation *as* mere play. For, one can still ask, *why* play at all if not for pleasure? Thus, the *Brahma-sūtra* commentators generally find it necessary to state that divine play is *not quite* like human play. Vijñānabhikṣu expresses this elegantly: "Although it is possible to imagine some slight purpose even in mundane plays, there cannot be any dependence on purpose in the actions of the Lord."[30] In this light, it is also a question if the illustration of a king playing ball is quite appropriate. Thus, Baladeva: "However, we do not accept the illustration of the king, because such play has happiness *as its result*."[31] From here, the argument takes two directions: play is either rejected or reconceived. Under this heading, we look at the first.

In his *Āgama-śāstra*, commenting on the *Māṇḍūkya Upaniṣad* teaching about the four states of the Self—which we will discuss in Chapter 7—the Vedāntin Gauḍapāda considers the question of world creation with respect to the third of these states. Gauḍapāda mentions the idea that creation is for the sake of play, but concludes that it is rather "the essential nature (*svabhāva*) of the Lord to create, for what craving could have he whose desires are fulfilled?"[32] The Naiyāyika Uddyotakara was, perhaps, the first to state the obvious: play cannot be the purpose for which God creates the world, because the purpose of play is *not* self-contained: play is not a self-teleological activity, it does have pleasure as a product external to itself, and thus it presupposes the lack of happiness. The Lord cannot seek pleasure because he has no misery. Like Gauḍapāda, Uddyotakara affirms that it is the essential or inherent nature of the Lord to create. "Just as earthen things naturally function in actions such as support, likewise the Lord operates in accordance with his essential nature. In other words, he is a principle the essential nature of which is to create."[33]

Śaṅkara acknowledged and absorbed this critique, and he moved to Brahman's inherent or essential nature, illustrated by respiration, as the preferable explanation of world creation, without explicitly distinguishing it from divine play in his *Brahma-sūtra* commentary:

> Just as activities such as inhalation and exhalation happen from intrinsic nature, without intending any external purpose, likewise God's engagement in creating the world, a mere play in character, proceeds from his intrinsic nature, without regard to any other purpose. . . . And, intrinsic nature cannot be questioned.[34]

This, however, was no more than lip service: commenting on Gauḍapāda's verse quoted earlier, Śaṅkara rejected play in favor of Brahman's essential nature.[35] In any case, respiration is a curious game, and I imagine it would not be the crowd's favorite at the Olympics. Vācaspati Miśra, therefore, distinguished actions of essential nature, such as respiration, from those of play, both of which he defended as reasonable with respect to world creation, along with a third kind that we may describe as "sheer purposelessness" or "hanging loose," or, even better, "doing random stuff" (*yadṛcchā*).[36]

So, why does Brahman create the world? Well, why does water flow, why vessels contain things? You don't question the thing's essential nature, and it is Brahman's essential nature to create, as the etymology of the word makes apparent: it is great, and it makes things grow. It is just what Brahman does. This, then, is an alternative theology of creation: world creation is not a play, *līlā*, but an expression of Brahman's inherent nature, *svabhāva*.

Why is respiration the ideal illustration of Brahman's inherent nature? Respiration in Vedānta is generally identified with the third state of the Self, called perfect calm (*samprasāda*), consisting of bliss, and characteristic of deep sleep.[37] It is a state in which consciousness persists—there is an agent regulating the metabolic processes of the body with the required knowledge of how to do that—but is not transitive in that the objects of waking and sleep are not present to awareness. It provides the ideal opportunity to argue for Brahman as a conscious entity, indeed omniscient in that it creates the world and regulates its functioning by governing the karma of the individual souls, without ever being aware of it and without any apparent external purpose. Gauḍapāda's aforementioned account of the origin of creation was developed precisely as an interpretation of this third state of the Self, described in the fifth verse of the *Māṇḍūkya Upaniṣad:*

> Where the one asleep does not desire anything, does not see dreams—that is deep sleep. The one in deep sleep, being single, is solid consciousness and enjoys bliss, for it consists of bliss, and is inclined towards awareness. This is the third state, that of *prājña*.

This account of creation as Brahman's essential nature is an eminently Advaita account, but it is not Śaṅkara's final word on the question of purpose. We will return to it at the end of the next chapter.

I should like to point out, though, that it was surely not Bādarāyaṇa's intention to affirm Brahman's essential nature instantiated by breathing as the *why* of creation, for he could have easily done so by referring to Yājñavalkya's teachings to Maitreyī in the *Bṛhad-āraṇyaka*, where creation and annihilation are called the exhalation and inhalation of the "great Being," Brahman:

> It is like this. As clouds of smoke billow from a fire lit with damp fuel, so indeed the Ṛgveda, Yajurveda, Sāmaveda, the Atharva-Āṅgirasa, histories, ancient tales, sciences, hidden teachings (*upaniṣad*), verses, aphorisms, explanations, glosses, sacrifices, oblations, offerings of food and drink, this world, the other world, and all beings—all these are the exhalation of this Immense Being. And they are the inhalation of that very Being.[38]

The idea that creation is Brahman's respiration is common in Hindu thought: that Bādarāyaṇa does not refer to it indicates that he either wants to stay in the context of purpose—while essential nature explains the *whence* of creation, it does not answer the question of the *why* of it—or that the omniscience of deep sleep is not quite to his liking.

Play as Brahman's Essential Nature

Śaṅkara's account of Brahman's essential nature was in response to Kumārila's objection that tied purposeful action with intelligence. Kumārila developed this idea as a grand theory of the purpose of ritual. Why do Vedic men perform ritual? Because they *understand* ritual will bring about desirable results in the future. No ritual would ever be done were it not for such understanding. But then, Kumārila characteristically turned this into a general philosophy of action which we may describe as utilitarianism. Don't people ever act out of other kinds of motives, such as love or parental affection? No, they don't. Even parents take care of their children expecting to be taken care of in old age.[39] This morphed into the doctrine of *iṣṭa-sādhanatā*, that scripture is about providing means for goals that are desirable to men.

Śaṅkara was very much an heir to Kumārila's doctrine, with some important divergences, one of which was to limit its scope to scripturally regulated action. Purpose that is tied to reason did not concern such actions that are "natural," common to humanity in general and not restricted to the world of the Vedas, for instance breathing or eating when you are hungry.[40] Breathing, then, provides the perfect illustration of an action that an intelligent being does, yet is not purposeful in the sense of being calculating or utilitarian. That surely overturns Kumārila's objection, but it also dispenses with the doctrine of creation as play. The continuation of consciousness in deep sleep is also not the ideal of omniscience for other Vedāntins, and Baladeva spells out this concern: "In the illustration of inhalation and exhalation, there would be the objection of loss of omniscience in states such as deep sleep."[41] Thus, the theology of essential nature as Śaṅkara presented it was not directly appealing to other Vedāntins, except for Bhāskara.

As we saw earlier, however, Śaṅkara imagined another possibility of a purposeless action performed by conscious agents: the behavior of mad men with deranged intelligence. He rejected this illustration, however, because it would compromise Brahman's omniscience: for omniscience, our Advaitin seems to have thought, it is better to vegetate and breathe than to be nuts. His turn of phrase, though, could also be interpreted as "drunk men," and in this sense, along with a new reading of the idea of essential nature, the illustration was appropriated by Madhva to salvage the doctrine of creation as Brahman's play.

Imagine a drunk man bursting with happiness who jumps up to dance and sing without intending any purpose. "Hari does not act with reference to any purpose such as creation, but out of pure joy, such as in the case of dancing of a drunk man. How could there be considerations of purpose on the part of him who is full of bliss?"[42] Madhva's account was explicitly based on the idea that creation is a manifestation of Brahman's essential nature: indeed, he quotes Gauḍapāda's conclusion on the question of origin that we cited earlier: "This is the essential nature of God, for how could he whose desires are fulfilled crave for anything?" Dancing and breathing, however, are very different expressions of a thing's essential nature. If Brahman is bliss, as Vedāntins including Gauḍapāda claim, then what Brahman does must be an expression of such bliss. The happy do not merely vegetate—they get up to dance and sing.

Unlike Śaṅkara, Madhva with his brief remarks does justice to Bādarāyaṇa's idea of creation as play—as we saw in the introduction, dancing and singing are paradigmatic actions of such kind—by shifting the onus from "for" to "out of," from play *for the sake* of happiness to play *as an expression of* happiness. One may nevertheless ask, is it not that Śaṅkara's objection is still valid? Drunk men *are* deranged, albeit temporarily, and that does not speak well for Brahman's omniscience. Baladeva, therefore, refines Madhva's account by rejecting the necessity of the drunk man trope for the illustration:

> God acts in the manner of a man drunk *with happiness*, who dances without regard to results but because of the overflowing of happiness. Therefore, play is in the sense of the essential nature of innate bliss. . . . This, moreover, does not compromise the Lord's omniscience, for we accept the illustration [of a drunk man] only with respect to play being the manifestation of bliss without intending any result.[43]

The illustration is not about *how* one has become happy. People are happy for various reasons and drinking and happiness are not invariantly related: sober men occasionally experience happiness too. Brahman, moreover, is *essentially* happy, requiring nothing extraneous to achieve such a state. This is, then, a third original reading of Bādarāyaṇa's reply: *līlā* as *svabhāva*, play as Brahman's essential nature. It is here rather than in Rāmānuja's account that we can talk about play as "total spontaneity."

Conclusion

Given Bādarāyaṇa's brevity, we cannot restrict ourselves to the two *sūtra*s to appreciate what he meant by creation as play. We may be certain that he did not have "essential nature as breathing" in mind. Historically, "essential nature" and "play" were contending accounts of world creation, and the absence of reference to Yājñavalkya is a strong *argumentum ex silentio*. On the other hand, Rāmānuja's theology of play was more an ontology of relations. Prime matter and the souls are always there for Brahman in a system that precludes outer gains because it is already all-encompassing: what could the ever-content and all-possessing Brahman gain by creating the world? Play becomes the perfect illustration of an autonomous action, one that is not driven by an extraneous *telos* yet requires objects of various kinds. In light of Bādarāyaṇa's multiple references to "intention," *abhidhyāna*, with respect to creation—as we have seen in the previous chapter—I am secure that Rāmānuja's argument that creation has a purpose—that of play—is on the mark.

But, Rāmānuja's brilliance aside, those of us who "would only believe in a god who knew how to dance" might still find Brahman's outpouring of bliss into the spectacle that is the world aesthetically, and perhaps emotionally, more satisfying.

Study Questions

1. Compare the three Vedāntic answers to the question of purpose and argue in favor of one of them.
2. Reflect on the Sāṅkhya doctrine of liberation as the teleological cause of creation: Can you think of a way to interpret it such that it is not liable to the refutation of Rāmānuja and Uddyotakara?
3. How might you argue against the claim, expressed by Vācaspati and other commentators, that a wholly good or compassionate God wouldn't create a world full of suffering *for the sake of others*?
4. What kinds of purposeless action that an intelligent being might do can you identify in the chapter? Can you think of others? Are they good cases against Kumārila's claim that no intelligent being does anything without a purpose?

Suggestions for Further Study

The reader may want to contrast my account with that presented in Lipner (1986, Chapter 5). Herman (1993, Chapter IX.3) analyzes the theology of play as part of the broader heading of which the two *sūtra*s are the first part. Chapter six in Dasti and Phillips (2017) provides an excellent translation of the most important texts-places on the Nyāya understanding of God. Kumārila's argument against the existence of God has been analyzed in Bilimoria (1990). The *sūtra*s covered in this and the next chapter, 2.1.31–4, have recently been usefully analyzed in Nicholson (2020), across several commentaries.

5

Brahman and the Problem of Evil

The Context

At this juncture of the *Brahma-sūtra*, after the account of creation as play, a variety of the theological problem of evil presents itself.[1] In contemporary philosophy of religion, the problem of evil is generally defined as an inconsistency between there being a God who has three essential characteristics—omnipotence, omniscience, and omnibenevolence—with the facticity of evil in the world. This is sometimes presented as a logical problem, as a contradiction between God's characteristics on the one hand and the presence of evil on the other: "A wholly good omnipotent being would eliminate evil completely; if there really are evils, then there cannot be any such being."[2] The very concept of an omnipotent and wholly good being does not allow for the *possibility* of evil, much as two plus two could not be five. Alternatively, it is argued that only some kinds and amounts of suffering are evidence that the world was not created by an omniscient, omnipotent, and wholly good being, although the two are not logically incompatible. Think, for instance, of *horrendous* suffering, such as the slow, intensely painful death of a trapped animal, or the raping and killing of a five-year-old girl; and *gratuitous* suffering, which has no evident purpose such as moral rectitude or personal transformation.[3] The business of theodicy, then, becomes to tackle one of the two variants of the problem of evil, the logical or the evidential.

In the *Brahma-sūtra*, the problem does not arise quite in the same way, although as we saw Brahman was defined as an omniscient and omnipotent being. The problem is set, rather, in cosmogenic terms: if Brahman had created the world, then he would be responsible both for the good and evil in the world—to be precise, for the *happiness* and *suffering* in their *various degrees* in animate life—and that would prima facie compromise Brahman's perfection of neutrality. This is in continuation of the creation-as-play argument, but once happiness and suffering have been introduced, the question of evil relative to God's benevolence specifically comes to the fore. As stated by Rāmānuja's imagined opponent: "A God full of compassion would not create a world full of suffering of various kinds, such as birth, old age, death, and hell; rather, he would create a world that has only happiness."[4] The business of theodicy or Brahman's defense, then, becomes to show that although Brahman is the first principle from which everything proceeds, he is not responsible for the varieties of good and evil and for the facticity of suffering.

All the while, the issue concerns strictly divine neutrality and justice, and Brahman's omnipotence is not directly questioned. The commentators, nevertheless, go on to raise issues concerning Brahman's omnipotence that stem directly from the proposed solution of divine justice. We will follow the course of the *sūtra*s and the commentaries, and along the way, we will also clarify the idea of "evil."

After Bādarāyaṇa's claim that creation is a mere game or play, one may ask how such a game produces the mess that is the world as we know it. Why does the game of creation feel like the Dinamo Zagreb versus Red Star Belgrade match of 1990, when hooligan fans of both teams clashed in a riot that provided the spark for the bloodiest conflict in Europe since World War II? Bādarāyaṇa's imagined opponent claims that two specific culpabilities would befall the playful Brahman: he would turn out to be partial and cruel. Rāmānuja's paraphrase in the *Vedānta-dīpa* may be usefully quoted at this point: "It is not possible for the Lord to have engaged in a world creation that is for the sole purpose of play, because through the creation of unequal classes such as gods, men etc. his being partial would follow, and through engendering unbearable suffering his being cruel would follow."[5]

How is partiality specifically defined? Several of the commentators point to the unequal distribution of happiness and suffering among created beings, instantiated by their general classes. Thus, Śaṅkara says that it would be prima facie partial for Brahman to create gods who enjoy absolute happiness, animals who suffer absolute misery, and men who get a mixed bag of both. One can imagine that the Brahmanical caste system of inborn hierarchy and slim prospects of individual social mobility would have been on the mind of our commentators, although none of them mentions it explicitly. While we would associate such partiality in granting happiness and suffering with the issue of divine justice—many theodicists have had to grapple with the question of uneven distribution of suffering—for Śaṅkara and Bhāskara partiality here points to a set of psychological states that we as humans are all too familiar with, such as affection, aversion, and folly, but are definitionally absent in God and the liberated souls.[6] Why do some have it better than others? If God is the creator, it must be that he likes some of us but is repulsed by others, or is just confused in how he makes things. Such a God would be, as Śaṅkara puts it, faulty like us ordinary folks.

Cruelty is tied specifically to this facticity of suffering and the question why there should be *any* of it. Before we tackle this second charge, it is apposite to ask what our Vedāntins mean under "suffering." What passes as suffering for which Brahman would be prima facie guilty? In the commentaries—and in Vedānta generally—the reference point on this is again Sāṅkhya. An oft-repeated definition is that suffering is the loss of the desirable and the encounter with the undesirable. There is nothing peculiarly Indian about this understanding, however, and suffering is more instructively analyzed with respect to the sphere in which it takes place. The *locus classicus* on this is the opening of the *Sāṅkhya-kārikā*, but Vedāntins mention it so often that we may take it as a "cultural given." "Because of the onslaught of three kinds of suffering, there arises the inquiry into the means of getting rid of them."[7] The three kinds of suffering alluded to in the *kārikā* are personal pain, one that has no immediately evident source beyond oneself—or perhaps we should say, that is experienced as private for instance a disease such as fever or the mental pain of depression; interpersonal suffering, coming from sentient life, from bedbugs to other men; and suffering from higher powers, such as heat and cold, floods, etc. Most significantly, however, four events or states are singled out as causing the most amount of suffering: birth, death, old age, and diseases of the leprosy or plague kind.[8] The birth-death cycle, involving the doctrine of transmigration that we will introduce shortly, suggests that *becoming* itself is suffering. And then, there is the idea of hell where particularly intense torment is experienced.[9]

All of this is alluded to by the commentators in tackling the charge that Brahman as the world creator would be guilty of cruelty, and it is precisely in this context that we come closest in Indian philosophy to rhetorically imagining evil in the narrow sense of character traits, actions, events, or people that are utterly despicable, in the order of the Holocaust, genocide, or Josef Mengele the angel of death. Let us take a stock of the more graphic commentaries for a good measure. Thus Śrīnivāsa:

> It would follow that a god who creates a world that is an abode of the three kinds of suffering and makes the souls enter prime matter at the time of universal destruction, although they do not mix with it, is merciless.[10]

Śaṅkara:

> Ordaining suffering and performing the function of universal destruction, the Lord would be so utterly cruel as to provoke the odium even of villains.[11]

And to paraphrase Rāmānuja:

> It is not possible for the wholly merciful, supreme, and perfect Lord to create the world of unbearable and utterly dreadful suffering of various kinds such as birth, old age, death, and hell, even for the sake of play, without being cruel.[12]

We will return to the idea of universal destruction shortly, but note for now: there is a time when the entire world is reabsorbed into Brahman and *all* sentient life is killed. To indulge in a hyperbole: a genocide if there ever was one.

The Theodicy of Karma

Bādarāyaṇa replies that the objection is unjustified "because of there being dependence." The commentarial concord, with one important exception that we will see shortly, is that Brahman in creating the world of diverse living beings depends on their individual karma. What is this karma? It is a complex phenomenon that we might begin delineating from two angles. On the one hand, it is the law or principle that no one should experience anything that has not been personally caused in the past, and that no deed should ever remain without a consequence.[13] This principle presupposes the idea of rebirth or transmigration, *punar-janma*: that is, that the soul has occupied other bodies in lives before its present birth, the deeds in which determine experiences in this life. While in popular—and poorly informed scholarly—accounts the principle is interpreted almost as a natural law akin to Newton's third law of motion, this is a vulgarization as far as our Brahmins are concerned. The principle does not say that, for instance, s/he who killed must be killed, but simply that no experience should be undeserved and no deed without a consequence. We will revisit the intricacies in Chapter 7, but for now we will take this as the minimal definition.

On the other hand, karma is the store in which these past deeds continue to exist in the form of seeds or potencies, waiting for an appropriate time to produce adequate results. The result on its part, the specific embodiment and one's resultant actions, produce further karmic potencies or seeds, in the manner that is described as circularity between the seed and the sprout. In this sense it is customary to call karma more specifically the "karmic stock" (*karmāśaya*) or "merit and demerit" (*puṇya* and *pāpa*), respectively resulting in the varieties of happiness and suffering that we introduced in the previous section.[14] This karmic stock envelops the soul and follows it in rebirth. While the principle of karma is how the karmic stock is created, it is the stock itself that is the direct causal factor determining rebirth and one's share of happiness and suffering.

Bādarāyaṇa, thus, argues that in creating the varieties of happiness and suffering, Brahman depends on karma, and he supports the argument with scriptural references. To translate *sūtra* 2.1.33: "[But then] partiality and cruelty [would follow on the part of Brahman].—No, because of there being dependence. Scripture shows thus."[15]

The scriptural references culled from the commentators present Brahman as a secondary agent, one acting in the causative verbal mode and called "instigator" (*prayojaka*) by the Sanskrit grammarians, the primary agent being the individual soul. Thus, for the first: "He himself makes him whom he wishes to raise from these worlds do good deeds, and him whom he wishes to bring down—bad deeds."[16] And, for the second: "One becomes meritorious by meritorious deeds, wretched by wretched deeds."[17] This idea of two agents calls for a clarification of the causal structure responsible for the production of animate life and its happiness and suffering. Two models of such relative causal efficacy emerge from the commentaries, but it would appear that they involve more verbal than substantive difference. Śaṅkara says that Brahman is the *general* or *common* cause (*sādhāraṇa-kāraṇa*) whereas karma is the *specific* or *unique* cause (*asādhāraṇa-kāraṇa*). The general cause operates across products, but precisely for this reason, it cannot determine the specific differences among them: an individuating factor is required, and that is the specific cause. Think of the growth of crops or plants: while all species require water and soil—in that sense we may describe them as necessary but insufficient causes—what precisely will grow on the soil depends on the seed. Brahman, thus, is like rain in Śaṅkara's example or soil and water in Sudarśana Sūri's example, whereas the karmic stock is like the seed.

Rāmānuja, on the other hand, quotes two verses from the *Viṣṇu Purāṇa* where Brahman is presented as the *nimitta-kāraṇa*, the *efficient* cause, whereas the capacities of the future created beings are the *upādāna-kāraṇa*, the *material* cause of what they will become. Thus, to use Śaṅkara's example, the rain would be the efficient cause whereas the seed, the material cause of the crop; likewise Brahman would be the efficient cause whereas the karmic stock—the material cause of becoming a god with pure happiness or a man with a mixture of happiness and suffering. Rāmānuja's commentator Sudarśana Sūri, however, treats this as purely a matter of verbal, not substantive, difference.[18]

Now, one may wonder why Brahman should be such a general or efficient cause: Why cannot karma be the sole causal factor exerting full efficacy over the varieties of creation? One obvious reason is the monistic ontology of the *Brahma-sūtra*: since Brahman is the only first principle, karma would have to be somewhere in the ontological continuum between Brahman and the world such that it be possible to describe karma as the proximate and Brahman as the distal cause. In this sense, the relative causality of Brahman and karma would be an instantiation of Bādarāyaṇa's general theory of preexistence of the effect in the cause, which, to remember, meant that the effect proceeds from the cause *but* with a surplus of some and deficiency of other characteristics. Thus, although Brahman is the sole first principle, it becomes possible to view Brahman and karma as distinct causal factors and to deliberate on their relative role. Because the karmic stock belongs immediately to the individual souls, the varieties of happiness and suffering would pertain solely to their ontological surplus, not to Brahman per se.

Although this ontologically must be the case, I think that something else is intended by calling Brahman the general or efficient cause. The context is not that of karma's originative relationship to Brahman—indeed, the karmic stock is already somewhat constituted—but of the relative causal efficacy with respect to the varieties of happiness and suffering and the classes of beings where they are experienced. The problem is that the karmic stock consists of *insentient potentials*, and for such potentials to fructify intelligent guidance is required. Additionally, an *omniscient intelligence* is necessary for the karmic coordination of total animate life. It is rather this role that Brahman performs with respect to the varieties of happiness and suffering of the individual souls—activating appropriate karmic seeds at an appropriate time and keeping the world's karmic "balance sheet"—and in that sense it is justified to describe Brahman as the efficient cause. Indeed, Naiyāyika's have developed this into a formal argument for the existence of God: since karma and similar causes are insentient, an intelligent cause is required for their functioning, just as the insentient axe requires an intelligent axe wielder.[19]

While Bādarāyaṇa's statement certainly addresses the problem of partiality, does it answer the question of cruelty and evil? It surely moves the full burden of responsibility to the individual, and with that, it makes suffering ultimately self-inflicted. It may be profitable at this point to pause and reflect on the idea of evil itself. We introduced earlier its restricted sense of utter moral depravity; however, in contemporary philosophy of religion evil is defined more broadly as "anything bad," such as physical or mental suffering, famine, or hurtful speech.[20] Nevertheless, a causal distinction is drawn between "natural" evil, for instance an earthquake or a tsunami over which human agents generally have no influence, and "moral" evil in which human agents bear the responsibility for the resultant suffering, for instance the aforementioned raping of the five-year-old girl. This distinction, however, is not particularly useful for our context, as ultimately there is no "natural" or any other kind of suffering that cannot be traced to a "moral" evil, to one's own fault or transgression done in the past, including previous lives. A more organic classification of "evil," therefore, would be into *suffering* on the one hand, further divided according to the three sources, and *bad karma*—wicked past deeds that have shaped one's *karmic stock*—on the other. Bādarāyaṇa's reference to the idea of karma, thus, seems to address the problem not only of partiality but of the facticity of evil as well: *nothing* that one may experience is undeserving; *every* experience is caused by some past action of the agent!

The Soul as Agent

It is apposite here before we continue with karma to pay one debt to Chapter 3 and briefly discuss Bādarāyaṇa's heading on the soul's characteristic of agency.[21] The background is again that of Sāṅkhya, where the soul is said to be an agent of experience, specifically of karma, but not of action. The underlying Sāṅkhya concern is soteriological—an *essentially* active soul could never become free of karma—but there is a soteriological price to pay as well. If the soul is not an agent, then it cannot exercise free will. How can, then, it ever become liberated? The Sāṅkhya reply is given in *Sāṅkhya-kārikā* 62: the soul *does not* become liberated, because it was never bound to begin with. It is only prime matter that binds and liberates itself. Even the soul's agency of experience is agency just "in a manner of speaking," because the soul is in mere proximity and not true union with prime matter.

The Sāṅkhya argument is bolstered by strong references, adduced by the commentators in presenting the prima facie view, from no less authoritative source than the *Bhagavad-gītā*, which says that it is the modes or *guṇa*s of prime matter that act, whereas the soul is merely the enjoyer of happiness and suffering, that is, of karma.[22]

There is again a major disagreement in the interpretation of the *adhikaraṇa*, and Śaṅkara and Bhāskara implicitly endorse the Sāṅkhya view, making the entire *adhikaraṇa* a prima facie view as it were. Their interpretation can be right only if their understanding of embodiment and liberation are shared by Bādarāyaṇa. We have seen how they are on their own with respect to the first, and in Chapter 7 a similar story will emerge with respect to the second. We side, therefore, with Nimbārka and Rāmānuja.

Bādarāyaṇa's argument about the soul's agency is theological, and its core is that for scriptural injunctions to make sense, the soul must be the agent, and the agent of action and experience must be identical.[23] This is based on a principle stated in *Mīmāṁsā-sūtra*: "The result of undertaking scripturally enjoined action belongs to the undertaker."[24] In Bādarāyaṇa's context, the principle specifically pertains to the attainment of *samādhi* or meditative absorption in which the vision of Brahman, whereupon liberation is consequent, obtains. If the soul has no agency in the meditative act, then it would not be entitled to the results of *samādhi* either.[25]

As we have seen earlier, the soul is not the only agent, and Bādarāyaṇa again affirms Brahman's crucial role: "[The agency of the soul], however, [comes] from the Supreme, because there are scriptural texts [to this effect]."[26] The texts identified by the commentators are those which we have seen in the case of Brahman's causative agency in the experience of karma, and similar dependence is stated here as well: not only does Brahman depend on karma in the domain of experience, but he also depends on the effort of the soul as the primary agent with respect to action, for otherwise injunctions and prohibitions would be useless.[27] Agency, then, must involve a degree of freedom, and while the experience of happiness and suffering are contingent on karma, karma is ultimately grounded in free will.

The "No Beginning" of Karma

However, the reference to karma does not necessarily address one issue taken up by the commentators: that of universal destruction. This provides a good occasion for us to tackle the last *sūtra* of concern, and for Bādarāyaṇa to clarify the last details about Brahman's causality. An objection is raised that the karma argument is faulty because karma is not individuated. That is, when Brahman creates the world, presumably all individual souls would start with a clean slate, without an initial karmic stock, such that it would be impossible to explain how subsequent differences appear. Bādarāyaṇa rejects this "because there is no beginning." What does this mean?

It is, in fact, possible to talk about Brahman's creation in two senses. We saw in Chapter 3 that Brahman is the sole first principle, but that prime matter as name-and-form and the individual souls are dependent ontological principles, whatever precisely this dependency is. To the degree that prime matter and the souls are different from Brahman, we may understand them as Brahman's products, not in a temporal but a logical sense: they are dependent yet non-created principles. The evolution of name-and form, on the other hand, is Brahman's temporal creation—as the Upaniṣadic account says, "in the beginning, this, the world, was just Being"—but such creation is also in a sense non-temporal: it happens in cycles of creation, duration, and reabsorption in Brahman, but without a beginning to the cycle series. What does this mean for the karma argument? There was no first instant at which the souls were "with a clean slate." As the commentators emphasize, there was no beginning to the flow of their karma, for which reason the problem of karmic individuation does not arise.

Bhāskara here eloquently extends the seed-and-sprout analogy, mentioned by most commentators, from the individual karmic stock to the world itself. The world of transmigration and varieties of happiness and suffering for the members of different classes of animate life is a product of karma—the classes of gods, men, and animals in the beginning of creation are populated by souls with appropriate karma—yet it is also the domain in which karma is created. "By the logic of the seed-and-sprout, the world creation depends on karma, and the creation of karma depends on the world."[28] The analogy is meant to illustrate the non-beginning discussed earlier by replacing the notion of linear with cyclical time. Now, this obviously raises the problem of what Indian philosophers call mutual dependence or ontological circularity—we saw it in the Sāṅkhya account of creation—and is known to us as the chicken-or-the-egg causality dilemma. Thus, charges Bhāskara's opponent:

> The seed-and-sprout illustration is not proper. How so? Because of mutual dependence. Was the seed first, or the sprout? It is not possible to ascertain therein which is prior and which posterior. The prior is the cause, while the posterior is the effect, that is how causality is established, but that cannot be done in this case.[29]

Now, Bhāskara's reply, it seems to me, amounts to claiming that the causal relationship is not between *the two genera* of karma and world categories, such that one may ask is *a* chicken prior to *an* egg or the other way around, but between *individual karmas in succession*. Pursuing the example, we readily observe that a seed arises from an anterior sprout and in turn becomes anterior to another sprout, in a perpetual succession that does not involve mutual dependence. Such a case of mutual dependence would arise if we had the two genera in mind, *two discrete things* that would perpetually chase after each other's tail, but we rather have *individual instances of the same continuum*. As we saw in the previous chapter, Vedāntins would not accept the seed and the sprout as two things in any case, but only as two states of the same thing. So, it is not that karma determines the classes of gods, men, and so on at the beginning of creation: they are potentials in Brahman, linguistic seeds that materialize when creation is current. Karma simply populates them in the new cycle and then the soul replenishes the karmic stock, but all the while, it is the soul that undergoes different states.

But, has Bhāskara answered the question about the *start* of this seed-sprout *series*? How can there be no first point of karma? Indeed, it has been argued that the karmic infinite regress ignores rather than solves the problem:

> The problem is quite general: how did the karmic process begin? What was the first wrong? Who was the original sufferer? This familiar objection points out that rebirth provides no solution at all, but simply pushes the problem back.[30]

It seems to me that the objections to there being no first point, as they have been stated, betray a Judeo-Christian cultural bias where we are accustomed to thinking about creation *ex nihilo* that happens in time. But it was clear even to Catholic theologians that creation in time is not a matter of reason but of revelation. If God is eternal, all that is required is that God be the first principle in a logical, not a temporal sense—indeed, in the *Viṣṇu Purāṇa*, time is a third principle, coeval with prime matter and the souls, as Brahman's direct creation[31]—and God could have just as well eternally created the world.[32] With that, the ball needs to be kicked back: How could karma have a first point in a creation that does not happen in time, *at a first point*, but has been going on in a circle for all eternity?

But, perhaps the uneasiness with "no beginning" can be stated better: beginningless karma on the face of it does not solve the original problem, that of karmic individuation. Granted the "flow of karma," as our commentators call it, hasn't a beginning, it is still unclear why an individual at any point becomes one thing rather than another. All other things being equal, how is the beginningless karmic flow differentiated if the souls are equal and Brahman is impartial? Put differently, the problem with origins is not necessarily one of *time*, but of *choice* to do one thing rather than another such that the countless karmic flows can be individuated.

It seems to me that a necessary entailment is that all individual souls are, in the final analysis, *unique* rather than *identical* members of the same class, each one with a touch of idiosyncrasy. This could be the reason why all theistic commentators insist on the beginningless nature not only of the karma-creation complex but of the individual souls as well, although it is only Madhva who explicitly vocalizes such a doctrine of ultimate uniqueness.[33] Notably, this solution does not work in Śaṅkara's case, where beginningless karma is not only the individuating factor of any temporal state, but *constitutive* of the individual soul itself, in what is a bad or impossible circularity. We will revisit this in Chapter 7.

Be that as it may, Bādarāyaṇa's final *sūtra* in full translation runs: "If it be said, 'no, because karma would not be individuated,' we reply, 'no, because it is beginningless. This makes sense and it is seen in scripture.'"[34] The reference to scripture helps Bādarāyaṇa portray the final details about Brahman's causality: creation is a cyclical evolution of name-and-form. "The creator fashioned the sun and the moon, just as he did before."[35] "He individuated in name-and-form that which was undeveloped in the beginning."[36] So, Brahman evolves its name-and-form, *itself* as the material cause, and places the individual souls in respective bodies where they can experience happiness and suffering according to their karmic stock. With respect to the initial creation, the karmic stock is sort of an accessory cause, but it is really the material cause of the future states of the souls, in which respect Brahman continues being the efficient cause, bringing karmic potentials to fruition. Karma is not, however, an accessory cause outside of Brahman: Bādarāyaṇa, we saw, rejected such a model of causality. In the *Bṛhad-āraṇyaka*, in fact, karma is the third component or mode of Brahman's being the material cause, such that we should really speak about *nāma rūpa karma*: "This, the world, is in fact a triad: name, form, and karma."[37] Finally, Brahman does this creation thing over and over, just as any interesting game ought to be played.

Parenthetically, we may now add the "final" final note in the story of words and universals. In every creation cycle, the offices of gods and sages in the "cosmic administration" are filled by different individuals, such that the words of the Vedas are truly denotive of classes. Cyclic creations are like elections, and "Indra" and "Vasiṣṭha" are not referential like "Barack Obama" or "Donald Trump," but like "President" or "Jester."

And it is perhaps here that we must seek the final answer about Brahman's alleged cruelty in the periodic total destructions on macrocosmic level, and in the cycle of transmigration as their microcosmic counterpart: these are scriptural facts, and we rest our case. Like any good game, the game of creation has timeouts, halftimes, and off-season. We may not understand it in the light of reason, but we will appreciate its aesthetic value: "Having withdrawn the objects in himself in the reverse order at universal destruction, Vāsudeva remains in silence, like a boy who has gathered up his toys."[38]

Karma and Brahman's Omnipotence

One glaring problem raised by this theodicy is that karma would seem to compromise Brahman's omnipotence. If Brahman *depends* on karma in the dispensation of happiness and suffering, then he cannot be an omnipotent being, since omnipotence, whatever it may otherwise mean, must at least connote independence. Thus, Wendy Doniger writes, "The flaws in this solution are immediately apparent. The hypothesis of karma violates the hypothesis of omnipotence and thus bypasses rather than resolves theodicy. If God is under the sway of karma, he is not omnipotent."[39]

The *Brahma-sūtra* seems to say explicitly that Brahman depends on karma: while *sāpekṣatva* literally means "having a regard for," it is true that the term is used primarily in a sense of deficiency. But perhaps it does not say this at all. In his cryptic fashion, Bādarāyaṇa simply says, "because of dependence." While the commentators are almost in unison that it is the Lord who depends on karma, Rāmānuja in fact comments that it is *the variegated creation* that depends on karma. His commentator Sudarśana Sūri clarifies: "Who depends on what? God does not depend on karma in the act of creation. The dependence on karma is only with respect to the created inequality."[40] In other words, karma is not a restriction of Brahman's creative power, but sort of an input that Brahman takes into account when creating. This certainly makes sense in light of the complex karmic causality that we described earlier. In this reading, then, Bādarāyaṇa does not say that Brahman *depends* on karma—that karma mandates Brahman how to create—but that the inequalities of happiness and suffering are contingent on karma. How that affects Brahman's omnipotence obviously depends on how one understands such "omnipotence" and on what ontological model one subscribes to.

With that, we should first clarify what bells would our "omnipotence" ring for Vedāntins. As we saw in Chapter 3, Brahman's literal "omnipotence," the characteristic of *sarva-śakti*, must be understood in the sense of cosmogenic and ontological omnipotence: Brahman is constitutively such an entity that contains all potential and all capacities to produce all things without requiring external stuff or agents. In that sense, karma must be understood as ultimately, but non-temporally, originating in Brahman, as Brahman's *śakti*, albeit vicariously through the individual souls. As such, karma must be Brahman's function and another feature of Brahman's omnipotence: it cannot compromise Brahman's omnipotence, as it is partially constitutive of it. Vijñānabhikṣu, in fact, says this explicitly: "But then, is it not the case that God who has regard for karma would lose his independence? Not so. Karma is not a hindrance to independence, because it is God's product and power."[41] God's dependence on karma would involve some form of ontological dualism, which is not the *Brahma-sūtra* doctrine.

It is not, therefore, with respect to such omnipotence that the commentators ask the question of dependence. Vācaspati's concern is whether the dependence on karma reflects poorly on God's "lordliness" or "majesty," the sovereignty to do as one pleases or exercise absolute freedom. The cultural image of such absolute freedom is the king—remember the ballgame—

who is superordinate to the laws of the land and can do whatever he wants: indeed, we will see in Chapter 7 that the highest human good, liberation, is understood just in those terms. That such a king distributes his gifts in dependence to the service or disservice of his subjects does not make him less powerful than he would otherwise be. Clearly, the king had chosen to adopt a principle to govern his action, although he is not obliged to do that and could, in virtue of his power, act indiscriminately.[42] Arguably, again, karma is a feature of Brahman's independence rather than its fault.

Keśava Kāśmīrī comes with a slightly different and more technically theological concern, prompted by the argument that Brahman is the general condition and karma the specific and decisive causal factor. In the conceptual apparatus of Vedic theology, at first appearance this would make karma the primary factor in the causal complex, the "boss," placing Brahman in a subordinate position and compromising his omnipotence. Vedic theologians have understood processes as consisting of one primary and an x number of subordinate causal factors. Without going into intricate details and specific disagreements, we may illustrate this with the technology of a ritual undertaking. The organizing principle of a ritual is the act of offering, but the act requires a myriad of other elements, for instance the material offering, its preparation, the required stuff, and so on. Since the operative factor for the attaining of the result is the act itself—much as, to banalize, kicking the ball would be decisive for scoring a goal—this makes the act primary, while all other causal factors are "for its sake." It is easy to imagine how in the process of allotment of happiness and suffering karma would be such a decisive and organizing factor, given the intention to place the burden of inequality on its shoulder, and Sudarśana Sūri states this distinctly: karma as the "specific cause" is the "primary causal factor," whereas the Lord as the "general condition" is the subordinate or "non-primary factor."

This, however, raises the abovementioned theological problem: Is karma Brahman's superordinate? Keśava argues against this by referring to Vācaspati's example. When a king decides to distribute rewards in conformity to service, he has not made himself subordinate to the principle. He is not serving *for the sake of the principle*, but rather uses the principle for his own sake.[43] The specific example, in fact, points to an old discussion in Śabara's commentary on the *Mīmāṁsā-sūtra* concerning the nature of the subordinate-superordinate relationship.[44] The *Mīmāṁsā-sūtra* defines a subordinate as "being for the sake of another" (*parārtha*), but it becomes important to clarify in what sense that is so. Imagine a master who buys a slave by birth, proposes Śabara (apologies for the moral depravity of the example). The slave is "for the sake" of the master, serving the master's needs. One may object, however, that such is not always the case: insofar as the master takes care of the slave, providing food and shelter, he becomes for the servant's sake, and one could say: subordinate. Śabara's final clarification, therefore, is to introduce the category of subordinate *absolutely* (*atyantaṁ parārtha*). While the master may be subordinate to the servant in a relative sense, the servant is subordinate absolutely in that the master has a use of him in feeding and providing shelter. In the case of ritual, then, although the act is predominant in terms of process, the beneficiary for whose sake the ritual is performed remains superordinate to the process itself. Following this logic, one could say that while Brahman as the general cause depends on karma, he in fact uses karma to distribute happiness and suffering in a just manner and remains superordinate to it. By that much, karma does not affect Brahman's omnipotence but is, again, its *modus operandi*.

Toward a Soteriological Theodicy

But, does this reaffirmation of omnipotence tackle the question, "why there should be evil *at all*?" If Brahman guides insentient karma while the responsibility for all good and bad experiences rests with the individual souls, it is still proper to ask, "Is Brahman compelled to coexist with karma and suffering, albeit on top of things, and if so, what does remain of his omnipotence? Wouldn't an omnipotent God be able to create a world without the possibility of evil?" While the theodicy of karma tackles the problem of partiality, it does not quite take up the question of the teleology of suffering.

One could say that Brahman does, in fact, "create" such a world, *brahmaloka* the domain of the liberated souls that we will encounter in Chapter 7, but the problem becomes all the more glaring in view of Bādarāyaṇa's theology of play which, I argued, rejects the prima facie Sāṅkhya doctrine that creation is for the purpose of liberation. This Sāṅkhya-like doctrine—that the world with all its suffering is meant to serve as the emancipation ground for the individual, sharing some similarity with what John Hick has called a "soul-making theodicy" following the tradition of St. Irenaeus—has had a place of pride in ancient Indian thought.[45] We need but think of the story of the Buddha and his four sights—an old man, a sick man, a corpse, and a renunciant—which set him on his journey toward enlightenment. Buddhist and Jaina sources also narrate the story of four ancient kings—Nimi, Dumukkha, Karaṇḍu, and Naggaji—who witness a scene that so strikingly illustrates the unavoidable suffering and strife in the world that they take up the life of mendicants on the spot and attain the state of solitary enlightened beings.[46]

My point is this: one could coherently argue that the omnibenevolent Brahman would have had a good use of suffering and evil that are necessary for the liberation of the eternally bound, imperfect but perfectible, souls. Yet, Bādarāyaṇa does not go there.

But, perhaps Bādarāyaṇa's rejection of Sāṅkhya concerns solely liberation as the final cause which is simultaneously the efficient cause of creation. Could liberation still be the final cause independently, and if so, have theodicean significance for Vedāntins? We saw Uddyotakara and Rāmānuja argue directly or through entailment that liberation cannot be the efficient cause because of vicious ontological circularity: liberation presupposes creation, yet it is supposed to set the world in motion. But, when Brahman creates in his playful exuberance and the individual souls have had their karma from the non-beginning of time, could it be that the world already constituted *is* for the sake of liberation? At least one commentator would happily reply in the affirmative.

The Śaiva theologian Śrīkaṇṭha in his commentary duly elaborates on the theology of play and karma, but then apparently switches gears when the following question is posed: since karma is insentient, it would not give an impetus to creation were it not for God to direct it. Why does God need to activate the karma of the individual souls? Why cannot they just remain unembodied and happy? Why would that omnibenevolent being put them in bodies and make karma unfold? Śrīkaṇṭha replies that unless this karma is consumed—and in Śaivism karma is consumed by a combination of human striving and divine grace—they cannot attain the supreme bliss of liberation. In other words, the souls cannot attain beatitude before they are rid of all karma. So, the omnibenevolent Śiva creates the world as the arena in which liberation becomes possible. He does that *for their sake*—so much for the theology of play—such that all individual souls would eventually attain liberation.[47] In doing so, he remains impartial like the sun that makes all things grow at their own pace. Those who work on their purity by engaging in Śaiva ritual and actively pursue liberation—those who place themselves in "Śiva's purifying fire"[48]—become free sooner than others, but eventually all will get there. That is how Śiva is, in fact, omnipotent, omnibenevolent, *and* just. It wouldn't be right for him to liberate all souls indiscriminately, to put an end to all suffering, but he can use karma to facilitate the "soul-making" on their part. Alternatively, the pursuit of liberation as an exercise of free will does not make sense unless such free will accommodates wrong choices.[49]

Omnipotence and Divine Justice

This argument of Śrīkāṇṭha is about a different impartiality on the part of Brahman, not concerning the just allotment of happiness and suffering but the success of soteriological aspirations. The issue is commonly discussed by Vedāntins, and it concerns yet again the matter of divine justice and omnipotence. If the law of karma is the means whereby Brahman remains just, and the condition of Brahman's omnipotence is that he must be able to break the law, what happens when he does, in fact, break it in affirmation of his omnipotence? What happens when he ceases being merely the administrator of karma and directly intervenes in the world, as the faithful hope he might? One such situation in the Hindu imaginary is the doctrine of *avatāra* or the incarnation, when God descends to earth and takes over the reins from the law of karma. Another one is the idea of divine grace, as when Śiva facilitates the consumption of karma and the attainment of liberation, or when Kṛṣṇa claims in the *Bhagavad-gītā* that he particularly cares for his devotees.[50] In such cases, does God remain just, or has he suspended his own instrument of justice, karma? The Śaiva argument that God simply responds to those who have placed themselves in his fire was perhaps the most common response to this question. Śaṅkara makes the same argument in his *Bhagavad-gītā* commentary. Whom God favors is a matter of who decides to approach him, just as fire gives warmth to those who get close. Such favoritism is not a case of partiality. Śaṅkara's commentator Ānandagiri gives the same illustration of the sun as Śrīkaṇṭha.[51]

One *Brahma-sūtra* commentator, nevertheless, was willing to call the spade a spade. The Vaiṣṇava theologian Baladeva argued that when God protects the faithful or his devotees, there is another "dependence" involved, not to the law of karma but to the law of *bhakti* or devotion, where the devotee attempts to forge a personal relationship with him on soteriological rather than karmic terms. Such *bhakti* is a function of God's inner, more essential *śakti* or faculty. And, where devotion is involved, of course God does not remain impartial! Baladeva rejects the reasoning that devotion can be reduced to karma so as to spare God of impartiality. Rather, in such cases the law of karma is suspended. And, he goes on to argue that this partiality is not a fault on the part of God: it is rather an embellishment. In other words, this is not God's warming effect over the devotee in the manner of the impartial fire, through proximity: an entirely different divine function is exercised![52]

This may leave us wondering, how can God be partial and impartial at the same time, and has divine justice been rejected at the expense of omnipotence? Baladeva's argument, however, should be read in the light of an ancient ontological doctrine that says that *any* entity may simultaneously bear mutually opposed properties. Think, for instance, of the question, is milk healthy. You will likely seek a clarification first: healthy for who? It is essential for babies but very bad for the lactose intolerant. Or, in Kumārila's old example: Does drinking alcohol cause bad karma? Again, it depends on who is drinking, and sometimes also what. A brahmin priest will generally create bad karma by having a few, but not his servant.[53] This means that things must have innate properties or faculties, *śakti*s, that are *constitutively relational*, and because a thing is never isolated, it is perfectly possible for it to bear mutually opposite properties at the same time, according as the specific relation. Baladeva was a follower of a Vedāntic tradition in which this became the central doctrine. It is perfectly reasonable for Brahman to possess mutually opposed properties. Asking whether his being partial compromises divine justice completely disregards Brahman's essential relationality, or, to use Charles Hartshorne's turn of phrase from his eponymous book, the "Divine relativity."[54] Brahman would be able to treat different individuals per the rules of karma or per the rules of *bhakti*, dependent on where they stand in relation to him. Such simultaneous partiality and impartiality would be just another instance of ontological omnipotence.

The Theodicy of Śaṅkara

But, perhaps our Śaivas and Vaiṣṇavas have brought us too far afield into theistic waters. To restore balance, I wish to end the chapter with an excursion outside of the few *sūtra*s and follow a lead of the *Brahma-sūtra*'s most celebrated commentator Śaṅkara. At the end of his comment on the theology of play, Śaṅkara makes the following crucial statement:

> It should never be forgotten that the Upaniṣadic statements of creation are not concerned with the absolute truth, because their scope is the common sphere of name-and-form superimposed by ignorance, and because their purpose is to present the unity of Brahman and the Self.[55]

Śaṅkara here refers to an idea which Advaitins share with Buddhist philosophers, that of two truths, a conventional truth of how things need to be so that the functioning of the world of various agents as well as soteriological aspirations may be possible, and an absolute truth of how things really are upon philosophical analysis or in the light of scripture. We cannot go into the details of this, but for Śaṅkara the Upaniṣadic accounts of creation can be read in two ways: through the lens of the conventional truth so as to explain how the world proceeds from Brahman the first principle; or through the lens of the absolute truth in which Brahman, omniscient and omnipotent under the requirements of causality, in the ultimate analysis ceases being that, because it is just the light of consciousness that does not admit of the discourse of causality at all. Brahman the great ground of Being is, really, *just* the inner Self, one and only for everyone, never really producing the world.

What Śaṅkara does with the above-cited statement seems prima facie to reject Bādarāyaṇa's account, and yet he goes on to interpret the *adhikaraṇa* in a manner presupposing the reality of creation. This had prompted Bimal Krishna Matilal to read Śaṅkara's statement in the following way:

> He does not say that since creation is nothing but superimposition of diversity through false belief, the question of the creator's being unjust and cruel does not arise. On the other hand he finds it important and necessary to justify the realist's (or the popular) notion of creation and the Creator God. One may wonder why. I believe that he did not reject realism outright, but having a firm footing in the realist's world he argued that the ultimate truth transcends the realists view of diversity and shows its ultimate unity with Brahman. Hence a defense of the ordinary notion of creation is also necessary.[56]

To be accurate, for Śaṅkara it is never about the unity of the *world* with Brahman, but only of the inner Self. The world as such is illusory pure and simple, but it has soteriological value. That aside, however, I wish to maintain that the question of the creator's being unjust and cruel *does not* arise if one were to follow the consequences of Śaṅkara's statement. What Śaṅkara does in the remainder of his *Brahma-sūtra* commentary on the section under analysis is going along with the standpoint of what is for him the conventional truth, because that is what Bādarāyaṇa does. A very different theology and theodicy would follow from Śaṅkara's standpoint of the absolute truth. Śaṅkara does reconsider the question of purpose in his comment on the *Bhagavad-gītā* 9.10, where he takes the stand of the absolute truth and argues that neither the question nor the answer concerning world creation is relevant.

To elaborate, if one were to assume that Brahman creates the world for his own pleasure, that would negate what Brahman really is, nothing more than the pure Self in virtue of which the empirical self, the individual soul, has a sense of self-identity. Brahman is just the light of consciousness, not an agent who would do anything for one's own benefit. Thus, Brahman does not have a positive attitude toward existent things, and in that sense, they are not objects to him. But, neither could it be said that the world was created for someone else. Things in the world exist only because they are objects of consciousness. For something to exist, it must exist *for* someone:

> All the activities in the world take place because things are objects of perception: "I enjoy in this; I see this; I hear this; I feel pleasure; I feel pain; I shall do this for that purpose; I shall learn this." All things, thus, begin in consciousness; they endure in consciousness; and end in consciousness.[57]

For a thing to exist for someone's benefit, it must exist for some consciousness. And yet, there is no conscious being other than Brahman.

One may argue that if Brahman as the pure Self is the only knower, this would make all the defects of the world objects to his consciousness, experienced by him the knower: Brahman itself would experience the suffering of the world. The point, however, is that Brahman's consciousness is never transitive; it never has objective content. Brahman is the knower just "in a manner of speaking," as one may say that fire gives warmth when it is heat that gives warmth. Knowledge is a process, and Brahman is never processual. The elements of the cognitive process—subject, object, instruments, cognition—are superimposed on Brahman by ignorance. All objectivity in the ultimate analysis is relevant on the level of conventional truth. There is no real relationship between the objects and consciousness, and the superimposition of what is phenomenal over consciousness is, ultimately, illusory. World creation is a magical show, but even that from the conventional standpoint: not only is Brahman not fooled by the magical show—*it is unaware of it,* for such awareness would compromise Brahman. We cannot import any positive content in the idea of Brahman as the knower, as consciousness, for when we do so Brahman is immediately relegated to conventional reality.

Thus, questions and answer concerning world creation are not proper from the standpoint of the absolute truth. If there is no duality and if Brahman is a pure subject with no objects of consciousness—in other words, if there is no world—it is irrelevant to speak about the problem of creation. This has massive theodicean consequences. If Brahman as the only knower is not aware of anything positive, there is no problem of suffering at all, for one cannot suffer that which one is not aware of. Śaṅkara's real theodicy, expressed from the standpoint of absolute truth, is that any and all theodicy is irrelevant. Speaking about creation and suffering just presupposes ignorance.

Study Questions

1. Evaluate the Vedāntic justification of God in the ways of evil (theodicy): is it a successful solution to the problem of evil?
2. Have Bādarāyaṇa's commentators successfully defended Brahman against the charge that the dependence on karma violates omnipotence?
3. Is Baladeva's account of God's partiality to his devotees a violation of divine justice? In other words, can *bhakti* or divine partiality as a consequence of Brahman's omnipotence run parallel to karma, without compromising divine justice?
4. Reflect on the social consequences of the theodicy of karma: can it accommodate aspirations for social justice, and if so, how?
5. Research how omnipotence is understood in contemporary philosophy of religion (a place to start is Hoffman and Rosenkrantz 2020) and reflect on how similar or different this understanding is from what is here (and in the third chapter) described as *ontological* omnipotence.

Suggestions for Further Study

McBrayer and Howard-Snyder (2013) is a readable guide on the problem of evil; particularly useful are chapters 1 (historical overview), 2 (on the logical problem of evil), 4 (on the evidential argument from evil), and 19 (on theodicy in India, written by Purushottama Bilimoria). Hick (2010, first published in 1966) is a classic on the problem of evil in Christian theology, in which two basic theodicies are traced: evil as a lack of good, and evil as a soul-making mechanism; the second can be favorably compared with forms of Vedāntic theodicies, as in the case of Śrīkaṇṭha. On the problem of evil in Indian philosophy, Herman (1993) is a thorough overview. Doniger (1980b) tackles the same question, but her focus is on Hindu mythology. Clooney (1989) is an analysis of the problem of evil in Advaita Vedānta, focused on the *sūtra*s that we cover in this chapter. Similar in scope is Matilal (1992), which the reader may contrast with my analyses here. Kaufman (2005) is a philosophical challenge to the doctrine of karma as a solution for the problem of evil. Much has been written on the history and the philosophical significance of karma in Hinduism. Good accounts are available in Halbfass (1991, chapter 9) and Doniger (1980a). Sprung (1973) is an edited volume on the idea of two truths, which I argued was significant for Śaṅkara's theodicy. Of the several papers, those by T. R. V. Murti, Richard W. Brooks, and J. G. Arapura are the most pertinent for Advaita Vedānta.

6

The Doctrine of Meditation on Brahman

In his discussion of liberation in the *Śloka-Vārttika*, the great Mīmāṁsaka Kumārila Bhaṭṭa argued that knowledge of the self as different from the body is for the sake of ritual: the engagement in performing a ritual is contingent on understanding that there is an eternal self which outlives the body and can enjoy the ritual results in the future. Knowledge of the self is not for-the-good-of-man, as Mīmāṁsakas say: it is not directly efficacious in bringing about the human good.[1]

This appears to have been, in fact, a long-standing Mīmāṁsā position. As far as we can infer from the *Brahma-sūtra,* the general Mīmāṁsā attitude toward the Upaniṣads was that they provide some esoteric knowledge whose purpose is to bring about a refinement or embellishment of particular ritual items. The scriptural justification of this principle was taken from a statement in the *Chāndogya*: "Only that which is performed with knowledge, with faith, and with an awareness of the hidden connections becomes truly potent."[2]

Two words are important in the *Chāndogya* statement: *vidyā*, translated as "knowledge," and *upaniṣad*, translated as "awareness of the hidden connections." The context of the passage is the *udgītha,* the central element of a Sāma Veda song, which is here identified with the syllable Oṁ, the understanding of which identity is supposed to fulfill all kinds of desire.[3] This knowledge embellishes the *udgītha* such that if it is chanted in a ritual with an understanding that it is Oṁ, the results of the ritual are enhanced. Early Mīmāṁsakas made this a principle that concerns the Upaniṣads generally: knowing the hidden connection of the *udgītha* with Oṁ embellishes the *udgītha* and enhances the ritual, and likewise knowing the self as distinct from matter embellishes that self which is the ritual agent.[4] If some independent result is said to follow from this knowledge of the self, such as liberation, that is a "ritual commercial break" where the Veda is trying to "sell" the taking up of such embellishments. Statements of such kind generally are meant for praise, *arthavāda*, and have no truth-value. The *Brahma-sūtra* puts this doctrine directly into Jaimini's mouth.[5]

The claim that all forms of esoteric knowledge in the Upaniṣads are for refinement of ritual items was rejected by Bādarāyaṇa as specific to the *udgītha* rather than general,[6] but Jaimini's particular assertion about knowledge of the self was a much more complex story. The claim that the self as an agent and the knowledge of the self as distinct from the body are for the sake of ritual was not directly controverted. What Bādarāyaṇa denied was that the Upaniṣads as a scriptural corpus are *really*, *only*, or even *primarily* about that. Śaṅkara is typically eloquent on this point: "Had the transmigrating soul *alone*—the embodied agent and experiencer—been taught in the Upaniṣads as merely distinct from the body, then the Upaniṣadic statement of results could have been a statement of praise in the aforementioned manner."[7]

That there is such an entity as a permanent self which survives death and can enjoy the results of ritual in the future is knowable from the Veda, as the Veda is the reliable warrant on supersensible matters; the Upaniṣads provide that knowledge, becoming subservient to ritual in that specific capacity. But, claimed Bādarāyaṇa, the Upaniṣads *primarily* teach a principle higher than this transmigrating self, in virtue of which they are the means of another, independent good of man, liberation. Because of this higher instruction, liberation cannot be explained away as mere talk and no substance.[8] This brings us to considering what this higher teaching is and how the *Brahma-sūtra* presented the Upaniṣads as a distinct canon that serves the human good.

And, it is important to be mindful of the "human good." One of the central and long-standing presuppositions of Vedic theology was that the purpose of the Veda was to provide for some human good that is not known by natural means. In the *Mīmāṁsā-sūtra*, this was the role of *dharma*. Śabara Svāmin defined *dharma* as that which brings human good, indeed the highest good (*niḥśreyasa*), and for the most part *dharma* was identified with ritual.[9] The *Brahma-sūtra*, again, puts this doctrine in Jaimini's mouth,[10] and the challenge for Bādarāyaṇa in defining the Upaniṣads as a canon distinct from the Brāhmaṇas of Mīmāṁsā was to show how the Upaniṣads serve the human good in a way different from or independent of ritual. This specific difference of the Upaniṣads was found in the doctrine of *vidyā* and *upāsana*, both of which I will translate as "meditation" for reasons to which I now turn.

Upaniṣadic Meditations and the Deep Structure of Ritual

Strictly speaking, *vidyā* refers to specific sections in the Upaniṣads that engage what Patrick Olivelle and others have described as "hidden connections" between two distinct things that are in some way understood as identical or related. These *vidyās* are either one-off, a distinct section in one Upaniṣad, or repeated throughout the canon, sometimes even in the same Vedic branch. By way of illustration of the first we may point to the well-known identification of the sacrificial horse and the Universe at the opening of the *Bṛhad-āraṇyaka*, which we will consider briefly later. An example of the second would be Śāṇḍilya's teachings about the entire world as Brahman, most prominent in the *Chāndogya* 3.14 but repeated in the *Śatapatha Brāhmaṇa* and in the *Bṛhad-āraṇyaka*, or the *Vaiśvānara-vidyā*, the teaching about the Self that is common to all, forming a part both of the *Chāndogya* (5.11–18) and the *Bṛhad-āraṇyaka* (5.9).

Bādarāyaṇa says that these *vidyās* constitute single, distinct units, whether they are one-off, restricted to one Vedic branch, or found throughout the canon, in the same way as sacrifices described in different Vedic texts are single ritual models. They aim at the same result, for instance attaining Brahman; they have the same form, for instance, they are about Vaiśvānara the universal Self and involve the same details; they start with the same injunction, for instance that one should meditate on this universal Self; and they share the same name, for instance *vaiśvānara-vidyā*. They are constituted as units by way of combining the details mentioned in different texts.[11]

The key textual locus in this regard is *Mīmāṁsā-sūtra* 2.4.9, which Bādarāyaṇa evidently references. The referenced text talks about how distinct rituals are formed as textual idealities by combining details pertaining to them from different locations in the Brāhmaṇas.[12] Whatever these *vidyās* turn out to be in the end, let us note very well now that they were understood from early on as the Upaniṣadic counterpart to Vedic ritual. They have an injunction that is supposed to introduce them as a practice, they aim at a result, and they have a procedure of performance.

Vedāntins of different backgrounds quite unanimously used the term "*upāsana*" as a synonym for *vidyā*, and it is here that we get an abundance of characterizations from which it is immediately apparent that the intended meaning of both terms, as well as a host of others, was that of meditation.[13] Here is a short selection taken from works of prominent Vedāntins:

> [Maṇḍana Miśra] A uniform stream of thought called contemplation (*dhyāna*), cultivation (*bhāvanā*), meditation (*upāsana*) . . .[14]
>
> [Śaṅkara] Meditation (*upāsana*) is a current of uniform thoughts, not mixed with dissimilar notions, concerning a scriptural object and in a scriptural manner.[15]
>
> [Śaṅkara] Meditation (*dhyāna*), to define it, is a stream of awareness fixed on objects such as Deities described in scriptures and

unbroken by [thoughts on] things of different kind. They call it concentration.[16]

[Śaṅkara] By meditation (*upāsana*), a direct perception of the object of meditation, such as the Lord, is achieved.[17]

[Sureśvara] Viewing an object as taught in Scripture and prolonged dwelling on that until one becomes identified with that, is, indeed, said to be meditation.[18]

[Rāmānuja] The teaching of Scripture is conveyed by means of the term "knowing" (*vedana*), which is synonymous with meditating (*dhyāna, upāsana*). That these terms are so synonymous appears from the fact that the verbs *vid, upās, dhyai* are in one and the same text used with reference to one and the same object of knowledge. . . . Now, *dhyai* means to think of something not in the way of mere representation (*smṛti*), but in the way of continued representation. And *upās* has the same meaning; for we see it used in the sense of thinking with uninterrupted concentration of the mind on the object. We therefore conclude that as the verb "vid" is used interchangeably with *dhyai* and *upās*, the mental activity referred to in texts such as "he knows Brahman" and the like is an often-repeated continuous representation.[19]

[Rāmānuja] For by meditation is understood thought directed upon one object and not disturbed by the ideas of other things.[20]

[Nimbārka] Since meditation (*upāsana*) is of the nature of contemplation (*dhyāna*) . . .[21]

[Śrīnivāsa] Contemplation, consisting of a continuous stream of thoughts having the form of the object contemplated, the synonyms of which are mentation (*vedana*) and meditation (*upāsana*).[22]

If any distinction at all should be drawn between the two, *vidyā* seems to stand more generally for the constituted textual ideality of an Upaniṣadic meditation, whereas *upāsana* indicates its facticity in practice. This, however, is a tenuous distinction and it should not be pursued consistently. Besides, several other words were used as full synonyms for *vidyā* and *upāsana*: *dhyāna, vedana, bhāvanā, darśana, dṛṣṭi, vijñāna*. Bādarāyaṇa exclusively used *vidyā*, but in the commentarial corpus *upāsana* became the term of art, and for a good reason: we will not fail to notice the related etymology of *upāsana* with *upaniṣad*. The unique feature of the Upaniṣads, then, was expressed in their title: they were texts of meditation as counterpart of ritual.

Let us briefly illustrate how an Upaniṣadic *vidyā/upāsana* would have looked like through the aforementioned identification of the sacrificial horse and the Universe and with the help of Śaṅkara and Sureśvara. In the opening of the *Bṛhad-āraṇyaka*, different limbs of the horse which is to be sacrificed in an Aśvamedha, the horse sacrifice, are identified with significant spatiotemporal elements and categories of the Vedic world: the horse's head is dawn; its torso is the year; its limbs and joints are the seasons, months, and fortnights; its feet are days and nights; its sight is the sun, its breath is the wind and its gaping mouth is the fire common to all men (i.e., the fire of digestion); its underbelly is the earth; its abdomen is the intermediate space and its flanks are the quarters; its bones are the stars; its flesh is the clouds; and its intestines are the rivers.

The description goes on, but it is already apparent that the horse is likened to categories of time and space on the one hand, and to elements of significance in the Vedic worldview on the other. Note, for instance, the complex of the sacrificial fire and the sun—the earthly and heavenly fire—which are related by the wind that carries sacrificial oblations from earth to heaven. What the Upaniṣad presented for Śaṅkara and Sureśvara was an identification of the sacrificial horse with the highest divinity of the Vedic worldview, Prajāpati, who was, as we have seen in Chapter 3, the soul behind the totality of both the natural and Vedic worlds. The meditation consists in *visualizing* these correlations: to be specific, it consists in *seeing* or *mentally assigning* these spatiotemporal and Vedic categories in or to a *specific horse*, one that is just about to be sacrificed in an actual ritual performance.[23]

Symbolic and Non-Symbolic Meditations

Two criteria of classifying the Upaniṣadic *vidyā*s can be inferred from the *Brahma-sūtra*. The *vidyā*s are, first, instruments of procuring something desirable to man: "From this [*vidyā*] there follows the attainment of a human good, because there is scriptural evidence to that account—thus Bādarāyaṇa."[24] They can, therefore, be classified in terms of the intended result. A second and a more basic criterion is the nature of the correspondence between the two things correlated in the meditation. This correlation can be either ontologically intended or based on a symbol.

The meditation on the sacrificial horse is a good example of the second: the head of the horse is not *really* dawn, but dawn is mentally imposed over the horse's head and meditated on as such in virtue of some resemblance between the two. Śaṅkara says, for instance, that *primacy* is a feature both of dawn and the horse's head, and this is a ground enough for the one to be visualized as the other.[25] In the commentarial corpus this kind of meditation became known as *pratīkopāsana,* symbolic meditation, the symbolic resemblance being the important factor even if an argument could be made for a real ontological relation.

For Bādarāyaṇa, *all* Upaniṣadic meditations other than the symbolic belonged to a single class, which we may provisionally call meditations on Brahman, *brahma-vidyā* or *brahmopāsana*. The distinction between the two kinds is drawn in *sūtra*s 4.1.4 and 4.3.14, the upshot of both being that the symbol-based meditations do not have the attaining of Brahman as their result.[26]

Bādarāyaṇa calls the symbolic meditations optional (*kāmya*), with a clear allusion to the optional, desire-based rituals that are performed for specific results.[27] Now, they are classified further as (1) performed within a broader ritual, or (2) performed independently. Bādarāyaṇa's term for the first was "meditations pertaining to subsidiary elements of a ritual" (*aṅgāvabaddha*), performed under the rubric of consecration or embellishment and meant to either enhance the result of the ritual or bring some added value.[28] The meditation on the sacrificial horse can again be adduced as an example. In the Aśvamedha sacrifice, the sacrificial horse would be classified under the category of subsidiary part, subordinate to the principal element that is the action of offering, and the whole ritual would be performed for a specific result. If the ritual, however, was accompanied by the meditation on the horse as Prajāpati as delineated earlier, then the horse would be embellished through that meditation and the ritual would bring for the sacrificer attainment of the highest heaven, the world of Prajāpati. The insertion of this meditation was optional, contingent on the desire of the sacrificer for another result, in the manner of the milking vessel or *go-dohana* which brings added value, a different result, to a ritual where otherwise an ordinary vessel was to be used. This meditation would be, thus, both optional and pertaining to a subsidiary element in the ritual (*kāmya* and *aṅgāvabaddha*).

Although these meditations pertained to elements subsidiary to a ritual, Vedāntins generally argue that the meditations themselves are not subsidiary to the ritual with which they were associated. They are units unto themselves and when combined with the respective ritual, it is the ritual that is subordinate to them, insofar as the result which was expected from the complex performance was the result associated with the meditation rather than the ritual. Śaṅkara and Sureśvara even claimed that the same meditation could be performed in a non-ritual context, as an option to the combined performance, still yielding the same result. The meditation on the Aśvamedha horse, for instance, could be performed outside of a ritual context and with no horse at all. If one did not have the requisite competence for an Aśvamedha, which was, we should note, a royal sacrifice, our Advaitins claimed that one could do the same meditation not on the horse *but on oneself*, on one's own head as dawn and the rest, and still attain the world of Prajāpati. This was, obviously, based on the "hidden connection" between the horse and Prajāpati the embodiment of the universe, *and* the "hidden connection" between the macrocosmic Prajāpati and the microcosmic ritualist that is so common to the worldview of the Vedas.[29]

The second group of optional meditations can be best defined negatively, through two characteristics: (1) they are *strictly* Upaniṣadic meditations, that is, *not* tied to ritual subsidiaries and *not* performed in a ritual context; (2) their results, however, are of the variety which ritual was thought to bring, and *not* the attainment of Brahman. Illustrations for these may be: "He who knows thus the wind as the child of the quarters will not mourn the loss of a son." "He who meditates on Brahman as name obtains freedom of movement as far as name reaches."[30] Such meditations are, in fact, interspersed in the Upaniṣads alongside the meditations for the attainment of Brahman, and from the two instances it is clear that they could be meditations on something either as Brahman or as some other divine principle. In either case the meditation was based on symbolic likeness, *pratīka*.

When Vedāntins talk about *pratīkopāsana*s, they generally have these independent Upaniṣadic meditations in mind, and even more restrictedly the meditations in which the symbolic counterpart is Brahman. It is clear, however, that the meditations on ritual subsidiaries were also understood as symbolic in nature. We may, thus, classify the optional meditations that do not end in attaining Brahman as pertaining to subsidiary ritual elements and as symbolic meditations, bearing in mind that in the second, the meditational counterpart could be either Brahman or something else.

Meditation on Brahman

I went into these details of classification of Upaniṣadic meditations not to bother the specialist or deter the proverbial general audience from reading on, but to bring home the following point: for Bādarāyaṇa, an Upaniṣadic meditation was either (1) symbolic and optional—related to a sacrificial element or independent—and resulting in an attainment other than Brahman; or (2) a meditation on Brahman proper. Once the first were properly identified and labeled, *all* the remaining Upaniṣadic meditations were meditations on Brahman, because they all result in attaining Brahman.

This is essentially a negative characterization, but in 4.1.3–4 it is combined with a positive one: a *brahma-vidyā* is a meditation on Brahman as one's Self. "As the Self, because that is what they admit and teach; but, not as a symbol, because the symbol is not the Self."[31] The commentaries, naturally, diverge in understanding the precise ontological relationship that undergirds the identification of Brahman with the Self, but we are prepared to cut through the net of disagreement if we simply recognize the doctrine of residence which we have introduced in Chapter 3: Brahman upon creating the world enters all beings, including the individual soul, becoming thus their Self. The two *sūtra*s are the soteriological application of the same doctrine. It is sufficient, therefore, to read Nimbārka's straightforward comment:

> "This is my Self,"[32] thus the ancients admit. "This is your Self,"[33] that is how they instruct students. Therefore, the aspirant after liberation should meditate on the Supreme Self as one's own Self. However, the Self is not to be intended in regard to a symbol, because the symbol is not the Self of the meditator.[34]

There are, in other words, texts in the Upaniṣads that identify one's Self with Brahman, and they constitute *brahma-vidyā,* meditations on Brahman; there are texts that identify something else with Brahman or with something else, such as the mind with Brahman or the *udgītha* with Oṁ, and they are not meditations on Brahman.

The negative characterization, however, was more basic, and that was to accommodate one Upaniṣadic locus that did not fit the Brahman-as-the-Self paradigm. It was the famed "knowledge of five fires" (*pañcāgni-vidyā*) from the *Chāndogya* 5.3–10 and *Bṛhad-āraṇyaka* 6.2, the two textual loci which introduce the notion of rebirth in the Vedic corpus. The knowledge of five fires was somewhat of an oddball for the *Brahma-sūtra* classification, because it does not relate two distinct things so that it could be a meditation on one thing as another. While the Upaniṣad describes it as a meditation on "austerity as faith," the passage is really a depiction of transmigration, *saṁsāra,* which was by some Vedāntins seen as a meditation on Brahman as an effect that is the world. Nimbārka, Śrīnivāsa, and Rāmānuja, on the other hand, interpret the *pañcāgni-vidyā* a meditation on "one's imperishable nature as having Brahman as its Self," that is, a meditation in which the object is not Brahman but the unchanging individual soul (more on this in the next chapter).[35] Whatever the case, the *pañcāgni-vidyā* promises the attainment of Brahman to those who know the process of rebirth through the same path which was associated with the common meditations on Brahman. Bādarāyaṇa, therefore, emphasized the "not as a symbol" principle: if a meditation is not symbolic and it promises the attainment of Brahman, it is a *brahma-vidyā.*

The attainment of Brahman was, in fact, "the higher instruction," the constituent in virtue of which the Upaniṣads facilitate some human good, as we have seen in *sūtra* 3.4.1 which we may quote again for good measure: "From this [*vidyā*] there follows the attainment of a human good, because there is scriptural evidence to that account—thus Bādarāyaṇa." The commentators have unanimously glossed the "higher instruction" as an instruction about the *Supreme Self* as opposed to the transmigrating enjoyer and ritual agent that the Mīmāṁsakas argued was the domain of the Upaniṣads, and they have also unanimously selected the famous statement "The knower of Brahman attains the Supreme" from *Taittirīya* 2.1.1 as the topical text about the human good referred to in the quoted *sūtra*. This provides the occasion to tackle the question of *brahma-vidyā* in some detail.

Let us attempt a definition first: in terms of scriptural theology, *brahma-vidyā* is the textual ideality of a specific meditation on Brahman, to be reconstructed through combining the meditational details of its various iterations as well as some other elements common to all *brahma-vidyā*s and to be applied optionally to the other *brahma vidyās* in an outlined procedure, resulting eventually in the attainment of Brahman. We are already familiar with the combination of details, but let us see how all of it was supposed to work.

A representative non-exhaustive list of prominent *brahma-vidyā*s and their respective Upaniṣadic loci reconstructed from the *Brahma-sūtra* commentaries would look like this:

- *Śāṇḍilya-vidyā* in *Chāndogya* 3.14 and *Śatapatha Brāhmaṇa* 10.3, with a few details in *Bṛhad-āraṇyaka* 5.6, the teaching of Śāṇḍilya about the innermost Self which is Brahman.
- *Bhūma-vidyā* in *Chāndogya* 7, the teaching of Sanat-kumāra to Nārada about Brahman that is plenitude (*bhūman*).
- *Sad-vidyā* in *Chāndogya* 6, the famous instruction of Uddālaka Āruṇi to his son Śvetaketu on how Being (*sat*) is everything, including the individual soul.
- *Upakosala-vidyā* in *Chāndogya* 4.10–15, the teaching of Upakosala Kāmalāyana to Satyakāma Jābāla about the person in the sun and in the eye.
- *Ānandamaya-vidyā* in *Taittirīya* 2, otherwise also known simply as *Brahma-vidyā*, and discussing the essential positive nature of Brahman.
- *Vaiśvānara-vidyā* in *Chāndogya* 5.11–18 and *Bṛhad-āraṇyaka* 5.9, the teaching of the king Aśvapati to six householder Brahmins about the Self which is common to all.
- *Akṣara-vidyā* in *Bṛhad-āraṇyaka* 3.8, Yājñavaklya's teaching to Gārgī about the imperishable Brahman.
- *Dahara-vidyā* in *Chāndogya* 8.1–6, containing the teaching about the small space in the city of Brahman, that is, the heart in the human body.

- *Madhu-vidyā* in *Bṛhad-āraṇyaka* 2.5, the teaching of Dadhyañc Ātharvaṇa to the two Aśvins about the brilliant immortal person within everything.
- *Pañcāgni-vidyā* in *Chāndogya* 5.3–10 and *Bṛhad-āraṇyaka* 6.2, delineating the process of rebirth.

In fact, a major part of the first book of the *Brahma-sūtra*, and more generally of the *Brahma-sūtra* project, was to go through these *vidyā*s or texts individually in order to establish that the meditational counterpart in them is, indeed, Brahman, and show that it is not one of the Sāṅkhya first principles. In the third book, Bādarāyaṇa's purpose is to establish the principles of unity undergirding unique individual *vidyā*s in different texts, the optionality of the different *brahma-vidyā*s, the possible aggregation of the non-Brahman meditations, and various exceptions to these principles. Bādarāyaṇa does not mention these individual *vidyā*s but he does name one of the non-*brahma-vidyā*s, so it is inferable that by his time the *vidyā* system was already standardized.[36]

Now, it will not escape the attention of the resident Upaniṣadic expert that this is a bit of a medley of texts and topics. Some work must be done not only to standardize the individual *vidyā*s but to normalize them across the board so that they all would be equal meditations that bring one to Brahman. A template *brahma-vidyā* had to be worked out to which they would all conform, yet keeping their individual details in virtue of which one of them could be practiced as per one's preferences but the result would be the same in all cases.

First of all, they would all have to aim at the attaining of Brahman through the so-called course of the gods or *deva-yāna* (on which more in the next chapter). In fact, it was precisely because of the *deva-yāna* that the *pañcāgni-vidyā,* which does not even mention Brahman as a counterpart to anything, made the *brahma-vidyā* cut: it promised those who know the secret of rebirth and meditate in the wilderness to ascend to the world of Brahman through the course of the gods.[37] The course, on the other hand, is not mentioned, for instance, in the *śāṇḍilya-vidyā, madhu-vidyā, vaiśvānara-vidyā,* so there it must be inserted. It *could* be inserted because there are direct statements from the Upaniṣads and related literature which associate knowing Brahman with ascending to Brahman via the divine path, for instance *Bhagavad-gītā* 8.24. These are taken as *generally applicable* whenever someone is a knower of Brahman, making the explicit mentions of the course in individual *vidyā*s *restatements* rather than their specific details. Thus, ascending through the course of the gods becomes a part of all *brahma-vidyā*s. By the principle of reciprocity, knowing Brahman is inserted in the *pañcāgni-vidyā:* if someone ascends through the *deva-yāna*, surely he must be a knower of Brahman.[38]

A second thing to normalize across the board was Brahman itself, and that was necessary so as to make sure that the object of meditation *and* the attained result were a match. A single conception of Brahman was to permeate the individual *vidyā*s, and so the notion of Brahman had to be standardized through inserting Brahman's "essential characteristics" that we have seen in Chapter 3. First to be inserted were Brahman's positive characteristics: Being, consciousness, limitless, and bliss.[39] There is a broader theological significance of this as well: the *Taittirīya* section where these positive characteristics are stated provides the paradigmatic meditation on Brahman (called, in fact, simply *brahma-vidyā*), since it gives the paradigmatic injunction—"The knower of Brahman attains the Supreme," *brahmavid āpnoti param*—that justifies all *vidyā-upāsana* as a means of human good. So, however Brahman is defined in this most important passage must be how Brahman is, and by that much this idea of Brahman must be included in all meditations on Brahman.

A second set of characteristics to be inserted universally in *brahma-vidyā*s were Brahman's negative attributes taken explicitly from Yājñavalkya's teachings to Gārgī about "the imperishable," known to us, again, from Chapter 3. Such insertion should prevent mistaking Brahman for any of the finite beings that are its perishable products.[40] The two key texts about Brahman, then, delineating its essential nature through a simultaneous application of *kataphatic* and *apophatic* discourse were to be included in all individual *brahma-vidyā*s.

We should not fail to note again that both insertions were justified by an appeal to a principle given in the *Mīmāṁsā-sūtra*, which stipulates that all characteristics essential to a primary element in a ritual—the definition of a primary being "that on which the attainment of the result depends"—follow that primary in all individual cases of application: "When the primary and the subsidiary diverge (belong to a different Veda), the relation to the Veda is through the primary because the subsidiary is for the sake of the primary."[41] Since Brahman is the primary element in all meditations on Brahman, its essential description given in the two respective texts follows Brahman in all meditations.

With these two additions, the concept of Brahman for the purposes of meditation would be complete. Conspicuously absent from this concept of Brahman is an emphasis on its causal role in relation to the world, which was so prominently placed at the very opening of the *Brahma-sūtra* (1.1.2): "Brahman is that from which proceed the creation, sustenance and dissolution of the world." This absence is a real giveaway of what *brahma-*

vidyā was about. Its aim was some attainment through self-assimilation. Through meditating on Brahman as one's Self one becomes Brahman in all respect, *except* for the ability to interfere with the creation of the world. So, Brahman's agency in creation was not emphasized in the constructed meditational concept not because it was not deemed essential to Brahman's nature, but because it was useless for meditational aspirations. But, we are getting ahead of ourselves: we will return to this question in the next chapter.

Once the different *vidyā*s have thus been normalized, whatever is left as characteristics of Brahman in the individual *vidyā*s is peculiar to them, not to be combined further. Thus, given that a *brahma-vidyā* as a kind of meditation correlates Brahman to the individual soul, its full-fledged formulation would have looked something like this:

> (P)(R,S)Brahman which is Being, knowledge, bliss, infinite, imperishable and thus different from its products, is my (Q)Self. [BV][42]

The predicate notations would stand for elements which are peculiar to the specific *brahma-vidyā*. P and Q would express the *specific* correlation. For instance, in the *Śāṇḍilya-vidyā* the relation would be between Brahman that is "larger than the earth, larger than the intermediate region, larger than the sky, larger even than all these worlds put together," and the Self "of mine that lies deep within my heart, smaller than a grain of rice or barley, smaller than a mustard seed, smaller even than a millet grain or a millet kernel."[43] R and S would signify features of Brahman characteristic to the individual *vidyā*, which could be of several kinds. Some would be specific characteristics of Brahman, but restricted to the *vidyā*s where they are mentioned. Again, in the *Śāṇḍilya* these would be "having true desires, true resolves, all actions, all smells and tastes" and the like. Other could be accidental properties that should facilitate concentration. For instance, in the *brahma-vidyā* of the *Taittirīya* (2.5), Brahman whose essence is bliss is described as having a body "whose head is pleasure, right side delight, left side thrill and torso joy." Because Brahman cannot be a composite entity, these are not real properties but are meant to facilitate concentration.[44] There may be other details to work out in the individual *vidyā*s, but the template would have looked something like that.

Because the attainment as their integral part in all of them is the same—Brahman through the course of the gods—only one should be practiced by an individual meditator: whereas the optional meditations which bring attainments of the same kind as ritual can be combined as one desires, the more the merrier, one *brahma-vidyā* would bring the same attainment as any other, and therefore they were theorized as options to one another: choose the one you fancy.[45]

The Practice of Meditation and Soteriological Causality

Now the question presents itself, how was a *brahma-vidyā* to be practiced? While Bādarāyaṇa clearly talks only about meditation as the means of attaining Brahman, all Vedāntin commentators have understood *brahma-vidyā* as consisting of three related processes. The topical text which became canonical for this division came from Yājñavalkya's teachings to Maitreyī in the *Bṛhad-āraṇyaka* (2.4.5 and 4.5.6): *ātmā vā are draṣṭavyaḥ śrotavyo mantavyo nididhyāsitavyaḥ,* "The Self, honey, is to be seen: it is to be heard about, pondered over and meditated upon." Vedāntins have universally interpreted the first gerundive, *draṣṭavya* or "to be seen," as stating the goal, namely that one should eventually achieve a vision of Brahman, whereas the other three as expressing the procedure: that goal can be accomplished through instruction in scripture, presumably so as to ascertain the meaning of the preferred *vidyā* that would become the textual ideality of one's meditational practice (*śravaṇa*); reflecting on the meaning of what was heard (*manana*); and meditation proper on Brahman as the constructed meditational object (*nididhyāsana*).

It is inferable that these three processes were supposed to be practiced sequentially. One hears from scripture first, clarifies the meaning of what was heard, and finally meditates: in terms of soteriological causality, the contribution of each preceding limb would be harnessed by the following.[46] From what we know from Śaṅkara's and Sureśvara's engagement with opponents, however, the first two were generally not discussed in pre-Śaṅkara Vedānta at all or very vaguely: meditation proper was *the* means, and Bādarāyaṇa's sole concern in the *Brahma-sūtra* is meditation. That seems quite natural, since the vision (*darśana*) as the goal and meditation (*dhyāna*) as the means were essentially the same thing, a vision of Brahman as the result achieved through vision as practice. Srinivasa Chari's observation may be profitably quoted on this point:

> Three stages are mentioned as preparatory to the vision of Brahman (*darśana*). These are *śravaṇa* or hearing, *manana* or reflection and *nididhyāsana* or meditation. . . . According to this teaching, *nididhyāsana* or *upāsanā* is the direct means to *mokṣa,* whereas *śravaṇa* and *manana* are subsidiary or *aṅga* to *upāsanā*.[47]

We have, thus, zeroed in on meditation proper. Bādarāyaṇa has several things to say on the practice of meditation. First, in terms of type of awareness, the meditation on Brahman is a fixed concentration on a notion or an idea: "Because meditation is of the nature of concentration."[48] This "fixed concentration" was a persistent feature of Vedāntic characterizations of meditation. We saw some of the definitions of *vidyā/upāsana* in the beginning, but it may be worthwhile to revisit a few: it is a repetition of the same thought or notion; it is a representational flow, focused mentation; a continuous flow of a uniform notion/thought of the meditational object; uniform stream of thought called contemplation, cultivation, and meditation.

In terms of content, the meditational thought that one would have mulled over would have been a self-identification with Brahman through a variation of the [BV] proposition that I formulated earlier in this chapter. As was generally characteristic of meditation in South Asia, meditation on Brahman was to be practiced strictly in a sitting posture, but there was no restriction in terms of place: it should be practiced "wherever concentration is possible."[49] This seems like a clear giveaway that the paradigmatic meditator on Brahman would have been a householder: he was not expected to renounce and meditate in seclusion.

Along the same lines, this meditation was to be accompanied by ritual and other religious observances. This primarily included the daily Agnihotra and practices such as charity and austerity for the members of the several soteriological vocations (*āśrama*s) of orthoprax Brahmanical society. These were the so-called obligatory actions (*nitya-karma*) that were binding for the members of the individual vocations. The vocations themselves were choices that a Vedic graduate was supposed to adopt at the end of his education in the *guru's* school. In the *Chāndogya* (2.23.1), three vocations with their respective obligatory actions are mentioned: the householders who perform sacrifices, Vedic recitation, and charity; the ascetics who do austerity; and a student who settles permanently in his teacher's home and serves the teacher.

Particularly interesting is the case about rituals as one of these obligatory actions. Mīmāṁsakas argued that certain rituals, such as the daily Agnihotra and the Darśa-pūrṇamāsa, were obligatory for everyone, including renunciants, for which claim they offered a negative justification. *Mīmāṁsā-sūtra* says that those who do not perform them would incur "fault," which in Śabara's reading meant "the loss of heaven." The problem was, however, that such rituals were generally classed as "optional" (*kāmya*), like the optional meditations that we saw earlier: they were grounded in a desire for attaining heaven. But, what if one had lost the desire for heaven and decides to pursue liberation instead? Śabara's argument was that Agnihotra and the like were still to be performed, in a simplified procedure and under a different injunction, such as "One should perform the fire ritual as long as one lives."[50] It was not all too meaningful, however, that the loss of heaven would happen when one had decided not to perform them, because the aspirants for liberation had precisely lost that desire for heaven. Kumārila, therefore, replaced the "loss of heaven" with bad karma or "downfall," "diminution" (*pratyavāya*) that would result unless the aspirants after liberation do ritual and their other obligatory actions.[51]

For Bādarāyaṇa, however, things were different. The purpose of ritual and the other obligatory actions was not to prevent bad karma, at least not in the context of meditation. Rather, they were supposed to *foster* the meditation on Brahman.[52] The scriptural statement that governed their practice was not that one should perform the fire ritual as long as one lives, but rather *Bṛhad-āraṇyaka* 4.4.22: "It is he that Brahmins seek to know by means of Vedic recitation, sacrifice, gift-giving, austerity and fasting."[53] This statement presents the obligatory actions as the means of attaining Brahman, but specifically as assistants to meditation: their soteriological causality is absorbed in meditation. Thus, the individual vocations were supposed to continue doing what they were doing before taking to meditation on Brahman, not because bad karma would follow otherwise, but because they *were* the means of liberation.[54] The injunctions about the lifelong performance of the daily fire offering and similar rituals pertained to those members of the vocations who were not after liberation.[55] Thus, Bādarāyaṇa and the commentators were typically Mīmāṁsic in turning the tables on Mīmāṁsā.

Bādarāyaṇa, in fact, went a step further. In arguing for the independence of meditation from ritual, he adduced in evidence the scriptural fact that there are those who do meditate but never light up the fire: that is, they take up renunciation without ever marrying. These were the Vājasaneyin renunciants from the same *Bṛhad-āraṇyaka* 4.4.22 that presented the obligatory duties of the soteriological vocations as fostering meditation and, thus, as means of attaining Brahman.[56] There is little doubt that Bādarāyaṇa wanted aspirants after liberation, renunciants or not, to do rituals, but he would not accept that bad karma would result from their non-performance.

Along with their vocational duties, all who aspired after liberation were expected to cultivate certain virtues which were stated in the *Bṛhad-āraṇyaka* immediately following the previous provision: "A man who knows this, therefore, becomes calm, composed, cool, patient and collected."[57] While these virtues are known to all students of Vedānta as one of the four requirements for beginning the inquiry into Brahman famously stated by Śaṅkara in the opening of his *Brahma-sūtra-bhāṣya*, the so-called six accomplishments (*ṣaṭ-sampatti*) that are calm, self-control, tolerance, and so on, in the *Brahma-sūtra* system of soteriological causality they were, just like the vocational duties, subsidiaries to meditation, but binding for *all* practitioners.[58]

Finally, meditation on Brahman was supposed to be practiced one's entire life.[59] This last stipulation is immediately relevant to considering the results of meditation, as it answered the question, what should one do when the meditational practice has borne fruit? The question was prompted by the assumption that there comes a point in time *during one's life* when the meditation has become perfect, at which stage one is a *vidvān,* a knower of Brahman.[60] The commentators do not say much about what this achievement was supposed to look like: Brahman becomes manifest in meditation which is of the nature of devotion, *bhakti*.[61] Bādarāyaṇa, in fact, says that Brahman becomes manifest in the manner of light, and so on, that appear through "repeated application," *abhyāsa*.[62] This seems entirely inspired by a section of the *Śvetāśvatara* (1.13–16), where the Self is said to be present in the body and in the individual soul as fire is present in firewood, oil in sesame seeds, or butter in curds. Though not visible, fire in firewood can be made to appear by the repeated rubbing of firesticks, and likewise Brahman that is like light can be made manifest in repeated meditation, by "rubbing" the body against the syllable Oṁ.

Brahman's function of residence is yet again soteriologically crucial, but the point about repeated meditation that should continue even upon the vision of Brahman is well captured by a lexeme that is characteristically used by the commentators, "steady recollection" (*dhruvānusmṛti*),[63] which suggests that the awareness of Brahman had to be maintained until the end of life. As we shall see in the next chapter, one is not liberated until reaching *brahma-loka*, Brahman's world, for which purpose the practice of meditation had to continue till one's final breath, along with Agnihotra and religious duties that nurture it. Meditation, thus, was something like the main obligatory action for the aspirants after liberation, much like sacrifice for the ritualists.

Conclusion

We saw in this chapter that the *Brahma-sūtra* challenge for charting its own space as an independent knowledge system was to overturn the Mīmāṁsā claim that the knowledge of the self presented in the Upaniṣads served the needs of ritual, insofar as it is required to know that there is an eternal self that outlives the body and can enjoy the results of ritual in the hereafter, and enhances the elements of the ritual and makes for better profits. Bādarāyaṇa's argument against this was that the Upaniṣads are not about the soul as the ritual agent but about a higher Self, Brahman. Consequent on this, the Upaniṣads have in their domain a means of the human good independent of ritual, namely, Upaniṣadic meditations.

Throughout the reconstruction, however, we witnessed the ghost of Mīmāṁsā perpetually lurking behind Brahman of the Upaniṣads. At the barest, the Upaniṣadic meditations were textual idealities formed on the ritual model, and the idea of a uniform notion of Brahman permeating all meditations was based on the Mīmāṁsā rule about the "characteristics of the principal element of a ritual that follow that principal everywhere." No less significant were the discussions about the soteriological efficacy of ritual, the justification of renunciation, and so on. This engagement with Mīmāṁsā will continue in the next chapter, when we move to the nature of liberation and the attainment of Brahman.

Study Questions

1. Describe Bādarāyaṇa's disagreement with Mīmāṁsā regarding the use of the Upaniṣadic knowledge.
2. What kinds of Upaniṣadic meditations are there? Can you work out a full classificatory scheme?
3. What is the difference between symbolic and non-symbolic meditations?
4. What is *brahma-vidyā*? How was a *brahma-vidyā* supposed to be worked out?
5. Think about the optional (*kāmya*) meditations and the optionality of various *brahma-vidyā*s: is the same *kind* of optionality involved in the two cases?
6. Briefly describe the practice of meditation on Brahman. Can you think of it in terms of "soteriological causality," that is, which elements were supposed to be directly efficacious and which indirectly?

Suggestions for Further Study

On the idea of "statements of praise" (*arthavāda*) in the Vedas that some Mīmāṁsakas applied to liberation, Harikai (1994) is a good reading. Olivelle (1998), Introduction, is an excellent reading on the Upaniṣadic "hidden connections" that inform the *Brahma-sūtra* idea of *vidyā,* meditation. The Mīmāṁsā attitude toward liberation is a complicated and contentious issue, but good places to start reading about it are McCrea (2013) and Taber (2007). On the combination of details in *brahma-vidyā* taken into an Advaita Vedānta direction, Clooney (1992) is a very good reading. Olivelle (1993) is a detailed history of the system of vocations (*āśrama*) that informs some of the *brahma-vidyā* practices.

7

The Individual Soul, Liberation, and Attainment of Brahman

Embodiment and Karma

Before we tackle the question of liberation and the attainment of Brahman, we must discharge our debts to Chapters 3 and 5, and finish the accounts of embodiment, transmigration, and karma. The Upaniṣadic origins of this complex of ideas—or one version of it, in any case—are found in a group of related texts that go by the name of *pañcāgni-vidyā*, "the knowledge of five fires," most important among which are *Chāndogya* 5.3–10 and *Bṛhad-āraṇyaka* 6.2. *Pañcāgni-vidyā* deals with both transmigration and liberation, and the first is taken up for systematization in *Brahma-sūtra* 3.1. As is the book's practice, the *Chāndogya* version provides the primary source.

The *pañcāgni-vidyā* presents rebirth as a cycle in which the Vedic gods as macrocosmic ritualists pour the transmigrating soul of the deceased terrestrial ritualist in five successive fires that are symbolic representations of juncture points in rebirth. The first fire is the "hereafter" in general terms, "the yonder world," but in a cosmic sense it is the sun, beyond which is the domain of liberation or "no return." The soul of the deceased ritualist who has been cremated—called "faith" by the Upaniṣad at the initial point but identified with "waters" at the ultimate point—is offered in this fire, from which it is born as "king Soma." King Soma is next poured in a raincloud, the second fire, from which rain is poured on earth, the third fire. A man, in which grain is poured, is the fourth fire, and the fifth fire is a woman in which semen is deposited. In this final or "fifth oblation," what was initially called "faith" but is now "waters" assumes the appellation "man," that is, receives "human" rebirth.

Once reborn, man's paths diverge. If he takes to life in wilderness, knows the five-fire doctrine, and knows that "faith is austerity"—for the *Brahma-sūtra*, if he practices *brahma-vidyā*—he takes "the course of the gods," the *deva-yāna*, and attains liberation.[1] If, on the other hand, he remains in the village and knows that "gift-giving is offering to gods and priests"[2]—if he continues his life as a ritualist—he becomes "king Soma" again through "the course of the forefathers," *pitṛ-yāna*, in a sphere identified with the moon: indeed, *soma* in the cosmic sense *is* the moon, the receptacle from which the gods drink soma juice.[3] There he enjoys until his stock depletes but is then reborn in the aforementioned downward course. Where he is reborn depends on his "conduct," *caraṇa*, while he was still on earth: if he did well, he is reborn in a family of the three higher classes, known to us from the end of Chapter 2, and gets another chance to take one of the two paths; if he was one of "rotten behavior," he is reborn from a "pig, a dog, or an outcaste woman."

There is a third possibility, called "the third state," for those who practice neither ritual in the village nor austerity in the forest: they are constantly reborn as "tiny creatures". *Bṛhad-āraṇyaka* specifies: as worms, insects, or snakes.[4]

This five-fire doctrine was very important for the *Brahma-sūtra*. Its systematization, to begin with, gives us an opportunity to round up Bādarāyaṇa's understanding of the embodied individual. Consonant with his *sat-kārya-vāda*, this embodied individual turns out to be a kernel that contains everything that is required for embodiment, including subtle forms of the elements that eventually make up its body. These subtle elements, denoted metonymically by "water" in the *pañcāgni-vidyā*, envelop the soul as it transmigrates from one body to another, and merely "evolve" or "transform" through stages: the soul does not "enter" matter during conception, but "manifests" in gross matter what it carries in subtle.[5] The "water" that the *pañcāgni-vidyā* talks about is the "triplicated" water, one element that contains portions of all others.[6] Śaṅkara offers an insightful reading why it is appropriate to call this complex of subtle elements "water" rather than, say, earth, reflecting the predominant character of grain that a man eats in the fourth oblation. On the one hand, it is the rebirth of a *ritualist* that is under discussion, one who had daily offered liquids in the sacrificial fire—*soma*, milk, and clarified butter—such that the *seed* created by the ritual takes a watery form: as Henk Bodewitz notes, the *pañcāgni-vidyā* is modeled not on any sacrifice but the Agnihotra, the main offering in which is milk.[7] On the other hand, the fifth oblation in which one properly becomes "man" is semen, a liquid substance. On both sides of the rebirth-process, the seed of embodiment is watery.[8] But, this is "vitamin water" we are talking about, one that contains all the other elements in itself.

The gods that "pour" the soul through the five junctures are its cognitive, active, and other faculties, *prāṇas*.[9] Indeed, as we have seen in Chapter 3, it is common for the Upaniṣads to identify the gods with the faculties of the macrocosmic Self and their representation in man. The faculties, then, also envelop the soul and lead it through transmigration, residing in the subtle forms of the elements.

And then, there is the karmic stock that also clings to the soul in seed form, waiting for appropriate conditions to fructify. We introduced the related ideas of karma and transmigration in Chapter 5, where we defined karma as a principle on the one hand—no experience should be undeserved and no action should be without consequence—and on the other hand as a stock of "seeds" created by one's action, waiting for appropriate circumstances to bear fruits. It is time now to flesh out this minimal definition. At least two *kinds* of action described in the *pañcāgni-vidyā* contribute to the formation of this karmic stock. First, there is action done in the ritual context—what the *Chāndogya* called "gift-giving is offering to gods and priests," *iṣṭāpūrte*—which is productive of what *Brahma-sūtra* commentators call "karma that gives results in the hereafter" (*āmuṣmika-phala*), in heaven that is here coterminous with the lunar sphere.[10] In later Brahmanical parlance, these are equivalent to the so-called *kāmya-karma*, optional rituals that are tied to specific attainments and good karma in general.

The second kind of action is the one called *caraṇa*, "conduct" or "behavior" by the Upaniṣad. The commentators gloss this as *cāritra, ācāra, vṛtta, śīla*, all of which points to habitual action that is expressive of character.[11] This action, to paraphrase Nimbārka and Śaṅkara, creates "karma that gives results in this world" (*aihika-phala*), experienced in rebirth after the fall from heaven.[12] We don't learn much more from the commentaries what kind of action this is—Śaṅkara talks about "Vedic conduct" (*śrauta-śīla*) and Rāmānuja about action "enjoined in *smṛti*"—yet at its barest it must be non-ritual action regulated by the wider Vedic canon, particularly the corpus on *dharma*.[13] Clearly, this corresponds more to the popular understanding of karma, where we think of the moral valence of actions and their underlying intentions. However, being scripturally regulated, it is not a form of autonomous or natural morality.

The two kinds of karmic stock are different not only in the sphere where they are experienced—the "here" and the "hereafter"—but in other ways too. The "heavenly karma" is exhausted at every "heavenly visit," while the "earthly karma" is "residual." This means that it must wait its turn—the heavenly karma of the dying ritualist always has precedence—and being related to habitual action, it seems to be constitutive more of continuous experience across lives. It is, nevertheless, important for Bādarāyaṇa to make clear that it is the stock in either case that determines rebirth and experience: habits and intentions don't matter as such, but only insofar as they translate to deeds that produce karmic seeds.[14] The "third state" would seem to include the suffering in hell described in *smṛti* literature:

this surely follows from Śaṅkara's interpretation, while in all other commentaries it is presented as part of the prima facie view, but not the part that is overturned.[15]

Bādarāyaṇa, then, was not intent on describing a doctrine of karma as a moral theory that governs humanity as such, or even more broadly animate life, nor with a general theory of rebirth. That is more of an afterthought, raised by the need to account for the rebirth of non-ritualists who are beyond the pale of the Vedas: if one becomes "man" in the fifth oblation, in sequence of falling from heaven, shouldn't non-ritualists also attain heaven? For, how else are they "human?" This conundrum is solved by relegating all those who do not perform ritual or meditation to the third state, and by severing the relation of the fifth oblation—semen—with impregnation as such. After all, scriptures are full of accounts of immaculate conceptions that do not require the pouring of semen, such that the fifth oblation is strictly applicable to ritualists falling from haven.[16] Good earthly karma also seems to be available only to those who are in the "Vedic world" or governed by its rules.

In other words, Bādarāyaṇa was concerned with those who take up *brahma-vidyā*, and they—male agents surely—were already part of the Vedic world, members of the three high classes, not merely of the "natural world" that includes bugs, snakes, doctrinal opponents, and ordinary folks. For such an agent, it is important to delineate the two kinds of karmic stock because liberation requires becoming free from both. We saw in the previous chapter that the character of ritual action could be changed such that it becomes useful for liberation rather than productive of good karma of the hereafter. Let us now finish the story of freedom from karma.

Liberation

We finished the previous chapter with the statement that there comes a time when the practitioner of *brahma-vidyā* achieves perfection of meditation and has experienced Brahman directly. While the vision itself is left undescribed, what follows is depicted in some detail. First, one becomes immediately free from the past karma which has not yet been activated, whereas the new karma that one would otherwise create does not stick.[17] The good karma is also gone without one having to experience another round of heavenly sojourn, though it seems that it remains active until death as it facilitates meditation. However, one must live through the karma that has already resulted in the present embodiment.[18] The text justifying this is the famous passage from the *Chāndogya*: "There is a delay for me here only until I am freed; but then I will arrive."[19]

Now, an important question concerns the nature of this delay: What does it mean that "there is a delay for me here," and how does that reflect on practice and the attainment of liberation? On this point, Śaṅkara gives an illustration derived from the *Sāṅkhya-kārikā*, which presents the delay as *karmic inertia*, and is a *locus classicus* on the later distinction between liberation while living (*jīvan-mukti*) and final liberation (*videha-mukti*):

> On the attainment of perfect knowledge, merit etc. are no longer causal, yet one remains embodied because of the force of past impressions, like the spinning of the potter's wheel.[20]

Śaṅkara's argument is that knowledge of Brahman arises with the help of certain products of ignorance.[21] Indeed, as we saw in Chapter 5, for Śaṅkara knowledge as cognitive content *is* predicated on ignorance, on the complex of subject, object, instruments, the cognitive act, and the cognition as their result. This has some soteriological significance as well: knowledge of Brahman, insofar as it is any positive awareness, must also be a product of ignorance. For this reason, such specific form of ignorance—the knowledge of Brahman—must remain subordinate to the last traces of karma that constitute embodiment, for there wouldn't be the liberating knowledge of Brahman without them. But, Śaṅkara's important point is that there is a *natural diminishing of the impulse* of karma that does not require the agent to do much more than simply "wait it out" until death. One is liberated for all practical purposes, but not just yet "absolutely."

This interpretation was rejected by other Vedāntins, and rightly so insofar as the *Brahma-sūtra* teaching is concerned. For Bādarāyaṇa, there was no such thing as liberation before death.[22] Still, this rejection of "liberation while living" might seem more verbal than substantive if we focus *solely* on what happens to karma upon the perfection of meditation: Just how are karmic inertia and the continuation of active karma until death really different? Indeed, even Bhāskara, the stern critic of the Advaita "liberation while living," had this to say:

> Liberation is inevitable for the knower of Brahman at death. There are two kinds of liberation: release from attachment, aversion, delusion, and their products such as madness during the state of living, and absolute liberation at death.[23]

Additionally, the critiques of "liberation while living" tended to focus on its ontological and epistemological impossibility on the Advaita model: How could one possibly know the non-dual Brahman yet remain embodied, in ignorance, that is, have the vision of non-duality and duality at the same time?[24] But, this critique goes somewhat past Śaṅkara's argument. The vision of non-duality is an approximation that happens within the context of ignorance, yet it is also one that has the power to stop all non-active karma. Something more is at stake.

The substantive difference—besides, of course, the nature of the intuited Brahman and the ultimate ontological status of the soul, which we will tackle shortly—concerns the continuation of one's meditative and other practice. For Bādarāyaṇa, upon the perfection of meditation and the vision of Brahman, one's practice was supposed to remain the same: one had to continue with meditation, with ritual, and with one's religious duties *for life*. The vision of Brahman that provides the liberating experience had to be actively nurtured until the end of life, because what happens at death was the decisive event: only then did the perfection of meditation translate to perfection of attainment, and one couldn't just "wait it out."[25]

Parenthetically, at the background of this disagreement was also one of the basic presuppositions of non-Advaita Vedic theology, that the Vedas are authoritative on undertakings that give future results, experienced post-mortem. "Liberation while living" in the Advaita Vedānta sense was an anathema. Śaṅkara rejected this doctrine, and for him liberation was not a "future attainment," but we cannot discuss that point here.

The Course of the Gods

Finally, when death comes, one's cognitive and active functions, life-breath, and the subtle elements forming together the subtle body progressively withdraw and gather around the soul, which at that point enters the heart and can exit through any of a number of channels connecting the embodied individual as a microcosm to the greater world.[26] These channels (*nāḍī*) are a common Upaniṣadic trope: they issue from the heart of the individual on the one side and from the sun on the other, forming a net of cosmic roads, "just as a long highway traverses both the villages, the one nearby and the one far away."[27] They are channels or veins within the body but sunrays without. *Prāṇa* flows through them as the pulsating breath-cum-functions of the macrocosmic body.[28] *Chāndogya* 8.6.6 says their number is 101. He who performed only ritual and associated religious action throughout life takes a lower channel and gradually attains the lunar sphere through the aforementioned course of the forefathers, known also as the "southern course" (*dakṣiṇāyana*), and eventually returns to earth when the good karma has been exhausted. For him, things have literally "gone south." For the knower of Brahman, on the other hand, a channel going through the top of the skull lights up, at which point begins his ascension through the course of the gods, called also the "northern course" (*uttarāyana*). His ascent is facilitated by the power of meditation and by Brahman who resides in the heart.[29] He never returns.

We don't need to query the history of the idea of the two courses. However, since they are described in various Upaniṣadic passages, for Bādarāyaṇa it was important to standardize the course of the gods because it forms an integral part of the paradigmatic *brahma-vidyā* as the course through which all knowers achieve Brahman.[30] The course of the gods delineates the progress of the knower of Brahman from entering the top channel to *brahma-loka*, Brahman's world, through a medley of intermediate stages of a heterogeneous character, temporal and other, such as "flame," "the waxing fortnight of thc moon," "lightning," various divinities, the sun and the moon, and so on. Karmarkar suggests that originally the course of the gods referred strictly to multiple paths through which the gods were thought to travel to earth to attend sacrifices and then back to heaven. These were described in superlative terms suggestive of light and increase of power (light, day, summer, the waxing moon, etc.) and associated with different divinities, but in the Upaniṣads and Vedānta the description assumed a literal sense.[31]

For Bādarāyaṇa, this medley of items became guiding agents or travel conductors—that is, divinities associated with each step—a specification required, according to the commentators, to preclude the possibility of their being identified with road signs or rest areas where the itinerant could refresh, "gas up," or have a little fun.[32] The ascent to the world to Brahman, then, was supposed to be more like a sleeper train voyage than a car ride.

Now, the course to the world of Brahman is standardized through combining the details mentioned in various textual loci, in the same way as the various details of individual meditations were combined. This works because the course is the same for all knowers, and different texts simply refer to it by mentioning a few of its characteristics.[33] And, when all the details are worked out, the course should look like this. When the knower of Brahman enters the top channel, he mounts the sun rays, which make a highway for the journey. It does not matter if he dies by day or night, in summer or winter, or at any other time mentioned in the Upaniṣads during which the sun is absent or week: sunrays are present at night because summer nights are hot, while in winter they are just "overpowered by frost" but still there.[34] What determines rebirth or its absence cannot be, in any case, a temporal contingency, as that would override one's karma and meditation. The first conductor that takes the course-of-the-gods itinerant is flame or light (*arciḥ*), which in the original accounts must have simply meant the cremation fire. Flame hands him over to a series of conductors identified by temporal names: "day," "the waxing fortnight," "the six months when the sun travels north," and "the year." From the "year" he reaches the world of the gods, specifically of Vāyu the god of air, and then the sun, moon, and lightning. The *Chāndogya* adds a charming detail: the sun is the gate to the hereafter and the password at the gate is Oṁ.[35] From that point on, past the lunar sphere—which is, remember, the domain of those who do ritual and are reborn—a "non-human person" that is associated with lightning comes for him and leads him to the world of Brahman, but successively assisted by Varuṇa, Indra, and Prajāpati.[36]

When he reaches the world of Brahman, there occurs an "entrance," says Bādarāyaṇa, which the commentators generally interpret as attaining liberation, with some disagreements on the details that are more exegetical than substantive.[37] Whatever the precise meaning, at the minimum the constituents of the subtle body of the knower—the subtle elements, faculties, *prāṇa*—merge back into Brahman and attain, says Bādarāyaṇa, "non-distinction" (*avibhāga*). The meaning of "non-distinction" is unclear from the commentaries, and for a good reason: Bādarāyaṇa surely intends to say that they go to the state prior to diversification of name-and-form, back to Brahman the cause, and what that means depends on what ontology one reads from or into the *Brahma-sūtra*.[38]

The Time of Liberation

To piggyback now on the question of the exact time of liberation, Bādarāyaṇa was emphatic that this precise point of "entrance" is the end of transmigration.[39] There is a background story to this, involving a competing Upaniṣadic account of liberation that is associated with the *Bṛhad-āraṇyaka* and its hero Yājñavalkya. In his teachings to king Janaka, Yājñavalkya presents the account of dying that we have been following so far: on deathbed, one's functions retract to the soul, one attains a state according to one's aspiration—of a forefather, of a Gandharva, of a god, or of Prajāpati—and is then reborn in accordance with one's karma. But then comes the twist: this course is for the man of desire. It does not apply to the desireless, the liberationist, whose functions do not depart in the stated manner. "Brahman he is, and to brahman he goes. . . . Then a mortal becomes immortal, and attains brahman in this world."[40]

This textual locus is the inspiration behind Śaṅkara's doctrine of two knowers, *vidvān*s, one who knows a "lower Brahman" and another one who knows a "higher Brahman," on which, under the next heading. Here the point is that in Yājñavalkya's teachings, final liberation does not seem to involve ascension to the top channel and a journey to the world of Brahman: the true knower is liberated upon the dawn of knowledge, right here and now. Yājñavalkya, for a good measure, ends his teaching to Janaka with the following statement:

> A man who knows this, therefore, becomes calm, composed, cool, patient, and collected. He sees the self (*ātman*) in just himself (*ātman*) and all things as the self. Evil does not pass across him, and he passes across all evil. He is not burnt by evil; he burns up all evil. He becomes a Brahmin—free from evil, free from stain, free from doubt. He is the world of brahman, Your Majesty, and I have taken you to him.[41]

Bādarāyaṇa was not impressed with this teaching, since it was opposed to the *Brahma-sūtra* normative account that was based on the *Chāndogya*. He therefore interpreted Yājñavalkya in the following manner. "Immortality in this world" stands for the aforementioned freedom from non-activated karma; it is "immortality without having burnt" the connection with the body, specifically the subtle body that continues to exist until one reaches the world of Brahman through the course of the gods. Were this not the case, one would drop dead upon the dawning of knowledge, and would lose all bodily warmth, which is a manifestation of the element of *tejas*, heat. Consequently, when Yājñavalkya said that the vital functions of the knower do not depart and the knower does not take the course of the gods, he meant that the vital functions do not depart *from the embodied soul*, not the body; they stay with the subtle body until the attainment of final liberation through the course of the gods.[42]

These several *sūtra*s prove to be one of the most difficult to interpret for Śaṅkara. Particularly on the last bit, on the non-departure of the vital functions, Śaṅkara breaks the *sūtra* in two and reads what is the conclusion in all other commentaries as the prima facie view, which he overturns in the second part—in a reading that is no doubt unjustified—to arrive at the exact opposite: the vital functions *do not* depart, and the knower *does not* take the course of the gods but attains liberation right here.[43] While his was surely the right interpretation of Yājñavalkya, it was not of Bādarāyaṇa the theologian, for whom all knowers of Brahman would have to take the course of the gods because it was the part and parcel of the *paradigmatic brahma-vidyā*, and for whom all Upaniṣads would have to speak with one voice, that of the *Chāndogya*.

Attaining Brahman

Now the question presents itself, what is this world of Brahman, and which Brahman is the *vidvān* led to by the "non-human person?" Let us see why this question arises.

The course of the gods delineated in the Upaniṣads provides a clue, particularly the eighth book of the *Chāndogya* on which the *Brahma-sūtra* account was based, but even more graphically the *Kauṣītaki Upaniṣad*, commonly referred to in the systematization of the course by the commentators. We may summarize what the Upaniṣad says on this with profit.[44] Once the knower of Brahman passes on from the world of Prajāpati toward *brahma-loka,* 500 celestial nymphs dispatched by Brahman, a few of which are individually named, greet him with garlands, lotions, cosmetic powders, clothes, and fruits. His first stop is at a lake by the name of Āra, which he must cross with his mind, and if his knowledge is imperfect he drowns there. A watchman greets him next as he comes to a river by the name of Vijarā, which he also must cross with his mind: should he succeed, this is the point at which his *saṁsāra*, embodiment, officially ends.

But the graphic description goes on:

> He then arrives at the tree Ilya, and the fragrance of *brahman* permeates him. Then he arrives at the plaza Sālajya, and the flavor of *brahman* permeates him. Then he arrives at the palace Aparājita, and the radiance of *brahman* permeates him. Then he arrives near the doorkeepers, Indra and Prajāpati, and they flee from him. Then he arrives at the hall Vibhu, and the glory of *brahman* permeates him.[45]

After some more heavenly adventures, the knower finally meets Brahman who sits on a throne, and presents himself before him. On Brahman's question: "Who are you?," *ko 'sīti*, he replies: "You are the Self of all beings, and I am who you are." After some more discussion, Brahman finally tells him: "You've truly attained my world, Mr. X, it is yours." I note here parenthetically that it is heartwarming to learn that Brahman on the throne asks the Brahman-to-be "Ko si ti," "Who are you?," in Serbian.

Now, already by the time of Bādarāyaṇa such graphic descriptions were not agreeable to all Vedāntins, and so there arises the question, to *which* Brahman precisely does the liberated soul go via the path of the gods. A certain Bādari is reported to have advanced the view that the *vidvān* is lead to Brahman the effect, *kārya-brahma*, Hiraṇyagarbha or Prajāpati the "collective individual" from Chapter 3. Since Brahman is omnipresent, Bādari claimed that actions such as motion and attainment are not possible in relation to him, and so the ultimate endpoint of the path of the gods must be the spatially determined Hiraṇyagarbha, who is called Brahman figuratively because of proximity, that is, because of being Brahman's first product. Bādari's reasoning was clearly related to the aforementioned account of "liberation here and now." Nevertheless, he accommodated the predominantly *Chāndogya* doctrine involving going to *brahma-loka* by the invention of the idea of gradual liberation that became very influential in later Vedānta: at the end of the creation cycle, Hiraṇyagarbha himself is liberated, and along with him the course-of-the-gods itinerant attains the supreme Brahman. In that sense, Hiraṇyagarbha may also be described as Brahman proper or "higher," although being the effected or "lower" Brahman.[46]

To these two Brahmans, Śaṅkara, as we mentioned under the previous heading, associated two *vidvān*s: one who takes the course of the gods, reaches Hiraṇyagarbha, and is eventually liberated if he attains true knowledge of Brahman in Hiraṇyagarbha's world, or is otherwise reborn in the next creation cycle; and another one who is liberated right here.

This view was opposed by Jaimini the *Chāndogya* master, who claimed that it must be the higher Brahman who is attained by those who meditate on it, because that is the primary meaning of the word "*brahma*."[47]

Bādarāyaṇa's conclusion on the matter is as transparent as it is mystifying. He rejects both views "because there is a fault in both ways," and instead says that the non-human person leads to Brahman those who do not meditate through symbols. This is an explicit reference to one of his cardinal doctrines—stated in *Brahma-sūtra* 4.1.3–4 and introduced by us in the previous chapter—that in a *brahma-vidyā* one must meditate on Brahman as one's Self, to the exclusion of symbolic meditations. We ought to remember here that Upaniṣadic meditations were based on the aspiration to turn oneself into the meditational object, and so if one's aspiration was to become the higher Brahman, then it is this higher Brahman that one ought to reach. Additionally, the Upaniṣads talk about different results related to the different kinds of meditation, *brahmopāsana* and *pratīkopāsana*, and the higher Brahman is described as the result of the first. From either point of the continuum—aspiration and attainment—it must be the higher Brahman that the itinerant is led to.[48]

This is very—and uncommonly so—transparent, an unmistakable link between two key *Brahma-sūtra* loci. The mystifying bit is, what exactly are the faults in the two rejected views? Indeed, how is Bādarāyaṇa's conclusion substantively different from Jaimini's claim, if one is led to the higher Brahman in any case? Ghate had proposed that Bādarāyaṇa had, in fact, accepted Jaimini's counter to Bādari as the conclusion and started another topic, about the eligible itinerant, rounding up thus the course-destination-traveler complex: by the course of the gods → to the higher Brahman → is led the meditator on Brahman as one's Self.[49]

This interpretation is appealing, although it does not fit fully the argumentative structure of the *Brahma-sūtra*, where Bādarāyaṇa intervenes in similar sequences of several teachers presenting prima facie views against which he gives his conclusion last. Let us see, therefore, how at least one of the commentators approached the issue of "double fault," as it will allow us to transition to the next heading. For Bhāskara, the proper reading was not "there *is* fault in both was," but "there *isn't* one," a reading allowed in the original Sanskrit.[50] In other words, *both* the attainment of Hiraṇyagarbha and of the higher Brahman were associated with the course of the gods in the Upaniṣads—and with the promise of liberation—for which reason siding exclusively either with Bādari or Jaimini wouldn't do. The saving grace was the aforementioned doctrine of gradual liberation, but with a twist different from Śaṅkara's: both *vidvāns*, of Brahman the effect and of the higher Brahman, do attain *brahma-loka*, but the first remains there with Hiraṇyagarbha until the end of the cycle and is then liberated, whereas the second crosses over to the highest attainment immediately upon arrival, passing with that across all temporal distinctions.[51]

The Knowledge of Small Space and Prajāpati's Teaching

Before we resume the discussion on the character of the attainment, however, we should briefly introduce the scriptural account on which the *Brahma-sūtra* systematization is based. This most important text is chapter eight of the *Chāndogya Upaniṣad*. The chapter has an interesting structure, as it is divided in two parts that share some material and are much intertwined, yet is clearly a ring-shaped whole. The first part, 8.1 to 8.6, is traditionally known as *dahara-vidyā* or "knowledge about the small space," whereas the second part, 8.7 to 8.15, is commonly referred to as *prajāpati-vākya*, "teachings of Prajāpati." The most important shared part is a statement that appears at the beginning of both: "This Self is free from evil, from old age and death, free from hunger and thirst, its desires and intentions are true." In the first part, though, this Self is additionally identified with a small space, "a lotus dwelling in the city of Brahman"—as we learn, the lotus dwelling is the human heart—in which are contained the earth and the sky, fire and air, the sun and the moon, all beings and desires, indeed: everything. One should search out and know distinctly this Self. That the whole chapter is structured as a ring, apart from the many shared elements, is clear from the end, where space—clearly an allusion to the small space of the beginning—is described as that which evolves name-and-form, Brahman the immortal Self. We will follow here the second part, but draw on the first as well.

The gods and the demons have heard that knowing the aforementioned Self makes one gain all the worlds and desirable objects, and have dispatched Indra and Virocana as their representatives to learn about it from Prajāpati. Prajāpati's instruction moves through three consecutive states of the Self, that of waking, dream, and deep sleep. Virocana is content with the first instruction: the body that one sees in reflective surfaces, adorned with ornaments and fine dress—the Self of the waking state—just *is* the Self that one should search out and know distinctly. Indra, however, is not convinced even after hearing about the Self that one experiences in deep sleep, although Prajāpati describes it in superlative terms, a state in which one is "totally collected and perfectly calm."

We will hear Indra's reasons shortly, but we should note now that this doctrine of three states of the Self was Yājñavalkya's, a prominent part of the *Bṛhad-āraṇyaka* (4.3). Yājñavalkya described the third state as liberation, reminiscent of the aforementioned opening definition of the Self, "beyond desires, free from evil, fearless," yet also one in which the Self, sentient though it remains, is not transitively conscious of anything because it has become everything: "There isn't a second reality here that he could see as something distinct and separate from himself."[52] Yājñavalkya insisted that just this is the world of Brahman. We have, in fact, already encountered this third state in Chapter 4: it was Śaṅkara's Brahman whose breathing creates the world as a manifestation of its essential nature.

Now, the third state proved to be important in the *Chāndogya* as well. Since the "small space" that is Brahman and contains everything is in the heart, and one in deep sleep becomes collected within the heart, withdrawing all cognitive faculties, one there comes close to the real Self. But the *Chāndogya* did not accept this third state of perfect calm as the final, and the true Self introduced in the beginning was not equivalent to Yājñavalkya's third state. Indra's dissatisfaction tells us why: he did not find it "appealing," or, as the *Chāndogya* puts it, "enjoyable," *bhogya*, because in it one is not aware of anything, including oneself. "One has become destroyed, as it were."[53] The state of non-transitive consciousness does not involve experience, and without objective consciousness, self-awareness is not possible either. Prajāpati, therefore, proceeds to tell Indra about a fourth state, in which "the perfectly calm Self rises from the body, reaches the highest light, and emerges in its true form."[54]

Part of the problem why the third state was not the final is that embodiment persists, and it is so because *prāṇa* or life-breath binds the self to the body, "like a draft animal that is yoked to a cart."[55] Remember: the Self of the third state was the one that "breathes out creation." In the fourth state, however, one becomes free from embodiment and from evil, bad karma, "like a horse shaking off its hair,"[56] and one attains the uncreated world of Brahman. But, more importantly, the fourth state unlike in Yājñavalkya's account does not involve the cessation of cognition: while Prajāpati agrees with Yājñavalkya that the Self remains an agent of awareness, he does not agree that no objects of experience are available to it, part of the reason being that the Self does have a "mind," which the Upaniṣad describes as "the divine eye" with which the Self can see things in the world of Brahman.[57]

With that, what happens when one had attained "the highest light" and had become, as the Upaniṣad says, "the final person?" Well, one frolics in the world of Brahman, "laughing, playing, and enjoying himself with women, carriages, or relatives."[58] Surely this is a different kind of play, *līlā*, than the "play" of breathing that is an expression of one's essential nature. More precisely, one had managed to uncover the "true desires and intentions" that belong to the Self in the small space, which the Upaniṣad illustrates with gusto: by the mere thought, one is able to summon or create fathers, mothers, brothers, sisters, friends, scents and garlands, food and drink, songs, women—in short, "whatever end or desirable object one may conceive, they appear to him merely through his intention."[59] He also gets absolute freedom of motion in whichever sphere he wants: "Those here in this world who depart after discovering the self and these real desires obtain complete freedom of movement in all the worlds."[60] Note these two, then: all desirable objects by the mere intention, and absolute freedom of motion.

Additionally, although this "final person" is not embodied, it "emerges in its own form," as we just saw. What does this mean? How is one without a body but with a form? What kind of an entity might this be? The Upaniṣad offers the following illustrations: the wind, the raincloud, lightning, and thunder. Howsoever one may interpret these images, clearly the intention isn't to say that upon discarding the body one remains shapeless, and perhaps we need to think about things that are not spatially determinate yet are not indeterminate either. The thunder may be the most useful illustration, a well-formed phenomenon, discernible sound, which is nevertheless not confined to one place but can be heard in a wide expanse.

Be that as it may, the chapter ends with the statement that he who had attained the world of Brahman does not return, repeating this twice for good measure. This is absolutely important for the *Brahma-sūtra*, as it provides the topical passage for the last *sūtra*, which Bādarāyaṇa also repeats twice:

"No return, because that is the statement; no return, because that is the statement."[61]

The Liberated Soul

Now, chapter four of the *Brahma-sūtra* is largely a commentary on *Chāndogya* 8. Bādarāyaṇa had, in fact, touched some of its elements even before, in chapter one on the "coherence" or *samanvaya* doctrine, that all Upaniṣadic passages are about Brahman. We should begin there. In a typical *samanvaya* manner, Bādarāyaṇa says that the small space in the *dahara-vidyā*, described as the Self free from evil, death, etc., of true desires and intentions, must be Brahman, because the stated characteristics fit Brahman only: in this small space everything is contained, and it is the dike that keeps the worlds—this one and *brahma-loka*—apart, lest they collide into one another.[62] But then, several problems arise, the pertinent for us being the following: in the subsequent text, the teachings of Prajāpati, the Self must be the individual soul rather than Brahman, because Prajāpati refers to it as "the person seen in the eye" and in reflective surfaces generally, and goes through its four states, the first three of which cannot pertain to Brahman. However, the two selves are described in identical terms, as free from evil, death, etc., of true desires and intentions. If so, shouldn't the reference of both sections be the same? That is, since in the second it is unmistakably the individual soul, not Brahman, Bādarāyaṇa must reject his *samanvaya* claim.[63] He replies, however, that Prajāpati's description of the soul refers not to the ordinary soul in transmigration, but to its "manifested nature," that is, its character in the state of liberation.[64] As a corollary, then, the descriptions of Brahman and of the liberated soul are identical.

What does this mean? How are Brahman and the liberated soul identical? For the likes of Śaṅkara and Bhāskara, upon liberation there *just is* Brahman, one and only, in which the soul had lost its individuality, including one of its defining characteristics from chapter three, its infinitesimal size. To piggyback now on our theodicy chapter, for Bhāskara and Śaṅkara (for the second, only from the conventional standpoint), karma was not only responsible for the vagaries of destiny, it was also a soul-making mechanism, in the ontological rather than soteriological sense. It was beginningless karma that organizes a section of name-and-form into an individual, a "causal" entity in its subtle state and "effected" entity when properly embodied, through all eternity in the manner of the seed-and-sprout, upon the background of Brahman. Do away with this karma, and name-and-form would fall off, leaving the one and only Brahman as the sole entity in liberation.

Now, obviously an ontology of this kind cannot be comfortable with the *Chāndogya* description of liberation in *brahma-loka*, the enjoyment with women and chariots. Yet, the *Brahma-sūtra* account was tied precisely to it, and the "liberation statement"—"he does not return"—was Bādarāyaṇa's grand conclusion. To return now to Bhāskara, we can appreciate why he found the idea of two knowers and two kinds of liberation appealing. First, that the embodied individual at the core was just Brahman made it possible to reject Bādari's express claim that one is lead to Brahman the effect, yet accept its implications. It was in any case the subtle body that travels to the world of Hiraṇyagarbha, not the omnipresent Brahman, and it was fine for the higher knower to be liberated upon reaching *and crossing beyond* this world, because that is how scripture wanted things to be: liberation not here and now, but through the course of the gods.[65] But, scripture did associate liberation with the lower knower, so he must be liberated as well, *after* enjoying with women and chariots. Were that not the case, the *Chāndogya* statement about non-return that clearly pertains to the lower knower, to Bhāskara's mind, would be false. And so, since liberation is scripturally determined, the ontology must be harmonized with the scriptural whims of soteriology. The idea of gradual liberation averts the objection of reason that liberation liable to change cannot be eternal.

But this does not seem to be Bādarāyaṇa's intention. He concludes the heading with a statement that the soul of *prajāpati-vākya* is an "imitation," or perhaps an image, reflection (*anukṛti*) of Brahman.[66] This suggests the notion of similarity or sameness rather than numeric identity. With this, let us forge into the final section of the *Brahma-sūtra*, where Bādarāyaṇa elaborates on this "manifested nature" of the soul, opening with the statement that upon attainment, upon rising from the state of perfect calm and attaining the "highest light," the soul emerges in its own nature or form. This manifested nature is liberation in which the individual soul has become non-distinct (*avibhāga*) from Brahman.[67] The remainder of the section clarifies this non-distinction, and it is evidently not numerical but qualitative identity. (Parenthetically, we should note that the "manifested nature" is mentioned in three *sūtra*s and three distinct contexts: 4.4.1 and 1.3.19, which both pick out the eighth chapter of the *Chāndogya*; and 3.1.4, which says that the essential nature of the soul is not manifested fully in the dream state and prior to liberation generally. This point is important methodologically, as mentioned in the Introduction, as it illustrates Bādarāyaṇa's consistency that facilitates the reconstruction of his philosophy.)

The first thing that needs clarifying is, which qualities does the liberated soul manifest? Jaimini argues—and Bādarāyaṇa agrees—that these are the qualities from the *dahara-vidyā* and *prajāpati-vākya*, most of which were negative and collectively coterminous with the freedom from karma, but also, crucially, the "true desires" and "true intentions," *satya-kāma* and *satya-saṅkalpa.*[68] The first just means attaining any desirable object, explicated again in the *Chāndogya* as the ability to see all of one's relatives and friends, to have food and drinks of one's choice, garlands and perfumes, women and chariots. The second pertains to the manner in which one may obtain such desirable objects: it is by *mere will* or *intention.*

I mentioned briefly the idea of *satya-saṅkalpa* in Chapters 3 and 4, and said that it signified the manner in which Brahman creates the world, Brahman's being omnipotent Being: Brahman creates through sheer will or mere intention. In liberation, the soul acquires the same ability, not quite to create worlds—we shall see why under the next heading—but to have relatives and enjoy things by sheer will.[69] Now, the characteristics of *satya-kāma* and *satya-saṅkalpa* immediately raise the question: How will the liberated soul enjoy such pleasures without a body? We saw that having a body was the problem of transmigration that the doctrine of *brahma-vidyā* was supposed to solve, and that upon liberation one severs the connection with the body and "emerges in one's own form," which Bādarāyaṇa interpreted as "manifested nature." But, enjoyment is predicated on appropriate cognitive instruments, and we also saw that in *brahma-loka* the mind, "the divine eye," was supposed to reemerge. The notion of *satya-saṅkalpa* was meant to address precisely this problem: just as Brahman creates the world in the manner of play through sheer will, not depending on separate effort, the liberated soul manifesting Brahman's characteristics can create bodies—*multiple bodies*, argues Jaimini—with cognitive faculties and all, in which to enjoy "true desires," desirable objects.[70]

But isn't this transmigration all over again, and doesn't it negate Prajāpati's statement about breaking embodiment for good? No, Rāmānuja argues: *satya-saṅkalpa* is precisely about this, creating bodies not contingent on karma but through sheer will, in the same manner of play in which Brahman creates the world![71] We should remember here the illustration of the king who plays ball just because he feels like it, for that is what one becomes in liberation: one's own sovereign, who gets to enjoy unrestrictedly the "good stuff" and move throughout all worlds, as the *dahara-vidyā* said, to meet whomever one likes.[72] So, liberation is best defined as full *sovereignty* or *majesty*—expressed in absolute freedom of motion—and unrestricted enjoyment in the manner of play, through mere will.

Now, can we say something more about the "own form" *qua* form that the soul manifests in liberation? We saw that the *Chāndogya* used the analogues of wind, cloud, lightening, and thunder, phenomena which are perceived as disembodied yet also "formed." Significant here is Bādarāyaṇa's former definition of the soul as *aṇu,* minute in size. Śaṅkara and Bhāskara, as we saw, thought that upon liberation, the soul loses this minuteness and becomes the omnipresent Brahman. The *Brahma-sūtra*, however, uses instead the image of a lamp, a point of light that enters things by spreading illumination.[73] With the characteristics of absolute freedom of motion and having no proper body, this illumination now is not confined to the body, as during transmigration, but must extend everywhere. This follows from the insistence of the commentators that the characteristic of "mere intention" excludes *all extraneous causes,* including actions such as going, simultaneous with the absolute freedom of motion.[74] The liberated soul, then, is like a lamp that enters bodies not by ensouling any of them exclusively, but by extending its unrestricted light, consciousness. It is this unlimited extension of the light of consciousness that facilitates enjoyment and freedom of motion.

This interpretation is further supported by the *Chāndogya* statement that the soul in liberation reaches the "highest light." We saw in Chapter 3 that Brahman being of the nature of light was reflected in all bodies: it was how Brahman's feature of residence was possible. The soul in liberation attains the same status, that of "the highest light," and the power to become reflected in multiple bodies that appear by its mere will, in which to experience pleasure. Bādarāyaṇa was serious about all of this, and arguably such unrestricted enjoyment of desirable objects in the manner of absolute sovereignty through sheer intention *just is* the individual soul manifesting the innate characteristic of bliss, becoming Brahman in full. To discharge now another debt to Chapter 3: bliss, *palpable enjoyment*, is the essential characteristic of Brahman, but also of the liberated soul: *satya-kāma* is just what *ānanda*, bliss, is. With respect to this, Hajime Nakamura writes: "The details of the description of this realm of liberation are almost unparalleled in the writings of any Indian school."[75]

Still, Jaimini's view about the positive characteristics in liberation was controverted by one Auḍulomi, who argued that the soul in liberation is only consciousness, because *just that* is its essential nature.[76] This view was tied to Yājñavalkya's account about the third state of the Self, or perhaps a fourth state which is for all purposes identical with the third, that of non-transitive consciousness, yet also final, involving no return to waking and dream.[77] In his teachings to Maitreyī,[78] Yājñavalkya described this state, the essential nature of the soul, as a "mass of awareness," *prajñāna-ghana*. This was the preferred soul of the Advaitins, under the provision that it is one only, but also—as recognized by Bhāskara—of Sāṅkhyas and Vaiśeṣikas (and Mīmāṁsakas, we should add), as plural.[79]

Now, Bādarāyaṇa does not refute Auḍulomi, but says that "even so, because of the existence of the former characteristics, owing to prior reference, there is no contradiction" between this view and that of Jaimini.[80] But how can that be? How can the liberated soul both *enjoy in bodies* through its own will, and be *just* pure, *nontransitive,* consciousness? The views diverge again. For Śaṅkara, the two descriptions pertain to the conventional reality of Brahman as the effect and the absolute reality of the higher Brahman respectively. Bhāskara explains it through his identity-and-difference ontology. Rāmānuja and Nimbārka advocate a synthesis of positive and negative characteristics, which really amounts to reaffirming Jaimini's view.

Perhaps something else is at play. To return briefly to the "double fault" issue and the question, to which Brahman is the liberated soul led, Rāmānuja and Nimbārka there introduce a distinction between two *vidvān*s, knowers of Brahman: those who meditate on the higher Brahman and are led to it, and those who meditate on their own essential nature as consciousness that is different from matter, *negatively identical* to Brahman's nature of the imperishable that we discussed in Chapters 3 and 6.[81] Bādari's view was wrong because those who intend to attain the higher Brahman would have been led to Brahman the effect, Hiranyagarbha, but Jaimini's view would have prevented the second kind of *vidvān*s from attaining the higher Brahman, because they don't quite meditate on it. We are reminded of the twelfth chapter of the *Bhagavad-gītā*, where Arjuna asks Kṛṣṇa about two kinds of yogis, those who venerate him with devotion and those who meditate on the imperishable. Kṛṣṇa accepts both: the first are the best, the second must toil hard, but both will attain him in the end.[82]

So, instead of a synthesis of consciousness with the positive characteristics of "true desires" and "true intentions," perhaps Bādarāyaṇa was ready to accept that some *vidvān*s in liberation remain just pure consciousness, though perfectly capable of transitive awareness.[83] If so, the possibility that we should entertain is that the uniform *brahma-vidyā* was not absolutely uniform after all, that is, that it had a stripped-down version focused solely on consciousness and the imperishable. But if such interpretation is right, there is no indication that these two views represent lower and higher attainments, of Brahman the effect and of the higher Brahman. More likely is that they were genuine options.

There are difficulties with this account, though, into which we cannot venture, and we must be content with it as a possible, by no means certain, interpretation.

The Final Ground of Difference

Be that as it may, to finish his treatise, Bādarāyaṇa takes up once again the opening text, the *Taittirīya* statement about Brahman being the first principle, "from which these beings proceed etc." If in liberation the soul had manifested the characteristic of bliss, one may wonder if it has become fully equal to Brahman. Bādarāyaṇa tackles this with an *adhikaraṇa* of five *sūtra*s, the content of which is somewhat hazy but the contours—the first and the last *sūtra*—clear.[84] Although the soul had become Brahman, there is a limit to this identity. It excludes its being the first principle, and generally the independent ability to interfere in the functioning of the world: identity is restricted to the characteristic of bliss.

To translate these two *sūtra*s: "The soul's being Brahman excludes the functions with regard to the world, because of the context and because the liberated soul is remote from it."[85] "And, because there is an indication of sameness that is restricted to enjoyment."[86] The topical passage of the first *sūtra* is the abovementioned *Taittirīya* statement, whereas the second is from the definition of Brahman that Bādarāyaṇa had followed throughout:

> Brahman is Being, consciousness, limitless. He who knows it as hidden in the heart (and in) the highest heaven attains all desires together with the wise Brahman.[87]

Śaṅkara says that this *adhikaraṇa* too is about the lower Brahman and the lower knower, who must be eventually reborn if he had not attained knowledge in *brahma-loka*. However, without these two references to the *Taittirīya*, there is no *Brahma-sūtra* for Bādarayaṇa to write, and Śaṅkara is surely not correct here. Let us, then, briefly reflect one more time on the beginning of the *Brahma-sūtra* and the definition of Brahman as the first principle, since the *adhikaraṇa* has important ontological ramifications.

To reiterate, liberation is an ontological apotheosis, a state where one is Brahman pure and simple, with one caveat: one manifests the characteristic of bliss, but not the functions of a creator God. For this reason, Brahman's creatorship was not part of the paradigmatic *brahma-vidyā*, as one's being Brahman did not include this property and wouldn't be of use to the meditator. Now, Advaita Vedāntins through history have tended to move the focus away from Brahman's being the first principle to its other features. Śaṅkara, for instance, argued that Brahman was underdetermined in this creative role, as there were other candidates for being the first principle, such as prime matter of Sāṅkhya or the atoms of Nyāya-Vaiśeṣika. Thus a more determinate definition of Brahman was required, that of Being, consciousness, bliss, infinite, distinguishing the true first principle from its competitors.[88] In later Advaita, this set was dubbed Brahman's "essential characteristics," *svarūpa-lakṣaṇa*, whereas creatorship became *taṭastha-lakṣaṇa*, a "marginal characteristic."

But if this is right, why begin the treatise with a marginal characteristic of the subject under discussion, as Advaitins had claimed, or one that was not important to the meditator, as we have argued here?

To revisit the opening, now, Bādarāyaṇa begins his treatise with the statement of Brahman's being the creator; proceeds to refute prime matter as the first principle by denying its having the characteristic of consciousness, yet tacitly affirming Being; refutes the individual soul's being the first principle by denying its having bliss, yet tacitly affirming Being and consciousness; gradually shows that the soul in liberation manifests the characteristic of bliss; and closes the treatise by reaffirming Brahman's being the first principle. To take a cue from M. T. Telivala, now, Bādarāyaṇa begins and ends the *Brahma-sūtra* with Brahman's creatorship not because this is a *general* feature, but because in his system it is Brahman's *unique* characteristic, *asādhāraṇa-dharma*, one that it does not share with prime matter or the souls and, therefore, the one that defines it most precisely.[89]

So, is that it? Is all there is to liberation creating bodies by mere wish; occupying them in the manner of light—that is, absolute freedom of motion—to enjoy desirable objects; and having one's relatives from prior embodiments appear to oneself? It seems it is all we can say with certainty. To return to the idea of *brahma-loka*, now, we saw that Śaṅkara and Bhāskara made it the world of Hiraṇyagarbha, at the expiration of which one would be finally liberated, or in Śaṅkara's case, reborn if failing to acquire knowledge of the pure Brahman. But the theists were not thrilled with this either: Rāmānuja, for instance, consistently depicts the place where the "true desires" are experienced as "the world of the forefathers etc.," that is, the heaven of the ritualists.[90] For them *brahma-loka* was just Brahman, or his non-material world, such as Vaikuṇṭha the heaven of Viṣṇu, beyond this world of corruption that includes the domain of Hiraṇyagarbha, the proper appellation of which was not *brahma* but *prajāpati-loka*.[91]

In either case, what Bādarāyaṇa directly described as liberation was more like a thirteenth salary for the commentarial tradition.

Arguably there was something more to liberation even for Bādarāyaṇa, but what that was hinges on understanding *sūtra* 4.4.19 of the "hazy content." To translate it provisionally: "And, not abiding in [the sphere of] transformation; for, scripture describes [this] situation as such."[92] Bhāskara and Śaṅkara interpret this, as we might expect, as referring to the higher form of Brahman—or a higher form of sovereignty—that the ultimately liberated soul attains, having lost distinct individuality. This is unlikely: the *adhikaraṇa* is about the ultimate distinction, as we just saw. Rāmānuja and Nimbārka, on the other hand, interpret the *sūtra* as pertaining to *another kind of bliss*, on top of the bliss enjoyed in the world of Hiraṇyagarbha and below. Nimbārka's paraphrase is concise enough to quote fully:

> The liberated soul intuits Brahman itself, which is freed from transformations such as birth, is the totality of innate, inconceivable, limitless qualities, and possessed of splendor. It is how scripture describes the situation of the liberated.[93]

The reference of what "scripture describes" is much more contextual with Rāmānuja and Nimbārka. The *Taittirīya* is the scriptural focus of the *adhikaraṇa*, and the *Taittirīya* describes liberation—fearlessness or *abhayam*, which is a synonym for liberation for all Vedāntins—as finding the "invisible, incorporeal, ineffable, and supportless essence."[94] Additionally, along with attaining all desires, the *Taittirīya* depicts the highest bliss, *ānanda* the essential characteristic of Brahman and the liberated soul, as a "hundred times greater than the bliss of Prajāpati," beyond the bliss of Brahman the effect in the *Brahma-sūtra* scheme of things.[95] We are reminded, thus, of the *Kauṣītaki* statement about the fragrance, brilliance, flavor, and glory of Brahman overwhelming the *brahma-loka* arrival.

If the liberated soul does intuit Brahman, we don't know how such experience is not one of change, transformation. Still, it is worth mentioning that the Viśiṣṭādvaita distinction between substantive changeless consciousness (*dharmi-jñāna*) and attributive transformed consciousness (*dharma-bhūta-jñāna*) was but a development of Bādarāyaṇa's theory of how the infinitesimal soul is conscious of a wider section than its minute extension, in the manner of the sun and its rays. So, perhaps the lamp that is the soul can illuminate and reveal Brahman even without being embodied and having the requisite senses: a direct intuition if there ever was one. And perhaps that is also how the unembodied Brahman sits on a throne to receive the Brahman-to-be: the highest light encountering the highest light. What is ultimately impossible for those whose mere intention is reality?

Settling Mīmāṁsā Scores

In lieu of a conclusion, let us finish with a brief reflection on the issue with which we opened Chapter 6. We saw that *vidyā* was modeled in the image of ritual, with an injunction, details of procedure, the whole shebang. In Mīmāṁsā, the main factor of a ritual was the action of sacrificing or offering, and the result was contingent on this main factor, the point being to remove the contingency of personal whim: no human or divine factor should govern the fruitfulness of one's undertaking. If the action was done properly, the result should follow just as it does in worldly action, such as agriculture.[96]

This brought the problem of impermanence: the ritual is an action, and the results produced by action are *not* permanent. As the *Chāndogya* put it, "as here in this world the possession of a territory won by action comes to an end, so in the hereafter a world won by merit comes to an end."[97] Ritual was also problematic in the specifically Indian understanding of permanence: it proceeded in the manner of combining elements to produce a new thing, and things that are got by composition can be broken apart. The *Muṇḍaka's* famous diatribe against ritual was along these lines: "Examining the world *piled up* through ritual, a Brahmin should become cognitively disengaged with it: what is not made cannot be got through what is made."[98]

Bādarāyaṇa, however, thoroughly reevaluated the category of the main factor against Jaimini, and replaced action with Brahman: "The result comes from Brahman, because that makes sense."[99] Brahman became the final court at which any Vedic enterprise is judged. The reasoning behind this was simple: Brahman is the repository of all desires which one could possibly obtain through action, and its intentions come true by necessity. Brahman is eternal, *imperishable,* and it is also one's Self, to be realized through meditation. If one could manifest one's being Brahman, one would obtain all desires *and* the requisite permanence.

In that sense, the study of Brahman was very much a continuation of the familiar Vedic aspirations. There isn't necessarily a different value system behind the *Brahma-sūtra*: the big discovery concerned the means.

Study Questions

1. What are the two kinds of karmic stock? Argue whether Bādarāyaṇa's theory of karma is universally applicable.
2. Summarize Bādarāyaṇa's account of liberation and identify where commentators like Śaṅkara and Bhāskara depart from it.
3. What is the distinction between liberation while living (*jīvan-mukti*) and final liberation (*videha-mukti*)? Where does Śaṅkara disagree with the other commentators concerning this distinction?
4. Describe the identity between Brahman and the liberated soul around the notion of "imitation."
5. What does it mean that the soul in liberation achieves "ontological apotheosis?" Research the idea of "apotheosis" (a good place to start is Turcan and Tomassi 2005: 437–40) and reflect on its applicability in Bādarāyaṇa's account of liberation.

6. How is it that the soul in liberation is unembodied yet possessing bodies?
7. Early Mīmāṁsā unlike Vedānta developed as a nontheistic tradition. Trace the reason for that in this chapter and elaborate.

Suggestions for Further Study

The complexities of the doctrine of five fires in the Vedic corpus are analyzed in Bodewitz (1996). The history of the idea of two courses—of the gods and the forefathers—is traced in Karmarkar (1925). Hock (2002) analyzes the *Bṛhad-āraṇyaka* account of embodiment and liberation, recognizing that it is different from and independent of the doctrine of five fires. Buchta (2016) provides a good analysis of the commentarial tradition on *Brahma-sūtra* 4.1.13–19, the *sūtra*s that tackle freedom from karma, and focuses on their devotional reinterpretation in the commentaries of Viṭṭhalanātha and Baladeva. The origin of the idea of "liberation while living" (*jīvan-mukti*) in Sāṅkhya is usefully presented in Jakubczak (2004). A detailed history of the same in Advaita Vedānta is available in Fort (1998), whereas Fort and Mumme (1996) is an excellent edited volume on *jīvan-mukti* in the wider setting of Vedānta. Fort (1990) is a useful reading on the four states of the Self, with a focus on Advaita Vedānta. On the meaning of *ānanda*, bliss, and particularly its association with palpable pleasure and orgasmic rapture, Olivelle (2011) is an exemplary philological study.

Notes

Introduction

1 Okita (2014a, Chapter 1).
2 Radhakrishnan (1960).
3 ChUBh, Introduction, vi.9.
4 Nakamura (1983: 426–8).
5 TU 2.1.1.
6 Doniger O'Flaherty (1981: 11).
7 I will generally quote the original Sanskrit of the *sūtra*s that I reference. For other quotations, I will include the Sanskrit only if that is philologically significant.
8 Thibaut (1890) is an introduction to his three-volume translation of the commentaries of Śaṅkara and Rāmānuja. It provides a summary of the entire BS and argues that Śaṅkara's system in many ways does not represent it accurately. Thibaut is much kinder to Rāmānuja, whom he finds a more reliable commentator. Along with the translation, which makes the two most important classical commentaries available in English for the first time, it is a landmark study on the BS system.

Telivala (1918) is a very learned, but densely written, evaluation of Śaṅkara's commentary on the BS as a misrepresentation of Bādarāyaṇa's doctrine, discussing a great number of *sūtra*s and drawing from many commentaries.

Karmarkar (1919–20, 1920–21) takes several commentaries—Śaṅkara, Rāmānuja, Keśava Kāśmīrī, and Vallabha—and attempts to adjudicate which of them "seems to have given a more natural explanation of the sūtras." It focuses on select *sūtra*s that deal with the common topics of Brahman, the world, and the soul, and favors the interpretations of Rāmānuja and Keśava. Similar in style is Ghate (1926), but covering the entire BS topic by topic, adding Madhva to the pool of commentators, and replacing Keśava with Nimbārka.

As must be evident from this brief description, all four studies are for the most part interested in ascertaining which commentator represents Bādarāyaṇa's system most accurately. Nakamura (1983: 425–532) is closer in format to my work, a synthetic study rather than a reading *sūtra* by *sūtra* or *adhikaraṇa* by *adhikaraṇa*, based on the commentaries of Śaṅkara, Bhāskara, and Rāmānuja. Nakamura has a predilection for Bhāskara's *bhedābheda* ontology.

Adams (1993) is an overview of the first chapter of the BS, helpful to the novice but of very limited use to the specialist. It generally does not tell more than is already obvious from the original and the few consulted commentaries, which have evidently been read only in translation. The contextualization is also limited, as I illustrate in nt.34 in Chapter 3, and the occasional references to Monier-Williams's Sanskrit Dictionary to adjudicate between the commentaries are simplistic (see nt.89 in Chapter 3 for illustration).

A general agreement in these studies is that, contra Śaṅkara and his tradition, the BS does not distinguish between higher and lower forms of knowledge, corresponding to two kinds of Brahman; and that the soul, though indistinguishable from Brahman, remains individual even in liberation.

Modi (1943, 1956) is an original attempt to read the second portion of the BS (from section 2 of Chapter 3 to the end) on the merit of the *sūtra*s themselves rather than their commentarial tradition, although Śaṅkara is the foil throughout. This has produced, in my opinion, mixed results: although many particular insights seem valid, the system teased out of the BS is dubious, and often the interpretations are exactly opposed to *every* traditional commentary, for instance on the all-important *sūtra* 3.3.33, and generally disjointed from the reception history of the *Brahma-sūtra*. I won't rely much on Modi's analysis, nor discuss specific disagreements with his interpretation, lest this book turns into "a series of angry footnotes" (as my Pali teacher Steve Collins used to say).

Sharma (1986) is a three-volume study of the commentaries of Śaṅkara, Rāmānuja, and Madhva, often drawing on the sub-commentarial tradition. Very rich in information, it is better read as an apologetic work of a member of Madhva's tradition. I have also found Roma Bose's translation of Nimbārka's and Śrīnivāsa's commentaries (2004, first published in 1940–41) very useful for quick overviews, as it provides brief notes on all points where Nimbārka and Śrīnivāsa disagree with Śaṅkara, Rāmānuja, Bhāskara, Śrīkaṇṭha, and Baladeva.

9 The literature on the issue of authorship is vast, and closely tied to the issue of the unity of the BS and the MS, discussed in nt.21 below. The details are omitted here, but the reader may consult Nakamura (1983: 369–424); Parpola (1981, 1994); Bronkhorst (2007); Aklujkar (2011); and pursue further references from there.

10 Uskokov (2022).

11 Deussen (1908: 27–9, 1912: 120–2).

12 Faddegon (1923).

13 Belvalkar (1918, 1927, 1929: 135–50).

14 For an extensive critique of Belvalkar's thesis, see Bhatkhande (1982).

15 Karmarkar (1921: 79).

16 Belvalkar (1929: 139–42); Karmarkar (1921).

17 Nakamura (1983: 435–6).

18 Hermann Jacobi (1911) argued that the relevant BS passage does not refute Buddhist idealism (Vijñānavāda) but Nāgārjuna's Mādhyamika. Others reject this (Nakamura 1983: 437, nt.7).

19 Nakamura (1983: 90–101).

20 Excellent introductions to the Vedic canon and the place of the Upaniṣads in it are available in Signe Cohen's guide (2018), especially the first seven chapters by Cohen and Dermot Killingly, and in Patrick Olivelle's Introduction to his edition and translation of the Upaniṣads (1998: 3–27).

21 The precise nature of the "prior-posterior," *pūrva-uttara*, relationship between the MS and BS is open to some conjecture, but two accounts are noteworthy. Hajime Nakamura (1983: 409–12) made the sensible suggestion that Vedānta was posterior to Mīmāṁsā in the sense that "the Vedānta Mīmāṁsā presupposed the ritual Mīmāṁsā as a precondition. The ritual Mīmāṁsā can be set up without necessarily presupposing the Vedānta Mīmāṁsā, but the Vedānta Mīmāṁsā, on the contrary, from the first assumes the ritual Mīmāṁsā as a precondition." This suggestion has an intuitive appeal, because understanding the BS is impossible without a good grip on principles of interpretation that can be learned only from the MS: the BS assumes a lot. This is close to what I call a minimal, *ideological* sense in which the MS and BS are evidently related, whatever historical circumstances otherwise were at play.

Another valuable suggestion has been made by Asko Parpola (1981 and 1994), who proposed that the names of the two disciplines had come from the names, or rather headings, of the two parts of one single work called *Mīmāṁsā-sūtra*. That is, initially the two *sūtra* compositions were two parts of a single *Mīmāṁsā-sūtra*, a first (*pūrva*) and a second (*uttara*) part respectively, and the present MS and BS as well as the two disciplines have evolved from the titles.

The outline of Parpola's argument goes something like this. There are in Sanskrit literature several works that are divided in two parts, *pūrva* and *uttara*, and a systematic practice of using such a nomenclature in the Sāma Veda. For instance, the *Jaiminīya Gṛhya-sūtra* has a *pūrva* and an *uttara/apara* part. Further, there is clearly the possibility that Jaimini had written a *Brahma-sūtra* himself, which would have been utilized and replaced by Bādarāyaṇa. In fact, Śaṅkara's student Sureśvara had ascribed *the* BS to Jaimini. While the Sureśvara argument has been put forward by several scholars in support of an earlier Jaimini BS, Parpola to his credit shows how reworking someone else's *sūtra* composition was a common practice in the early post-Vedic period: if Bādarāyaṇa had used and replaced Jaimini's work, he would not have been the first to do a thing of this kind. Next, it is well known that the MS and BS quote several Vedic scholars or teachers, including Jaimini and Bādarāyaṇa, numerous times; the *analysis* of these quotations shows that Bādarāyaṇa is later than Jaimini and had reworked his BS. The brevity of the present BS also supports its later date, as the Śrauta-sūtras tend to abbreviate when taking material from another Śrauta-sūtra. Finally, the BS clearly refers to the MS five times, using the phrase "*tad uktam*," "that has already been explained."

The rest of Parpola's work is a highly instructive analysis of the teacher quotations in the two *Sūtra*s, which suggests that Jaimini was a central character in both, and that "Bādarāyaṇa evidently is a teacher who has intruded into the Mīmāṁsāsūtra after its original composition." Parpola makes a strong case for his claim. His studies are the most thorough engagement with the early history of the two *mīmāṁsā*s and the best *historical* explanation put forward so far.

Johannes Bronkhorst (2007), however, claimed relatively recently that the view according to which Vedānta was in the beginning inseparably linked to *pūrva-mīmāṁsā* contradicts some facts. Namely, the tradition of Mīmāṁsā up to and including Śabara and Prabhākara shows no awareness of liberation. "Śabara's *Bhāṣya* deals with Vedic ritual, which as a rule leads to heaven." Vedānta, on the other hand, "has, presumably from its beginning, been about liberation through knowledge of Brahma." If the two were one in the beginning, where did liberation in early Mīmāṁsā disappear? Having set the issue in these terms, the absence and presence of liberation from the beginning, Bronkhorst does not really tackle it. He reviews the arguments about the unity of the two schools that have been made in secondary literature and attempts to show that the evidence, which is, it bears mentioning, all circumstantial, does not support such unity. He does not examine just what heaven and liberation were in the two *śāstra*s—were they really incommensurable—and he hardly engages with the *sūtra*s at all. He is also wrong that Prabhākara shows no awareness of liberation. (Uskokov 2019: 206)

Unlike Parpola's contextualization of Mīmāṁsā in the whole range of *sūtra* literature, Bronkhorst's work concerns solely with secondhand material. His challenge is, thus, weak, and even his reading of the circumstantial evidence is often faulty, as demonstrated by Ashok Aklujkar (2011). Bronkhorst (2014) makes a brief reply to Aklujkar, which the reader may also wish to consult. I intend to take up the issue, specifically the argument that Mīmāṁsā and Vedānta had started from two disparate presuppositions—heaven and liberation—in a future publication.

22 For the intellectual presuppositions of Mīmāṁsā, see Clooney (1990).

23 For Sāṅkhya, see Larson (1979).

24 For Nyāya-Vaiśeṣika, see Dasti and Phillips (2017).

25 ŚBSBh 1.1.2, i.11.

26 Bhāmatī 1.1.1, p.47.

27 MBSBh Introduction, p.10.

28 antaryāmy adhidaivādi-lokādiṣu tad-dharma-vyapadeśāt; na ca smārtam atad-dharmābhilāpāt; śārīraś cobhaye 'pi hi bhedenainam adhīyate.

29 See Garge (1952: 2, fn.3); Parpola (1981: 158–62).

30 Particularly the ritual *sūtra*s and the *dharma-sūtra*s are straightforward.
31 Nakamura (1983: 440).
32 Nakamura (1974), Parpola (1981, 1994).
33 āsīnaḥ sambhavāt; dhyānāc ca; acalatvaṁ cāpekṣya; smaranti ca; yatraikāgratā tatrāviśeṣāt; 4.1.7–11.
34 To be sure, I am *not* suggesting that we should read *any sūtra* without commentaries, and I have never done that; much more than just the meaning of the *sūtra* is to be derived from them, and even when a clear meaning emerges from the *sūtra*s themselves, I cannot imagine how one may orient oneself in the work without dependence on commentaries. My point is, rather, that interpreting many *sūtra*s is more straightforward than otherwise claimed, that their meaning is evident, and that and this is methodologically significant.
35 The "mention of difference," *bheda-vyapadeśāt*, is in 1.1.18, 1.1.22, 1.3.5.
36 It may be objected that a work such as the BS, which had developed through time and does not have an author in the traditional sense, is prone to terminological inconsistencies. However, one of the reasons I had decided to refer to the author as "Bādarāyaṇa" was precisely to reject an alleged absence of authorial intention. That is to say, I take it that whoever redacted the final text of the BS is responsible for its consistency.
37 Ingalls (1954).
38 It is to be noted that both Thibaut (1890: lxxxvi–vii) and Nakamura (1983: 455–65) observed a remarkable consistency between the commentaries. Nakamura in particular found that of the 555 *sūtra*s, the interpretations of Śaṅkara, Bhāskara, and Rāmānuja differ on approximately 209 (1983: 458). In other words, on about 63 percent of the BS text there is full commentarial unison. While it is possible that competing oral traditions of the BS were in place but had died out, and that what is found in the available commentaries is reflective just of one tradition of interpretation, precariously little would remain of writing a book on the BS if we do not include commentarial unison in our hermeneutic toolbox.

Chapter 1

1 See nt.8 in the Introduction.
2 On the notion of *mahā-vākya*, see Uskokov (2018c), chapter 10.
3 Notes 8 and 21 in the Introduction may be read as a sketch in this direction.
4 Pollock (2006).
5 For an overview of pre-Śaṅkara Vedāntins and BS commentators, see Nakamura (2004: 3–208) and Pandey (1983).
6 This division is a commonplace in scholarship. However, Lawrence McCrea (2015) had argued that insofar as the two are conceived *as schools* rather than positions on a wide spectrum of Vedānta, *Bhāmatī* and *Vivaraṇa*

become prominent only in the sixteenth century and arguably under the doxographic influence of a Dvaita Vedāntin, Vyāsatīrtha.

7 Śaṅkara's reliability as a commentator before "he inserts unnecessary interpolations and ideas of his own" has been rightly noted by Nakamura (1983: 459–60).

8 ŚBSBh 4.1.7.

9 ChU 6.8.7ff.

10 BĀU 1.4.10.

11 My brief reconstruction of Śaṅkara's ontology here is based on my dissertation research (Uskokov 2018c); important primary references that the reader may wish to consult include ŚBSBh 2.1.14 2.1.22, 4.1.2; TUBh 2.1.1; BĀUBh 3.9.28.7.

12 The continuity of Śaṅkara's Vedānta with the doctrines of some teachers cited in the BS was noted by Telivala (1918: 92).

13 It has been argued that ignorance did not have a cosmological sense in Śaṅkara's system (Hacker 1995: 67–70), and that such sense was introduced by Śaṅkara's followers. I have argued before the American Oriental Society (Annual Meeting 2021) that this is a wrong interpretation, and will publish my argument in a future paper.

14 BhBSBh 2.1.13, 2.1.18.

15 BhBSBh 2.1.27.

16 BhBSBh 1.4.22, 2.1.13.

17 BhBSBh 1.4.26.

18 VAS §63, p.227–8.

19 Carman (1974: 124–33).

20 RŚBh 2.1.14.

21 McCrea (2014: 83).

22 Vrajlal (1964: 435–55).

23 Vrajlal (1964: 472–9).

24 Vrajlal (1964: 456–67).

25 Ghate (1926: 168).

26 Sharma (1997: 79–88).

27 Sharma (1997: 89–137).

28 NVPS and ŚVK 1.2.5–6, 1.2.8, 1.2.12, 1.2.21, 1.3.5, 1.3.43, 1.4.3, 1.4.9, 1.4.11, 1.4.20–1, 1.4.26; 2.1.6–7, 2.1.13–4, 2.1.22; 3.2.27–8; 4.1.3.

29 The section on Vijñānabhikṣu is largely indebted to Nicholson (2010).

30 "New logic" or *navya-nyāya* is a development of the traditional Nyāya school of philosophy, the primary interest of which was theory of knowledge. For a contextualization of Vijñānabhikṣu in the context of *navya-nyāya*, see Nicholson (2010), especially chapter 3.

31 T. S. Rukmani had just recently published a translation of the first five *sūtra*s of the *Vijñānāmṛta*, which is not yet available in U.S. libraries or from U.S. book vendors.

32 The section on Baladeva is largely indebted to Okita (2014a).

33 The origin is rather the *Viṣṇu Purāṇa*, mediated by Baladeva's teacher Rādhādāmodara; see Okita (2014a: 142–53).
34 For a historically nuanced discussion, see Okita (2014a: 234–52).
35 On this work, see Clooney (2020).
36 VNM 1.1, commentary.
37 VNM 1.9–10.
38 VNM 1.2.
39 On this work, see Srinivasa Chari (2008).
40 This work is studied and translated in Veezhinathan (1972).
41 Minkowski (2011).
42 The literature on the date of the *Bhāgavata* is extensive. For an entry point, see Uskokov (2022). On the *Bhāgavata Purāṇa,* see Valpey and Gupta (2017). On the *Bhāgavata* as a work of Vedānta, see Chattopadhyay (1992); Gupta (2007); Venkatkrishnan (2015).
43 Translation Gupta and Valpey (2017: 200).
44 BhP 12.13.12, 15.
45 Elkman (1986: 90–8).
46 Chattopadhyay (1992: 217–18).
47 The full title is *Vedānta-darśanam-bhāgavata-bhāṣyopetam*, "*Brahma-sūtra* with *Bhāgavata* as its commentary." Śāstri (1979).
48 Venkatkrishnan (2015).
49 Marfatia (1967): 43–8.

Chapter 2

1 śāstra-yonitvāt.
2 BĀU 3.9.26.
3 Ibid., 3.6.1, Olivelle (1998: 85).
4 The sustained discourse on "Hindu Theology" originates with Catholic theologians working in India, particularly Richard de Smet. However, it is the work of Francis Clooney that is largely responsible for Hindu theology becoming both a common mode of discourse and itself an object of deliberation in contemporary academia.
5 von Stietencron: (2006: 1879–83).
6 "The Vedic injunction only, and not any sense organ, can intimate a past, present and future thing that is subtle, concealed, remote or similar in kind." MSBh 1.1.2, i.13.
7 "That which is not immediately knowable and is not established even by that (i.e., analogical inference) is established through valid testimony." SK 6. Gauḍapāda (p.52) gives the following instances of such things: "Indra is the king of the gods; there is the land of the Northern Kurus; there are nymphs in heaven."

8 kāma-kāreṇa caike; 3.4.15. "And some [Vedic schools] [say that ritual is given up] voluntarily." The "some" refers to the Vājasaneyins, the followers of Yājñavalkya. The reference is to BĀU 4.4.22 (Olivelle 1998: 125): "It is he, on knowing whom a man becomes a sage. It is when they desire him as their world that wandering ascetics undertake the ascetic life of wandering. It was when they knew this that men of old did not desire offspring, reasoning: 'Ours is this self, and it is our world. What then is the use of offspring for us?'"

9 ChU 2.23.1.

10 parāmarśaṁ jaiminir acodanāc cāpavadati hi; 3.4.18. "Jaimini says [that there is only] a mention [of such renouncers], since there is no injunction; and [scripture] condemns [renunciation]."

11 anuṣṭheyaṁ bādarāyaṇaḥ sāmya-śruteḥ; vidhir vā dhāraṇa-vat; 3.4.19–20. "[The practice of renunciation different from the life of the stay-at-home] is to be observed, thinks Bādarāyaṇa, because of the direct statement of sameness. Or, it is an injunction, as in the case of holding." The "holding" according to the commentators refers to a case in the description of the Agnihotra ritual where an apparent mere mention or repetition must be read as an injunction.

12 SK 44 with commentaries.

13 Copleston (1993a: 314–18).

14 Copleston (1993b: 313).

15 We will talk about material and efficient causality in Chapters 3 and 4.

16 ChU 6.2.3, Olivelle (1998: 247).

17 nānumānam atac-chabdāt; 1.3.3. "It (the abode of heaven and earth, introduced in 1.3.1) is not the inferred principle, because there are words that do not express it."

ānumānikam apy ekeṣām iti cen na śarīra-rūpaka-vinyasta-gṛhīter darśayati ca; 1.4.1. "If it be said, 'the inferential one too [is mentioned in texts] of some schools,' [we say] no, because the word is mentioned in the simile of the body. The text also shows this." It is not necessary to expound on the context. Śaṅkara's commentary is illustrative of the rest: ānumānikam api anumāna-nirūpitam api pradhānam; ŚBSBh 1.4.1, i.226. "'Inferential' refers to prime matter that is ascertained by inference."

18 1.1.5–12, particularly the following: īkṣater nāśabdam; 1.1.5. "Because of seeing, the non-scriptural [prime matter] is not [intended]." gauṇaś cen nātma-śabdāt; 1.1.6. "[Objection:] The word is used in a figurative meaning. [Reply:] No, because the term 'Self' is used." tan-niṣṭhasya mokoṣopadeśāt; 1.1.7. "Because liberation is mentioned of him who is intent on that (the Self)." gati-sāmānyāt; 1.1.11. "Because of sameness of understanding [of Brahman as sentient in all Upaniṣads]."

19 ānandamayo 'bhyāsāt.

20 TU 2.2–5, discussed in 1.1.13–20. The argument to "repetition" pertains to the culmination of Brahman's being bliss in TU 2.8.

On Brahman's "gladdening" the soul: tad-dhetu-vyapadeśāc ca; 1.1.15. "Because of the designation of being the cause of that (i.e., the bliss of the individual soul)." This is a reference to TU 2.7.1: raso vai saḥ rasaṁ hy evāyaṁ labdhvānandī bhavati . . . eṣa hy evānandayāti, "It surely is the essence, for having attained this essence one becomes blissful. . . . For this (essence, *rasa*) alone causes bliss."

21 tat tu samanvayāt.

22 ŚBSBh 2.1.3, ii.288.

23 tarkāpratiṣṭhānād apy anyathānumeyam iti ced evam apy anirmokṣa-prasaṅgaḥ; 2.1.11. "And, because reasoning is without [final firm] ground. If it be objected, 'One can infer otherwise,' then non-release will follow." etena śiṣṭāparigrahā api vyākhyātaḥ; 2.1.12. "By this, [the doctrines] not accepted by the learned Vedic men have been refuted as well." śrutes tu śabda-mūlatvāt; 2.1.26. "Because of hearing. For [Brahman's causality] is rooted in scripture." The non-release in 2.1.11 is interpreted by the commentators mostly in the sense of the persistence of inconclusiveness in pursuing causal relations inferentially with respect to what is supersensible.

24 sarva-dharmopapatteś ca; 2.1.35. "And, because all attributes are appropriate." Nimbārka's comment is short and to the point: "Because all attributes of a cause fit only in Brahman, all contradiction is avoided." sva-pakṣa-doṣāc ca; 2.1.10. "And because of the fault in its own view." This is repeated almost in identical terms in 2.1.28: sva-pakṣe doṣāc ca.

25 na vilakṣaṇatvād asya tathātvaṁ ca śabdāt; 2.1.4. "[Brahman is] not [the cause], because the world is different [from it], and because such being the case is [known] from scripture."

26 dṛśyate tu; 2.1.6. "But, it is seen."

27 asad iti cen na pratiṣedha-mātratvāt; 2.1.7. "If it be said, [then the effect] is non-existent [in the cause], [we reply] no, because it is merely a negation [of the restriction that the characteristics must be identical]."

28 BSBh 2.2.24, ii.388.

29 McCrea (2013: 141–2).

30 See ĀDhS 1.4.8–10, 1.12.10–11; GDhS 3.36; BDhS 1.6.

31 The MS does use *smṛti* elsewhere than the third chapter of book one, which is traditionally known as "the *smṛti* chapter."

32 MSBh 1.3.1.

33 Brick (2006).

34 See 1.3.28; 3.2.24; 4.4.18, 20, with the commentaries.

35 ŚBSBh 1.3.28, i.191.

36 BhBSBh 1.3.28, p.105.

37 MSBh 4.1.3, iv.1199.

38 BhBSBh 1.1.7, p.36.

39 autpattikas tu śabdasyārthena sambandhas tasya jñānam upadeśo 'vyatirekaś cārthe 'nupalabdhe, tat pramāṇaṁ bādarāyaṇasya, anapekṣatvāt.

40 In translating *pramāṇa* as "reliable warrant," I follow the practice of Dan Arnold. See his *Buddhists, Brahmins, and Belief* (2005), particularly p.60.

41 The six are perception (*pratyakṣa*), inference (*anumāna*), scripture (*śāstra*), resemblance (*upamāna*), postulation (*arthāpatti*) and absence (*abhāva*).
42 MSBh 1.1.5. i.37, quoting the Vṛttikāra.
43 Ibid.
44 "You do not understand the defeated-defeater relation. Here what is defeated is the vision 'there are hundreds of herds of elephants on the fingertip,' which is (in the domain of) another reliable warrant. Not, however, 'hundreds of herds of elephants.'" Bṛhatī 1.1.2, i.24–6.
45 ṚV 1.1.2. i.32.
46 "Now, in *gauḥ*, what is the word? It is the phonemes *g, au, ḥ*—thus says the venerable Upavarṣa. . . . From the phonemes an impression is produced, and from the impression, there follows the cognition of meaning. Therefore the phonemes are the cause of cognition of meaning. . . . Therefore, *gauḥ* the word which begins in *g* and ends in *ḥ* is just the phonemes. There is no word separate from them." MSBh 1.1.5, i.45.
47 apauruṣeyaḥ śabdasyārthena sambandhas; MSBh 1.1.5, i.41. "The word-meaning relationship is non-personal." Likewise in MSBh 1.1.5, i.52–53: "'Therefore, we think someone, a person, created a word-reference relation and composed the Veda in order to employ this relation.'—On this, it is now said, it is proven, because the relationship is non-personal." In both cases quoting the Vṛttikāra.
48 See 1.1.28; 1.1.31; 1.2.27; 1.3.8; 2.3.28; 2.4.9; 2.4.19; 3.4.48; 4.1.1. In all cases, the reference is to something *specific* said in scripture, as specific as a grammatical case ending.
49 See Biswas (1996), particularly the following: "The term *upadeśa* broadly conveys: whatever is pronounced by the original teacher Pāṇini, and some times by Kātyāyana and Patañjali also. It also means: the basic metalinguistic-form of grammatical-element, may be a letter, an affix, an augment, a substitute, a root, or a *Prātipadika*" (p.xiii).
50 MS 1.3.24–29.
51 MSBh 1.1.2, i.17.
52 MSBh 1.1.5, i.42, quoting the Vṛttikāra.
53 MSBh 1.3.24–29.
54 Venkataramiah (1948: 203–7).
55 See his long commentary on MS 1.2.7 in the *Tantra-vārttika*.
56 "When actions are not known, it is not possible to state the distinction of what forms of knowledge combine with them and what do not, because there is no understanding of what should be rejected or accepted." BhBSBh 1.1.1, p.3.

Chapter 3

1 janmādy asya yataḥ.
2 Griswold (1900).

3 Brereton (2004).
4 Gonda (1950: 58).
5 VP 3.3.22.
6 TUBh 2.1.1., vi.59.
7 ŚBhGBh 3.15, xi.91.
8 anādi-nidhanaṁ brahma śabda-tattvaṁ yad akṣaram |
vivartate 'rtha-bhāvena prakriyā jagato yataḥ. VPBK 1.
"Brahman is without beginning and end, imperishable, and substantively verbal. It apparently transforms in things and processes, being thus the source of world creation."
9 TU 2.1.1.
10 TU 2.9.1.
11 The heading *sūtra* (3.3.11) here is ānandādayaḥ pradhānasya, "[The characteristics of] bliss etc. [should be included everywhere because] they are of the principal." This is in the section on how Upaniṣadic meditations are formed, and the remaining *sūtra*s are less important for our present purpose.
12 RŚBh 3.3.13, iii.856–7.
13 BĀU 3.3.8, Olivelle (1998: 91).
14 MU 1.1.7, Olivelle (1998: 437).
15 akṣara-dhiyāṁ tv avarodhaḥ sāmānya-tad-bhāvābhyām aupasada-vat tad uktam; 3.3.33. "But there is inclusion of ideas about the imperishable, because of generality and being that; as in the case of Upasad; that has been said." As I mentioned in the Introduction, *tad uktam*, "that has been said," always refers to the MS. This too is primarily about how meditations on Brahman are formed, and will be discussed in detail in Chapter 6.
16 1.3.12.
17 RŚBh 3.3.33, iii.882–5.
18 Here is just an illustration from Śaṅkara's commentary on 3.3.33, on the two kinds of characteristics: tatra vidhi-rūpāṇi viśeṣaṇāni cintitāni, iha pratiṣedha-rūpāṇīti viśeṣaḥ; ŚBhBh 3.15, iii.672. "There (in 3.3.11) the affirmative characteristics were considered, whereas here—the negatory; this is the distinction."
19 2.3.1–15.
20 TU 2.1.1.
21 This is discussed in 2.3.1–6. To the objection that the *Taittirīya* text (2.1.1.) about the origination of space must be read as figurative rather than literal, because space cannot originate and because then the ChU account would be compromised (*sūtra* 2.3.3), Bādarāyaṇa replies that this would compromise the ChU thesis (6.1.3) that by knowing the one thing, Being that is Brahman, everything else would be known. Insofar as space does exist, if it did not originate from Brahman it would not be known by knowing Brahman.
22 ākāṣo 'rthāntara-vyapadeśāt; 1.3.42. "Brahman is space, because there is a predication of 'other things.'" This refers to ChU 8.14.1, where space is described as Brahman that evolves name-and-form, in which all things

are contained. Since this is part of the first chapter where Brahman is established as the reference of various terms in Upaniṣadic passages, most of the commentaries identify the alternative reference that is rejected with the "elemental space," *bhūtākāśa*.

23 SK 3 with commentaries.

24 na ca guṇādīnāṁ pṛthag-utpattir vaktavyā. dravyotpattau cotpatti-siddhis, tad-ananyatvāt; BhBSBh 2.3.9, p.p.220. "Separate origination of qualities should not be affirmed. They originate with the origination of substance, being non-different from it." The qualities talked about here are sound, touch, and so on.

25 The entire BS 2.4 is concerned with their origination.

26 2.3.15; 2.4.12 with the commentaries. The topical passage on the mind, *manas*, is BĀU 1.5.3, which identifies it with phenomena such as desire, resolution, doubt, and so on. Generally in Indian philosophy *manas* is the organ of cognition of internal states, such as memory, and there is no reason to think that Bādarāyaṇa understands it in any different sense. As a faculty, it should not be confused with the soul.

27 1.1.32, 1.4.17, 2.4.8.

28 2.4.13.

29 RŚBh 2.4.17, iii.767.

30 2.3.15.

31 2.1.2 is interpreted in some commentaries as an explicit repudiation of *mahat* and other Sāṅkhya principles that are not seen in the Upaniṣads.

32 2.4.19, ŚVK thereon, p.761.

33 Clooney (1988).

34 śabda iti cen nātaḥ prabhavāt pratyakṣānumānābhyām; 1.3.28.

The account that follows is based on the so-called *devatādhikaraṇa*, 1.3.26–30. With respect to this *adhikaraṇa*, Adams (1993: 101) comments: "This section reveals little about Bādarāyaṇa's own theology, other than that he believes that the gods are eligible for seeking the Brahman." In fact, what Bādarāyaṇa does in this *adhikaraṇa* is predicated on MS 1.1.5, *attributed to him*, as we have discussed in Chapter 2. Little else tells us *more* about his own theology than this section.

35 1.3.30, 2.4.19.

36 4.3.6. I will discuss this *sūtra* and its *adhikaraṇa* in Chapter 7.

37 See, for instance, the phrase "samaṣṭi-vyaṣṭi-rūpeṇa hiraṇyagarbhena," in ŚBSBh and BhBSBh on 2.4.13.

38 The pertinent *sūtra* here is 1.3.30: samāna-nāma-rūpatvāc cāvṛttāv apy avirodho darśanāt smṛteś ca. "And, because of the name-and-form being the same, there is no contradiction with respect to repetition. That is known from perception and memory."

Bhāskara: vidyamānasya cābhivyāktī-karaṇa-mātraṁ sṛṣṭiḥ. katham? samāna-nāma-rūpatvāt. kalpāntarātītair indrādibhiḥ kalpādau sṛjyamānānāṁ nāma-vācakaḥ śabdo rūpam ākṛtiḥ; BhBSBh 1.3.30, p.110.

"Creation is just the manifestation of an existent thing. How so? Because the name-and-form are the same; that is, the name, i.e. words, and the form, i.e. universals, of the things that are created at the beginning of the *kalpa* through Indras etc. that have passed in the previous *kalpa*." A *kalpa* is a creation cycle, on which in Chapter 5.

Śrīnivāsa: tadā vedās tad-vācakās tat-tad-ākṛtayaś ca tasminn ekībhūya tiṣṭhanti; ŚVK 1.3.30, p.237. "Then (in the state of dissolution, prior to creation) the Vedas, their words, and the universals denoted by them are merged in one and reside in Him (the Lord)."

Rāmānuja: indra-vasiṣṭhādīnāṁ tat-tad-ākāra-vācitvaṁ tat-tac-chabdena tat-tad-artha-smṛti-pūrvikā ca tat-tad-artha-sṛṣṭiḥ . . . vedasya nityatvam upapadyate; RŚBh 1.3.28, ii.448. "Because words such as Indra and Vasiṣṭha, of gods and sages, are expressive of the respective form / universal, and the creation of the respective object is preceded by the memory of the object by means of the word . . . the eternal nature of the Veda makes sense."

Śaṅkara: ata eva niyatākṛter devāder jagato veda-śabda-prabhavatvāt veda-śabda-nityatvam api pratyetavyam; ŚBSBh 1.3.29, i.197. "Therefore, because the world consisting of gods and other things that have fixed forms originates from the words of the Vedas, the eternity of the Vedas too should be acknowledged."

39 anādi-nidhanā nityā vāg utsṛṣṭā svayambhuvā |
ādau vedamayī divyā yataḥ sarvāḥ pravṛttayaḥ. In the Critical Edition, the first line is the second part of MBh 12.224.55; the second line has been taken as unauthentic. Cited in ŚBSBh 1.3.28, i.191, BhBSBh 1,3,28, p.106; RŚBh 1.3.27, ii.447; NVPS 1.3.28, p.230; ŚVK 1.3.28, p.232.

"The Self-born emanated in the beginning the eternal, divine Vedic speech, without origin and end, from which all actions proceed."

sarveṣāṁ tu sa nāmāni karmāṇi ca pṛthak pṛthak |
veda-śabdebhya evādau pṛthak saṁsthāś ca nirmame. Manu 1.21. Cited in ŚBSBh 1.3.28, i.191, BhBSBh 1,3,28, p.106; RŚBh 1.3.27, ii.447; ŚVK 1.3.28, p.232.

"In the beginning through the words of the Veda alone, he fashioned for all of them specific names and activities, as also specific stations" (Translation Olivelle 2005: 88).

nāma-rūpaṁ ca bhūtānāṁ kṛtyānāṁ ca prapañcanam |
veda-śabdebhya evādau devādīnāṁ cakāra saḥ. VP 1.5.63. Cited as such in RŚBh 1.3.27, ii.448. Śaṅkara, Bhāskara, and Śrīnivāsa read instead *Kūrma Purāṇa* 1.2.28cd-29ab, which has minor differences.

40 See 4.4.18 with the commentaries.

41 2.4.14–18.

42 Mīmāṁsakas eventually moved much closer to this Vedāntic account. Thus Kumārila accepts partial destructions and recreation of the world involved in the so-called *manvantara* periods, reigns of a Manu, such that names

of some Vedic sages such as Manu are positions occupied by different individuals in every *manvantara* cycle. See his comment on MS 1.3.7 in the *Tantra-vārttika*.

43 RŚBh 2.3.13, iii.714.

44 tad-abhidhyānād eva tu tal-liṅgāt saḥ; 2.3.13. "But on the account of his will, and because of the indication, it is he."

45 sañjñā-mūrti-kḷptis tu trivṛt-kurvata upadeśāt; 2.4.19.

46 Indeed, the entire second section of chapter one is informed by ideas about Brahman's residence.

47 BĀU 3.7.23, Olivelle (1998: 89).

48 guhāṁ praviṣṭāv ātmānau hi tad-darśanāt; viśeṣanāc ca; 1.2.11–12. "Two souls have entered the cave, because that is seen. And because of specification."

49 MU 3.1.1–2; ŚU 4.6–7.

50 1.3.7.

51 1.2.21, translated in the Introduction and cited there in nt.28.

52 AA 1.4.30; in Sharma (2000: 240–2).

53 1.4.23–27.

54 TU 2.7.

55 MU 1.1.6, 3.1.3.

56 ātma-kṛteḥ pariṇāmāt.

57 This reading seems justified in light of the entire section four of chapter one, particularly *sūtra*s 1.4.8–10, where the *Śvetāśvatara* (ŚU 1.3, 4.5, 4.10) doctrine about the so-called unborn prime matter is taken up for discussion. Bādarāyaṇa says (1.4.9) that this unborn prime matter is the same as the collective of the three creative principles of the ChU, which can be metonymically identified with the entirety of Brahman's primary creation.

58 NVPS 1.4.26, p.356; BhBSBh 1.4.26, p.144.
On *bhogya-śakti:* aupaniṣadaṁ brahma tu ekam eva bhogya-śaktiṁ vikṣipyākāśādy-acetana-rūpeṇa pariṇāmayate; ŚVK 2.1.26, p.463, following Bhāskara. "Brahman of the Upaniṣads, one only, transforms into the insentient space etc., by projecting its capacity of being the object of experience."

59 ŚU 1.3 uses the term "*devātma-śakti*," God's own power, and famously in 6.8, parāsya śaktir vividhaiva śrūyate svābhāvikī jñāna-bala-kriyā ca, "The power of the supreme is heard to be diverse, the inherent working of knowledge and strength," quoted by several commentators on 1.4.26.

60 SK 9.

61 SK 11.

62 ŚBSBh 1.4.23, i.269.

63 2.1.4, see nt.25 in Chapter 2.

64 2.1.6, see nt.26 in Chapter 2.

65 The commentators on Pāṇini's *sūtra* on *prakṛti* (1.4.30), discussed earlier, have, in fact, presented the scorpion as a *sahakāri*, an "associated" or

"accessory cause"—of which the classical examples are the wheel and the stick used by the potter the efficient cause to make a pot out of clay the material cause—precisely because it is *not present* in the effect. See Sharma (2000: 241).

66 BhBSBh 2.1.6, p.151.

67 RŚBh 2.1.6, ii.566.

68 upasaṁhāra-darśanān neti cen na kṣīravad dhi; 2.1.23. "If it be said [Brahman] is not [the cause] because of aggregate [of causes], we say no, for it is like milk."

69 sarvopetā ca sā tad-darśanāt; 2.1.29. "And Brahman is endowed with everything, because it is seen [in scripture]."

70 ChU 3.14.4, Olivelle (1998: 209).

71 ŚBSBh 1.2.22, i.128; ŚBSBh 1.4.9, i.242.

72 samavāyābhypagamāc ca sāmyād anavasthiteḥ; 2.2.13. "[The Vaiśeṣika account of causality is wrong] because they accept inherence, since there would be infinite regress because of sameness [of inherence as absolutely different from the entities it relates]."

73 kṛtsna-prasaktir niravayavatva-śabda-kopo vā; 2.1.25. "[But then, if Brahman transforms], the unwanted consequence of wholesale [transformation] would follow, or the statements about [Brahman] being partless would be compromised."

74 ubhaya-vyapadeśāt tv ahi-kuṇḍala-vat; prakāśāśrayavad vā tejastvāt; pūrva-vad vā; 3.2.27–9. "[Prima facie view:] Because of the mention of both, like in the case of the serpent and the coil. [Second prima facie view:] Or, like illumination and its basis, because of having light. [Conclusion:] Rather, as before."

Sūtras 3.2.27–9 are variously interpreted by the commentators, and here I follow for the most part Rāmānuja, Nimbārka, and Śrīnivāsa, agreeing with Karmarkar (1919–20: 115–21) that this is the preferred reading. "As before" refers back to section one of chapter two, the arguments from scripture (2.1.26), but also 2.1.24, 27 (see the next note).

75 devādi-vat api loke; ātmani caivaṁ vicitrāś ca hi; 2.1.24, 27. "It is like the [creation] of gods etc. in the world. And, because such fabulous [modifications] are seen in the soul as well." The interpretations differ, but the upshot is that Brahman has fabulous creative powers.

76 prākṛtaitāvattvaṁ hi pratiṣedhati tato bravīti ca bhūyaḥ; 3.3.22. "For, it denies so-much-ness related to the topic, and then speaks further." This refers to BĀU 2.3, which talks about two forms or appearances of Brahman, one with shape (*mūrta*) and one shapeless (*amūrta*). These are clearly the visible and invisible elements (air and ether). The section ends with the statement that by the rule *neti neti,* "not thus, not thus," it follows that there is nothing beyond "not," but also that this beyond bears the name "the real of the real," *satyasya satyam*. So the question is, naturally, is there any form of Brahman beyond the phenomenal world. The *sūtra*, then, says

that the negation pertains to Brahman being that much, that is, limited to the shaped and shapeless.

77 parābhidhyānāt tu tirohitaṁ tato hy asya bandha-viparyayau; deha-yogād vā so 'pi; 3.2.5–6. "But, it is concealed by the desire of the Supreme. Thus his bondage and release make sense. Or that [concealment] is because of association with the body."

78 Along with 3.2.5, it is in 2.3.13 (see nt.44 above) and 1.4.24: abhidhyopadeśāc ca. "And, because of the statement of intention." All three refer to ChU 6.2.3, tad aikṣata bahu syāṁ prajāyeya, "It (Being) reflected, how about I become many, procreate myself."

79 adhikaṁ tu bheda-nirdeśāt; 2.1.21. "But [Brahman is] something more, because difference is specified." Also 3.4.8, which we will discuss in Chapter 6.

80 aṁśo nānā-vyapadeśād anyathā cāpi dāśa-kitavāditvam adhīyata eke; 2.3.42. "[The soul is] a part, because of the designation "many," and otherwise too (i.e., identical). Some read that [Brahman is] of the nature of anglers, gamblers, etc."

81 aśmādi-vac ca tad-anupapattiḥ; 2.1.22. "[The souls are] like stones etc. Thus, there is impossibility of that (i.e., Brahman doing what is not beneficial)." The *sūtra* follows 2.1.21 cited in nt.79, and the context is of Brahman being liable to transmigration if some Upaniṣadic texts that state identity between Brahman and the soul are read solely through the lens of identity.

82 MU 2.1.1, Olivelle (1998: 443).

83 pratijñā-siddher liṅgam āśmarathyaḥ; 1.4.20.

84 nātmāśruter nityatvāc ca tābhyaḥ; 2.3.17. "The self [does not originate], because it is eternal, known from those [scriptural statements]."

85 utkramatiṣyata evaṁ-bhāvād ity auḍulomiḥ; 1.4.21. "Because the one who is about to depart being like that – thus Auḍulomi."

86 avasthiter iti kāśakṛtsnaḥ; 1.4.22. "Because of residence, thus Kāśakṛtsna."

87 Cf. BhBSBh 1.4.22, p.111: tathā hi śrutir *anena jīvenātmanānupraviśya nāma-rūpe vyākaravāṇi* (ChU 6.3.2) iti parasyaiva jīva-rūpeṇāvasthānaṁ darśayati, "In 'How about I enter with the living soul and manifest name-and-form,' scripture demonstrates a condition of the Supreme itself as the living soul." The consequence of this: para eva sākṣād jīvaḥ, "The Supreme itself is directly the individual soul."

88 Ibid., p. 138.

89 See 1.2.18, 2.3.24. It bears mention that Thibaut (1890: xcix–c) had already recognized that Bādarāyaṇa throughout the BS uses *avasthiti* in the sense of "permanent abiding," which is a reason to side with Rāmānuja's reading of the *sūtra* against Śaṅkara. Nakamura (1983: 372–9) dissents by preferring Bhāskara's interpretation, but he is wrong and inaccurate in his references. Adams (1993: 119) also thinks that Rāmānuja's reading is right, but his reason is bizarre: such is the meaning listed in Monier-Williams's Sanskrit

to English dictionary, but even then, he is looking at the wrong entry (*avasthita* instead of *avasthiti*).

90 NVPS 1.4.22.

91 2.3.44.

92 BhG 15.7, van Buitenen (1981: 131).

93 Uskokov (2019: 202–3).

94 jño 'ta eva; 2.3.18. "For this reason, it is a knower." See nt.84 for the preceding *sūtra*, picked up by "for this reason."

95 2.3.19–31. This is a controversial *adhikaraṇa*, with Śaṅkara and Bhāskara standing on one side in thinking that the soul is ultimately omnipresent (*vibhu*), while for everyone else it is minute (*aṇu*). Contemporary scholarship has sided with the second (Thibaut 1890: liv–lvi; Telivala 1918: 32–40; Karmarkar 1920–21: 36–44; Ghate 1926: 93–8; Nakamura 1983: 506–7, however, sides with Bhāskara), and I concur. I shall revisit Śaṅkara and Bhāskara in Chapter 7.

96 3.2.11–14. The lead *sutra* here is: na sthānato pi parasyobhaya-liṅgaṁ sarvatra hi; 3.2.11. "Not even by residence does the highest have both sets of characteristics, because it is omnipresent." This is a very important *sūtra* interpreted in a variety of ways. Śaṅkara introduces the distinction of Brahman with and without distinguishing qualities (*saviśeṣa* vs. *nirviśeṣa*), that is the higher and lower Brahman that I mentioned in Chapter 1, to argue that Brahman can never have such a dual nature, that is, it must be without distinguishing qualities. Rāmānuja introduces his idea of *ubhaya-liṅgatva*, that Brahman *has* two sets of characteristics, positive and negative, that we saw at the beginning of the chapter, So, for him the *sūtra* runs: "Not even by residence [is Brahman defiled, like the soul], for Brahman *has* dual characteristics, as it is everywhere." Śaṅkara's reading is non-contextual to the previous topic, and the distinction that he introduces here is not seen anywhere else in the BS. While Rāmānuja's interpretation is not materially wrong—Brahman *does* have the positive and negative characteristics, as we discussed earlier—the syntax of the *sūtra* becomes quite strained. To me it is patent that *ubhaya-liṅgam* does not refer to either, but simply negates that the dual nature *of the soul*, which was discussed just in the foregoing section, pertains to Brahman as well. While the soul has such a dual nature—that of Brahman, which is concealed but is manifested in liberation, *and* that of embodiment—Brahman does not have the faults of embodiment even through residence in "places." Brahman's residence in places was discussed in 1.2.14; it refers to residence in objects of veneration in Upaniṣadic meditations, such as the heart.

97 arūpavad eva hi tat-pradhānatvāt; 3.2.14. "For, it is only without form, because it is the principal [agent of diversification of name-and-form]."

98 3.2.15–21. In particular, 3.2.18: ata eva copamā sūryakādi-vat. "For this reason, a simile, like the sun etc."

Chapter 4

1 Nietzsche (2006: 29).
2 Couture (2018).
3 Smith (1996: 17–18).
4 Herman (1993: 264ff).
5 Lipner (1986: 92–3).
6 See, for instance, Dasti and Phillips (2017, Chapter Six).
7 BĀU 4.3.21, Olivelle (1998: 115).
8 Bhāskara's statement (BhBSBh 2.1.32, p.178) is fairly representative: "A different objection is now advanced: The supreme divinity does not engage in creation, for the Upaniṣads say that all its desires are fulfilled. Consequently, it has no purpose to do anything."
9 Bhāmatī 2.1.32; RVD and RŚBh 2.1.32; KKP 2.1.31; BGBh 2.1.32. Keśava Kāśmīrī is particularly succinct and clear: "It is again objected: Brahman could not be the cause, since all action has purpose, and Brahman, all its desires being fulfilled, could not have a purpose. If Brahman acts for its own sake, that will compromise its having all desires fulfilled. Alternatively, if Brahman creates for the sake of others, creating a world full of endless suffering would compromise its compassion."
10 na prayojanavattvāt; 2.1.31.

There is no substantive difference in what the challenge comes down to in the various commentaries, although there are some interesting variations in the readings of the *sūtra*. Śaṅkara and Bhāskara read this and the next *sūtra* as a separate *adhikaraṇa*, whereas for all others the *adhikaraṇa* continues until the end of the chapter (additional four *sūtra*s, or three in Nimbārka's counting that we are following here). Madhva does not read the *sūtra* as presenting a prima facie view, but he does presuppose the same prima facie view as the other commentaries and reads under this *sūtra* what others read under the next.
11 SK 56–62, 66, and the commentaries thereon, particularly Gauḍapāda and Vācaspati Miśra, go at length in developing this doctrine *specifically against* God as the efficient or Brahman as the material cause of creation. *Kārikā* 66 is particularly significant: "'I have seen her,' thinks the one, indifferent. 'I have been seen,' thinks the other, and she desists. Although there is still union of the two, there is no longer purpose of creation." Vācaspati on the "purpose" (*prayojana*): "Purpose is the reason why prime matter engages in creation; without a purpose for the soul (*puruṣārtha*), creation does not take place."
12 Uddyotakara, NBhV 4.1.21, pp. 433–4.
13 RŚBh 2.1.10, ii.576.
14 Verses 43ff. On Kumārila's argument, see Bilimoria (1990).
15 jagac casṛjatas tasya kiṁ nāmeṣṭaṁ na sidhyati |
prayojanam anuddiśya na mando 'pi pravartate. ŚV SĀP 54cd–55.

16 ŚBSBh 2.1.32, ii.339–40.
17 RŚBh 2.1.32, ii.639.
18 lokavat tu līlā-kaivalyam; 2.1.32.
19 RVD 2.1.33, i.240.
20 VABh 2.1.33, ii.97–8.
21 BhBSBh 2.1.33, p.179.
22 KKP 2.1.32, p.476.
23 "Brahman engages in the creation of the world in the manner of those who have no desires, i.e. have accomplished everything for themselves and others and are well-disposed because they have done their business, yet act just for the fun of it, without reference to a purpose even if some future purpose does remain." Bhāmatī 2.1.33, p.481.
24 Lipner (1986: 93).
25 ŚBSBh 3.2.2, iii.562. Rāmānuja too is aware of this when he interprets Yājñavalkya's teaching to Maitreyī that the Self is not "for desires," but that "desires" are for the Self (BĀU 2.4.4, 4.5.6): "They are desired; therefore, they are desires: attainments of what is dear to the Self" (RŚBh 1.4.19, ii.526).
26 Gethin (2001: 191–2); Webster (2005: 122–5).
27 RVS 2.1.33, pp.160–1. The descriptor "of three modes" pertains to prime matter having three modes or *guṇas*—being (*sattva*), impulse (*rajas*), and inertia (*tamas*)—through which it creates the world and permeates its every nook and corner.

Of his three commentaries on the BS, the shortest *Vedānta-sāra* is the most useful for appreciating Rāmānuja's understanding of this *sūtra*.

28 VP 1.2.18 with Śrīdhara.
29 Cf., also, the famous statement of Heraclitus, Fragment B52: "Eternity is a child at play: the kingdom is a child's" (Barnes 1987: 102).
30 VVABh 2.1.33, p.160.
31 BGBh 2.1.33, p.110.
32 bhogārthaṁ sṛṣtir ity anye krīḍārtham iti cāpare |
devasyaiṣa svabhāvo 'yam āpta-kāmasya kā spṛhā. ĀŚ 1.9.
33 NBhV 4.1.21, pp.438.
34 ŚBSBh 2.1.33, ii.340–1.
35 ĀŚBh 1.9, v.103.
36 Bhāmatī 2.1.33, p.481–2.
37 1.3.8–9 with the commentaries.
38 BĀU 4.5.11, Olivelle (1998: 129).
39 See his ŚV ĀV 53: "With regard to this there just isn't such a notion. Moreover, the engagement in bearing sons is for one's own good, but even that does not work in your case."

In the context, Kumārila's statement is in reply to a Buddhist argument that karma does not need to presuppose self-identity through time: the agent and the experiencer, being merely a complex of instances in the causal process at distinct points of time, may nevertheless be related by karma, and the one may act for the benefit of the other, just as parents act for the future success of their sons even though they know them as different (verses 51–2).

40 This is a recurrent distinction in Śaṅkara's works. See, for instance, his commentary on BĀU 1.3.1.

41 BGBh 2.1.33, p.110.

42 MBSBh 2.1.33, p.466. Hari is a name of Viṣṇu, the personal divinity who is Brahman in Madhva's theology.

43 BGBh 2.1.33, p.110.

Chapter 5

1 The *theological* problem of evil is commonly distinguished from other problems of evil, such as the psychological (the need for ultimate comfort), the cognitive (the need to understand the *why* of suffering and injustice), or the practical (the need to get rid of it), and so on. It pertains to a prima facie conflict between the facticity of evil and the existence of a supreme being, i.e. a conflict possible only in theism and for a theology.

2 Mackie (1982: 150).

3 Oppy (2013); Herman (1993).

4 RŚBh 2.1.32, ii.639.

5 RVD 2.1.34, i.241–2.

6 ŚBSBh 2.1.34; BhBSBh 2.1.34.

7 duḥkha-trayābhighātāj jijñāsā tad-abhighātake hetau |
dṛṣṭe sāpārthā cen naikāntātyantato 'bhāvāt. SK 1. See the commentaries of Gauḍapāda and Vācaspati on how the three kinds of suffering are conceptualized.

In the context, it is mentioned explicitly by Śrīnivāsa (ŚVK 2.1.33).

8 BhG 13.11 is the *locus classicus* on this, alluded to in RŚBh 2.1.33; BGBh 2.1.33.

9 Bhāmatī 2.1.34; BhBSBh 2.1.34; RŚBh 2.1.34.

10 ŚVK 2.1.33, p.477.

11 ŚBSBh 2.1.34, ii.342.

12 RVD 2.1.34, i.241–2.

13 In the commentaries, this is expressed negatively: if there is no karma, then the undesired consequence of "getting what hasn't been done and losing what has been done" would follow (akṛtābhyāgama-kṛta-vipraṇāśa-prasaṅgaḥ; ŚBSBh 2.1.35; likewise RVD 2.1.35; RŚBh 2.1.35; VABh 2.1.35).

14 Vācaspati's locution *pāpa-puṇya-karmāśaya*, "the karmic stock of merit and demerit," is along those lines (Bhāmatī 2.1.34, p.482).

15 vaiṣamya-nairghṛṇye na sāpekṣatvāt tathā hi darśayati; 2.1.33.

16 KauU 3.8, quoted in ŚBSBh 3.1.34; BBSBh 2.1.34; ŚVK 2.1.33; KKP 2.1.33; VABh 2.1.34; BGBh 2.1.34.
17 BĀU 3.2.13, quoted in ŚBSBh 3.1.34; NVPS 2.1.33; KKP 2.1.33; VABh 2.1.34; similar is BĀU 4.4.5, quoted in RŚBh 2.1.34; ŚVK 2.1.33; KKP 2.1.33.
18 "In the action of creating things, he is merely the efficient cause (*nimitta*), whereas the material cause (*pradhāna*) are the capacities of the things themselves. Except for this efficient cause, nothing more is required, best of ascetics: a thing becomes what it is by its own capacity." VP 1.4.51–52, cited in RŚBh 2.1.34, ii.641.

Sudarśana Sūri: "That he is merely the efficient cause means that he is not the material cause, as it is said in the verse itself in 'being the material cause.' It is like in the statement 'Just be the instrument, Arjuna' (BhG 11.33). The material/primary cause is the unique cause, whereas the common cause is incidental/non-primary." SŚP 2.1.34, iv.464.

NB that *pradhāna* involves an ambiguity between "material" and "principal," which "material" as opposed to "incidental" expresses well.
19 Vattanky (1993: 30ff).
20 Hickson (2013).
21 2.3.32–9.
22 BhG 3.27, 13.21, 14.19. On the *guṇa*s, see nt.27 in the previous chapter.
23 kartā śāstrārthavattvāt; 2.3.32. "It is an agent, because scripture has meaning."
24 śāstra-phalaṁ prayoktari; MS 3.7.18. Cited in RŚBh 2.3.33.
25 samādhy-abhāvāc ca; 2.3.38. "And, because there would be no *samādhi*."
26 parāt tu tac-chruteḥ; 2.3.40.
27 kṛta-prayatnāpekṣas tu vihita-pratiṣiddhāvaiyarthyādibhyaḥ; 2.3.41. "But depending on the effort made, because what is enjoined and prohibited is not futile etc."
28 BhBSBh 2.1.36, p.180.
29 BhBSBh 2.1.36, p.180–1.
30 Kaufman (2005: 22).
31 "The soul is the first form of the supreme Brahman; the non-manifest and the manifest are another two forms, and so is time." VP 1.2.15.
32 See, for instance, Copleston (1993b, Chapter XXXVI), on St. Thomas Aquinas's argument that creation in time does not follow from reason but from scripture. The followers of Averroes went even further in claiming that creation in time was impossible.
33 Sharma (1997: 90–4).
34 na karmāvibhāgād iti cen nānāditvād upapadyate cāpy upalabhyate ca; 2.1.34.
35 Ṛg Veda 10.190.3, quoted in ŚBSBh 2.1.36; BhBSBh 2.1.36; RŚBh 2.1.35; NVPS 2.1.34.
36 BĀU 1.4.7, quoted in RŚBh 2.1.35.
37 BĀU 1.6.1.
38 ŚVK 1.3.30, p.237.

39 Doniger (1980b: 14).
40 SŚP 2.1.34, iv.463–4.
41 VVABh 2.1.34, p.161.
42 Bhāmatī 2.1.34.
43 KKP 2.1.33.
44 See MS 3.1.2: śeṣaḥ parārthatvāt. "Subordinate, because of being for the sake of another." See Śabara thereon.
45 Hick (2010).

In a recent study, and a fine specimen of cross-cultural philosophy, Ilievski (2020) makes a similar argument for a soteriological theodicy that moves away from the anthropocentric focus—the assumption that men are there for happiness and pleasure, and if they experience suffering this prima facie is a problem for theism—to the issue of the purpose of creation and the possibility that God intends something different than an imagined paradise on earth. In such a soteriological theodicy, the question of God's benevolence is not adjudicated by the amount of happiness and suffering, but by the success of soteriological aspirations, in which light suffering could prove to be an asset rather than a liability, for instance as a deterrent from the pursuit of pleasure or as a catalyst of dispassion.
46 Wiltshire (1990, chapter 3).
47 Into a similar direction has gone Madhva's interpreter Jayatīrtha, who argues that while *self*-purpose is rejected from creation, Brahman does create the world for the sake of *others*. See Sharma i.400, nt.2 (and pp. 339–404). Sharma typically ascribes whatever Jayatīrtha says to Madhva himself.
48 I borrow this phrase from Richard H. Davis's wonderful *Ritual in an Oscillating Universe* (1991: 27).
49 ŚKBSBh 2.1.35.
50 BhG 9.29.
51 See ŚBhGBh 9.29 and Ānandagiri thereon.
52 BGBh 2.1.36.
53 See his *Śloka-vārttika* on the *Codanā-sūtra* 252cd–255ab (Kataoka 2011: 500–3).
54 Hartshorne (1969).
55 ŚBSBh 2.1.33, ii.341.
56 Matilal (1992: 363–4).
57 ŚBhGBh 9.10, xi.260.

Chapter 6

1 "The statement 'the self should be known' is not enjoined for liberation; it only indicates that self-knowledge is the cause of taking up action. Once it is understood that its purpose terminates in something else (i.e., ritual), the promise of result (i.e., liberation) must be read as a statement of praise, for there is no result over and above heaven." ŚV SĀP 103–4.

2 ChU 1.1.10, Olivelle (1998: 171).
3 The *udgītha* is the second and principal element of the five parts of a *sāman* melody in which verses are sung. The *udgītha* begins in Oṁ. See Sen 1978: 53, 118 (entry on *sāman*).
4 All the BS commentators make ChU 1.1.10 the topical text of BS 3.4.4 and illustrative of a general Mīmāṁsā attitude toward all Upaniṣadic *vidyā*s. Someśvara under TV 1.3.29 invokes the same text in justifying Kumārila's claim that discriminative knowledge of the Self serves the purpose of ritual.
5 śeṣatvāt puruṣārtha-vādo yathānyeṣv iti jaiminiḥ; 3.4.2. "Because [the agent is] subsidiary [to the action], [the statement of results is just] talk of the good of man, as in other cases; thus Jaimini."
6 asārvatrikī; 3.4.10. "Non-universal." NVPS, p.1102: *yad eva vidyayā* iti śrutir na sarva-vidyā-viṣayā; "The ChU text 'Only that which is performed with knowledge etc.' is not included in all forms of meditation."
7 ŚBSBh 3.4.8, iii.721.
8 adhikopadeśāt tu bādarāyaṇasyaivaṁ tad-darśanāt; 3.4.8. "But, because of teaching of what is superior; thus Bādarāyaṇa's [view], because it is seen [in scripture]."

With 2.1.21, discussed in Chapter 3, this is the second time where Brahman is described as "superior" or "more" (*adhika*) than the individual transmigrating soul. This, again, illustrates the consistency in terminology that is methodologically important.

9 Under MS 1.1.2 (i.11, 13), Śabara describes *dharma* as that category, consisting of sacrifices such as Jyotiṣṭoma, which relates man to the highest good, *niḥśreyasa*.
10 dharmaṁ jaiminir ata eva; 3.2.40. "*Dharma* [in the form of merit] [is whence the result comes from], thus [says] Jaimini, for the same reason (i.e., scriptural statements to that effect)."
11 sarva-vedānta-pratyayaṁ codanādy-aviśeṣāt; 3.3.1. "The understanding from all Upaniṣadic texts [is uniform], because the injunction etc. are identical." NVPS thereon, p.920: "Although a meditation is described in several places, it is one only, because of uniformity of injunction and the rest."
12 See Śabara on MS 2.4.9, ii.635–6: "The act in all branches and Brāhmaṇa texts is one, because of uniformity of relation to purpose—we cognize the same act enjoined for the same purpose; because of uniformity of form in terms of offertories and deities; because the same human effort is enjoined; because of uniformity of name."
13 Bādarāyaṇa does not use the term "*upāsana*," nor the all-important lexeme "*brahma-vidyā,*" but he uses the term "*vidyā*" throughout in the sense of distinct Upaniṣadic units, and names one of them, *puruṣa-vidyā,* in 3.3.24.
14 BrS p.74.
15 TUBh 1.3.2–4, vi.17.
16 ChUBh 7.6.2, vii, 431.
17 ŚBSBh 3.3.59, iii.710.

18 TUBhV 1.66, Balasubramanian (1984: 237).
19 RŚBh 4.1.1, Thibaut (1904: 716).
20 RŚBh 4.1.8, Thibaut (1904: 721).
21 NVPS 4.1.8, pp.1119–1200.
22 ŚVK 4.1.8, p.1200.
23 See BĀUBh on 1.1 and BĀUBhVAB thereon, ii.299–300.
24 puruṣārtho 'taḥ śabdād iti bādarāyaṇaḥ; 3.4.1.
25 See BĀUBh 1.1.1, viii.9. "Dawn, the period relating to Brahman, . . . is the horse's head because of primacy; and, the head is predominant among the parts of the body."
26 na pratīke na hi saḥ; 4.1.4. "Not in the symbol, for that is not him." I will discuss 4.3.14 later. Cf. also VPS on 3.3.58, where these meditations are called brahma-prāpti-vyatirikta-phala, "having results other than the attainment of Brahman."
27 3.3.58–64 with the commentaries.
28 3.3.53.
29 BĀUBhVAB, verse 4.
30 ChU 3.15.2, 7.1.5, discussed in the commentaries on 4.1.4.
31 ātmeti tūpagachanti; 4.1.3. *Sūtra* 4.1.4 quoted in nt.26.
32 ChU 3.14.3.
33 BĀU 3.4.1.
34 NVPS 4.1.3–4, p. 1190, 4.
35 4.3.14–15 with the commentaries.
36 puruṣa-vidyāyām api cetareṣām anamnānāt; 3.3.24. "Also in *Puruṣa-vidyā*, because other [qualities] are not mentioned."
37 ChU 5.10.1–2.
38 aniyamaḥ sarveṣām avirodhaḥ śabdānumānābhyām, 3.3.31. "No restriction, [the course belongs to] all [meditations]; [there is] no contradiction, through the evidence of scripture and inference." The commentaries are quite unanimous, again.
39 3.3.11, see nt.11 in Chapter 3.
40 3.3.33, see nt.15 in Chapter 3.
41 guṇa-mukhya-vyatikrame tad-arthatvān mukhyena veda-saṁyogaḥ; MS 3.3.9.
42 I should like to emphasize that this formulation is not meant to be a logical notation expressing a relation, but a template with variables.
43 ChU 3.14.3, Olivelle (1998: 209), slightly modified.
44 priya-śirastvādy-aprāptir upacayāpacayau hi bhede, 3.3.12. "Non-obtainment [in the universal meditational concept of Brahman of qualities] such as 'having pleasure as its head,' because addition and subtraction [are possible] in [the context of] duality."
45 vikalpo 'viśiṣṭa-phalatvāt; kāmyās tu yathākāmaṁ samuccīyeran na vā pūrva-hetv-abhāvāt, 3.3.57–8. "There is option, because the result is the same. But, the optional-volitional meditations may be combined or not promiscuously, because the previous reason does not obtain."

46 There are numerous references to this effect in Śaṅkara's works and in Maṇḍana Miśra's *Brahma-siddhi*.
47 Srinivasa Chari (2002: 283).
48 4.1.8, see nt.33 in the Introduction.
49 4.1.7, 11, see nt.33 in the Introduction.
50 "The *śruti* text says that a fault follows from the omission of the principal ritual act: 'He who is a performer of Darśa-pūrṇamāsa is certainly cut from heaven if he fails to perform the ritual on a full moon or a new moon.' Speaking about a fault when the principal act is not performed, the *śruti* text shows that the act is obligatory." MSBh 6.3.3, iv.1411.
51 nitya-naimittike kuryāt pratyavāya-jihāsayā; ŚV SĀP 110cd. "One should perform the obligatory rites with the intention of warding off diminution."
52 agnihotrādi tu tat-kāryāyaiva tad-darśanāt; 4.1.16. "But, Agnihotras and the rest are for that effect, because that is seen." Cf. ŚVK thereon, p. 1214: "There is no question of ceasing the duties of one's *āśrama*, such as Agnihotra, charity, austerity, etc., through meditation. They must be observed because they nurture meditation, since we see in the ritual texts that they give rise to knowledge." Also, sahakāritvena ca; 3.4.33. "And, as being assistants."
53 Olivelle (1998: 125).
54 sarvāpekṣā ca yajñādi-śruter aśva-vat, 3.4.26. "[Meditation] depends on all [*āśrama* duties], as per the text about sacrifice and the rest, in the manner of the horse." The horse is interpreted differently, but Nimbārka's is the simplest: "as one depends on a horse for going." The "text about sacrifice" is BĀU 4.4.22.
55 vihitatvāt cāśrama-karmāpi; 3.4.32. "Because they are enjoined even as *āśrama*-duties."
56 3.4.15, see nt.8 in Chapter 2.
57 BĀU 4.4.23, Olivelle (1998: 127).
58 śama-damādy-upetaḥ syāt tathāpi tu tad-vidhes tad-aṅgatayā teṣām avaśyānuṣṭeyatvāt; 3.4.27. "Still, he should be possessed of calm, self-control, etc., since they are to be practiced mandatorily on the strength of being subsidiary to meditation as per the injunction."
59 āvṛttir asakṛd upadeśāt; 4.1.1. "[There should be] repetition [of meditation] more than once, because such is the instruction." ā prayāṇāt tatrāpi dṛṣṭam; 4.1.12. "Until death, for it is seen in scriptures [that it is done] even then."
60 api saṁrādhane pratyakṣānumānabhyām; 3.2.24. "And [Brahman is revealed] in perfect meditation, because of [the evidence] of perception and inference (that is, *śruti* and *smṛti*)."
61 Nimbārka: bhakti-yoge dhyāne; Śaṅkara: bhakti-dhyāna-praṇidhānādy-anuṣṭhānam; Bhāskara: bhaktiḥ, dhyānādinā paricaryā; Rāmānuja: samyak-prīṇane bhakti-rūpāpanne; Śrīnivāsa: nididhyāsana-lakṣaṇe bhakti-yoge. All comments on 3.2.24 and the meaning of *saṁrādhana*.

62 prakāśādi-vac cāvaiśeṣyaṁ prakāśaś ca karmaṇy abhyāsāt; 3.2.25. "And as in the case of light etc., there is non-distinction. And the light [appears] in the act [of meditation] through practice."
63 This lexeme is commonly associated with Rāmānuja, but Śrīnivāsa uses it as well. See, for instance, his comment on 4.1.13.

Chapter 7

1 The BĀU (6.2.15) version has, rather, "truth is austerity."
2 Or, in the BĀU (6.2.16) version, practices sacrifice, gift-giving, and austerity.
3 Renou (1957: 70–1).
4 BĀU 6.2.16.
5 tad-antara-pratipattau raṁhati sampariṣvaktaḥ praśna-nirūpaṇābhyām; 3.1.1. "In attaining the next [body], [the soul] goes enveloped [by the subtle elements], because of questions and expositions."
6 tryātmakatvāt tu bhūyastvāt; 3.1.2. "[The mention of water is] through preponderance, because of being threefold."
7 Bodewitz (1996).
8 ŚBSBh 3.1.2.
9 A point made in the commentaries on 3.1.1, 3.
10 kṛtātyāye 'nuśayavān dṛṣṭa-smṛtibhyāṁ yathetam anevaṁ ca; 3.1.8. "Upon the passing away of works, [the soul descends] possessing the remainder [of karma], according to *śruti* and *smṛti*, just as it had come and not thus (i.e., in a different way)." See the commentaries on the details of the karmic remainder.
11 caraṇād iti cen na tad-upalakṣaṇārtho 'ti kārṣṇājiniḥ; 3.1.9. "If [it is said], because of conduct, [we reply] no, because [*caraṇa*] connotes works figuratively—thus Kārṣṇājini." See the commentaries on the meaning of *caraṇa*.
12 NVPS 3.1.8; ŚBSBh 3.1.8.
13 ŚBSBh 3.1.9; RŚBh 3.1.9.
14 3.1.9–11 with the commentaries.
15 3.1.12–16 with the commentaries.
16 3.1.17–21 with the commentaries.
17 tad-adhigame uttara-pūrvāghayor aśleṣa-vināśau tad-vyapadeśāt; 4.1.13. "On the attainment of that, prior and posterior karma does not stick and is destroyed, because there is mention of that."
18 itarasyāpy evam-asaṁśleśa pāte tu; 4.1.14. "Of the other (i.e., good karma), there is likewise non-clinging, but at death." anārabdha-kārye eva tu pūrve tad-avadheḥ; 4.1.15. "But, only those two that have started bearing fruits, because the other has a term."
19 ChU 6.14.2, Olivelle (1998: 257).

20 SK 67.
21 ŚBSBh 4.1.15.
22 Such is the force of BS 4.1.15 with the commentaries other than Śaṅkara.
23 BhBSBh 4.1.14, p.224.
24 BhBSBh 4.1.15; Fort (1998: 77–80) and Uskokov (2020: 75–7).
25 4.1.12, see nt.59 in Chapter 6.

An informative discussion on the origins of the doctrine of "liberation while living," *jīvan-mukti*, is available in Slaje (2007: 127–30), who argues that originally it meant liberation while remaining engaged in social and other action, throughout one's life.

26 vāṅ manasi darśanāc chabdāc ca; ata eva sarvāṇy anu; tan manaḥ prāṇa uttarāt; so 'dhyakṣe tad-upagamādibhyaḥ; bhūteṣu tac-chruteḥ; naikasmin darśayato hi; samānā cāsṛty-upakramād amṛtatvaṁ cānupoṣya; 4.2.1–7. "Speech [merges] in the mind, because it is seen, and scripture says so. All other [functions] follow. The mind merges in *prāṇa*, on the account of what follows [in the text]. *Prāṇa* merges in the ruler [the individual soul], because of statements of approaching that. In the elements, because that is stated. Not in one [but in their triplicated form], because [that follows] from scripture. The same [for the knower and the non-knower] until ascending the path; and, immortality without having burned."
27 ChU 8.6.2, Olivelle (1998: 279).
28 ChU 8.6; BĀU 4.3.
29 tadoko'gra-jvalanaṁ tat-prakāśita-dvāro vidyā-sāmarthyāt tac-cheṣa-gaty-anusmṛti-yogāc ca hārdānugṛhītaḥ śatādhikayā; 4.2.16. "Then there is lightening of the forepart of his abode, the door being illuminated by him (Brahman), through the power of meditation. By the application of recollection on the path that is an integral part [of *brahma-vidyā*], favored by the one in the heart, [the knower departs] through the hundred and first."
30 Important loci in which the path is discussed, or which are otherwise relevant, include ChU 4.15–5; 5.10.1–2; 8.5–6; BĀU 5.10; 6.2.15; 4.3–4; KauU 1.3; MU 1.2.11; and BhG 8.24–5.
31 Karmarkar (1925: 461).
32 ātivāhikās tal-liṅgāt; 4.3.4. "They are conductors, because there is such an indication." Cf. ŚVK p.1278: "They could be road signs, like trees or mountains . . . or places of pleasure." Likewise, Rāmānuja, Bhāskara and Śaṅkara, who is characteristically most elaborate.
33 arcir-ādinā tat-pratīteḥ; 4.3.1. "By the [path] beginning in light, that being known." All the commentators here make the point that the path is constructed by combining all its iterations in various texts.
34 raśmy-anusārī; niśi neti cen na sambandhasya yāvad-deha-bhāvitvād darśayati ca; ataś cāyane 'pi dakṣiṇe; 4.2.17–19. "Following the sunrays. If it be said, 'but not at night,' then no, because the relation [of the knower with his karma] lasts only as long as the body, as scripture shows. Therefore, also during the southern course of the sun."

35 ChU 8.6.5.
36 4.3.1–5 with the commentaries.
37 tad-apīteḥ saṁsāra-vyapadeśāt; 4.2.8. "Because of the reference to transmigration until entering that." SVK, p.1268: "Entering means attaining the nature of Brahman, and this takes place when one has attained a particular region through the path beginning with light. Prior to that, the soul is subject to transmigratory existence." Likewise, Rāmānuja.
38 tāni pare tathā hy āha; avibhāgo vacanāt; 4.2.14–15. "They (the elements) [merge] in the Supreme, because it is said so. Non-distinction, because of the statement."
39 4.2.8. See nt.37 in this chapter.
40 BĀU 4.4.6–7, Olivelle (1998: 121).
41 Ibid., Olivelle (1998: 127).
42 sūkṣmaṁ pramāṇataś ca tathopalabdheḥ; nopamardenātaḥ; asyaiva copapatter ūṣmā; pratiṣedhād iti cen na śārīrāt spaṣṭo hy ekeṣām; smaryate ca; 4.2.9–13. "And the subtle body [still persists], because that is seen from [scriptural] proof. [The immortality] is not through destruction [of the relation to a body]. On the appropriateness [of the subtle body], heat [is present]. If [it be objected], because of denial, [we say] no, [because the departure is denied] from the embodied soul, [which] is clear [from the reading] of some. And, it is remembered."

The Sanskrit of the text under discussion, BĀU 4.4.6 in the Kāṇva reading, is: athākāmayamāno yo 'kāmo niṣkāma āpta-kāma ātma-kāmo na tasya prāṇā utkrāmanti. "Now, a man who does not desire—who is without desires, who is freed from desires, whose desires are fulfilled, whose only desire is his self—his vital functions (*prāṇa*) do not depart" (Olivelle 1998: 121). The "some," *ekeṣām*, in *sūtra* 4.2.12 refers to the less common Mādhyandina text of the BĀU, where instead of the genitive *tasya* the ablative *tasmāt* is read, na tasmāt prāṇā utkrāmanti, "the functions do not depart from him."
43 ŚBSBh 4.2.12–13. On why Śaṅkara's reading is not justified, see Ghate (1926: 151–2).
44 This is from the first book of the Upaniṣad, specifically chapters three through seven.
45 KṣU 1.5, Olivelle (1998: 329–31).
46 kāryaṁ bādarir asya gaty-upapatteḥ; viśeṣatatvāc ca; sāmīpyāt tu tad-vyapadeśaḥ; kāryātyaye tad-adhyakṣeṇa sahātaḥ paraṁ abhidhānāt; smṛteś ca; 4.3.6–10. "To Brahman the effect, says Bādari, because going is possible only in regard to him. And, because of his being qualified. And, [Hiraṇyagarbha] may be called that [Brahman] because of proximity to it. At the expiration of Brahman the effect, [the soul] along with the ruler [of Brahman the effect] attains the higher, because of the statement. And, it is remembered."
47 paraṁ jaiminir mukhyatvāt; darśanāc ca; na ca kārye pratipatty-abhisandhiḥ; 4.3.11–13. "The higher, says Jaimini, because of primary

meaning. And, because it is seen [in scripture]. And, the intention of attaining is not with respect to the Brahman that is the effect."

"Seen in scripture" refers to the ChU (8.34) mention of *paraṁ jyotiḥ* in atha ya eṣa samprasādo 'smāc charīrāt samutthāya paraṁ jyotir upasampadya svena rūpeṇābhiniṣpadyate. "This serene one who, after he rises up from the body and reaches the highest light, emerges in his own true appearance." (Olivelle 1998: 227). This is an immensely important passage for the BS doctrine of the attainment, and we will discuss it further in the text.

48 apratīkālambanān nayatīti bādarāyaṇa ubhayathā doṣāt tat-kratuś ca; viśeṣaṁ ca darśayati; 4.3.14–15. "He leads those who do not depend on symbols—thus Bādarāyaṇa, because there is a fault in both ways; also, [he leads him] whose intention is that. And, [scripture] shows the difference [concerning results]."

49 Ghate (1926: 159–60).

50 ubhayathā doṣāt or ubhayathādoṣāt, which in a manuscript would be written in the same way. Śaṅkara also reads like Bhāskara.

51 BhBSBh 4.3.14.

52 BĀU 4.3.23.

53 ChU 8.11.2.

54 Ibid., 8.3.4.

55 Ibid., 8.12.3.

56 Ibid., 8.13.1.

57 Ibid., 8.12.5.

58 Ibid., 8.12.3, Olivelle (1998: 285).

59 Ibid., 8.2.10.

60 Ibid., 8.1.6, Olivelle (1998: 275).

61 anāvṛttiḥ śabdād anāvṛttiḥ śabdāt; 4.4.22.

62 dahara uttarebhyaḥ; gati-śabdābhyāṁ tathā hi dṛṣṭaṁ liṅgaṁ ca; dhṛteś ca mahimno 'syāsminn upalabdheḥ; prasiddhaś ca. 1.3.14–17. "[Brahman is] the small space, because of what follows. From the fact of motion and [the use of] the word [*brahma-loka*, it is Brahman]. It is likewise seen, and there is an indicatory mark. And, because of holding [the worlds in place, he is Brahman], since his greatness is seen [in another passage]. And, it is well-known [that Brahman is called 'space']."

63 itara-parāmarśāt sa iti cen nāsambhavāt; 1.3.18. "If it be said that because of the mention of the other (the individual soul), [it must be the individual soul], [we say] no, because of impossibility."

64 uttarāc ced āvirbhūta-svarūpas tu; 1.3.19. "If [it be argued that it is the individual soul] because of the following [section,] [we reply] no, it is a manifestation of intrinsic nature."

65 BhBSBh 4.3.14, 4.4.22.

66 anukṛtes tasya ca; api ca smaryate. 1.3.22–23. "And, because of [the soul's being] the imitation of that (i.e. Brahman). And, it is so remembered." That

the soul is Brahman's "imitation" is perhaps also how we should interpret 2.3.49, *ābhāsa eva ca*, "And, an appearance," which is one of the most contentious *sūtra*s in the text. See Ghate (1926: 104–5) and Nakamura (1983: 450–1).

Śaṅkara and Bhāskara read this as a separate *adhikaraṇa*, but their interpretation is not contextual, as Ghate recognizes (1926: 67–8).

67 sampadyāvirbhāvaḥ svena śabdāt; muktaḥ pratijñānāt; ātmā prakaraṇāt; avibhāgena dṛṣṭatvāt; 4.4.1–4. "[The soul] manifests its own form having come [to Brahman], because the word *svena,* 'own,' is used. Released, because that is the promise. It is the Self, because that is the context. As non-divided, because it is seen."

68 brāhmeṇa jaiminir upanyāsādibhyaḥ; 4.4.5. "Jaimini [says that] it [manifests] with the qualities of Brahman, because of reference etc."

69 saṅkalpād eva tac-chruteḥ; 4.4.8. "By the mere will, because of that statement."

70 abhāvaṁ bādarir āha hy evam; bhāvaṁ jaiminir vikalpāmananāt. 4.10–11. "Absence [of a body], [says] Bādari, for [scripture] says thus. Presence [of a body], [says] Jaimini, because of the statement of optionality."

The "optionality" is a reference to ChU 7.26.2, which says that he who "sees rightly" and "sees no death," apparently a reference to liberation, "is single, threefold, fivefold."

71 RŚBh 4.4.8–11.

72 ata evānanyādipatiḥ; 4.4.9. "For this very reason (i.e., because of getting everything by mere will), [the attainment is a state] without having another as a master."

73 pradīpa-vad āveśas tathā hi darśayati; 4.4.15. "There is entrance, in the manner of a lamp, for [scripture] shows thus."

74 Commentaries on 4.4.8.

75 Nakamura (1983: 531).

76 citi tan-mātreṇa tad-ātmakatvād ity auḍulomiḥ; 4.4.6. "Auḍulomi says, in consciousness, because its essence is only to that extend."

77 This was explicitly developed as a different fourth state, *turīya*, in the first chapter of *Māṇḍūkya Upaniṣad* and Gauḍapāda's *kārikā* thereon.

78 BĀU 4.5.13.

79 BhBSBh 4.4.6.

80 evam apy upanyāsāt pūrva-bhāvād avirodhaṁ bādarāyanaḥ; 4.4.7.

81 RŚBh 4.3.14; NVPS 4.3.14.

82 BhG 12.1–4.

83 If so, this would be like the Bhāṭṭa Mīmāṁsā view of liberation, as developed by Pārthasārathi Miśra. See Ram-Prasad (2007: 133–46). But *sūtra* 4.4.13 insists that even without a body, the liberated soul may have transitive consciousness, like in a dream. tanv-abhāve sandhya-vad upapatteḥ. "In the absence of a body, as in dream, because it is possible."

84 4.4.17–21. I think Modi (1943: 457) is right that the last *sūtra*, 4.4.22, should be read as a separate *adhikaraṇa.*

85 jagad-vyāpāra-varjaṁ prakaraṇād asannihitatvāc ca; 4.1.17.
86 bhoga-mātra-sāmya-liṅgāc ca; 4.1.21.
87 TU 2.1.1.
88 ŚBSBh 1.1.4; TUBh 3.1.1.
89 Telivala (1918: 11–12).
90 RŚBh 4.4.13–14.
91 See, for instance, ŚVK 1.2.17; the Vaiṣṇava commentaries on 1.3.13 (Rāmānuja, Nimbārka, Śrīnivāsa); Ghate (1926: 160).
92 vikārāvartti ca tathā hi sthitim āha; 4.4.19.
93 NVPS 4.4.19, p.1354.
94 TU 2.7.1.
95 TU 2.7.1–2.8.
96 See 3.2.40 in nt.10 in Chapter 6. Cf. NVPS, p.914: "*Dharma* is the cause of the result, thinks Jaimini, because only that makes sense, as in agriculture and the like."
97 8.1.6, Olivelle (1998: 275).
98 MU 1.2.12.
99 phalam ata upapatteḥ; 3.2.38.

References

Prose sources, including commentaries, are quoted with text and page number. In multivolume editions, the volume and page are given together. For instance: (1) BhBSBh 2.1.6, p.211, stands for Bhāskara's commentary on the *Brahma-sūtra*, on *sūtra* 6 of *adhyāya* 2, *pāda* 1, on page 211 in the reference volume; (2) RŚBh 3.3.13, iii.856–7 stands for Rāmānuja's *Śrībhāṣya* on the BS, on sūtra 13 of *adhyāya* 3, *pāda* 3, pages 856–7 in the third part of the reference volume. Page numbers are not given in citations, where direct quotation or close paraphrase is not provided. *Sūtra*s, verses, and prose sections of the Upaniṣads are quoted only by text number. The *Brahma-sūtra* is referenced according to Nimbārka's commentary, as printed in Brahmacārin 1904; few typos have been silently corrected. The primary sources and translations are listed in the general bibliography and are arranged according to the Sanskrit alphabet.

List of Primary Sources

Ānandagiri. Commentary (*ṭīkā*) on Śaṅkara's commentary on the BhG. Text Āgaśe 1934.

Āpastamba Dharma-sūtra. Text and translation Olivelle 2000.

Īśvarakṛṣṇa. *Sāṅkhya-kārikā*. Text and translation Mainkar 1972.
Commentaries: Gauḍapāda, Mainkar 1972; Vācaspati Miśra, Jha 1896.

Uddyotakara. *Nyāya-bhāṣya-vārttika*. Text Thakur 1997. Translation Jha 1984.

Kumārila Bhaṭṭa.
Śloka-vārttika. Text Rai 1993. Translation Jha 1907.
Tantra-vārttika. Text Gosvāmī 1984. Translation Jha 1983.

Keśava Kāśmīrī. *Kaustubha-prabhā* commentary on BS. Text Brahmacārin 1904.

Kauṣītaki Upaniṣad. Text and translation Olivelle 1998.

Gauḍapāda. *Āgama-śāstra*. Text and translation Bhattacharya 1989.

Gautama Dharma-sūtra. Text and translation Olivelle 2000.

Chāndogya Upaniṣad. Text and translation Olivelle 1998.

Jaimini. *Mīmāṁsā-sūtra*. Text Abhyankar and Joshi 1929. Translation Jha 1933.

Taittirīya Upaniṣad. Text and translation Olivelle 1998.

Nimbārka. *Vedānta-pārijāta-saurabha* commentary on BS. Text Brahmacārin 1904. Translation Bose 2004.

Pāṇini. *Aṣṭādhyāyī*, First Adhyāya. Text and translation Sharma 2000.

Prabhākara. *Bṛhatī* commentary on Śabara's commentary on the MS. Text Ramanatha Sastri 1934.

Baladeva Vidyābhūṣna. *Govinda-bhāṣya* commentary on BS. Text Kṛṣṇadasa Baba 1965. Translation Vasu 2002.
Bādarāyaṇa. *Brahma-sūtra*. Text Brahmacārin 1904.
Bṛhad-āraṇyaka Upaniṣad. Text and translation Olivelle 1998.
Baudhāyana Dharma-sūtra. Text and translation Olivelle 2000.
Bhagavad-gītā. Text Āgaśe 1934. Translation van Buitenen 1981.
Bhartṛhari. *Vākyapadīya, Brahma-kāṇda*. Text Subramania Iyer 1966. Translation Subramania Iyer 1965.
Bhāgavata Purāṇa. Text Shastri 1983.
Bhāratītīrtha. *Vaiyāsika-nyāya-mālā*. Text Pandit 1891.
Bhāskara. Commentary on BS. Text Kato 2011 (Chapters 1–2), Dvivedin 1915 (Chapters 3–4).
Maṇḍana Miśra. *Brahma-siddhi*. Text Sastri 1984.
Madhva. Commentary (*bhāṣya*) on BS. Text Gopālakṛṣṇācārya 1900. Translation Subba Rau 1904.
Manu-smṛti. Text and translation Olivelle 2005.
Mahābhārata. Text Sukthankar 1927.
Muṇḍaka Upaniṣad. Text and translation Olivelle 1998.
Rāmānuja
Vedānta-dīpa commentary on BS. Text and translation Anantha Rangacharya 2005.
Vedānta-sāra commentary on BS. Text and translation Krishnamacharya and Narasimha Ayyangar 1979.
Vedārtha-saṅgraha. Text and translation van Buitenen 1956.
Śrībhāṣya commentary on BS. Text and translation Karmarkar 1959–1964. Translation Thibaut 1904.
Śaṅkara Bhagavatpāda
Commentary on Gauḍapāda's ĀŚ. Text *The Works of Sri Sankaracharya*, 1910, volume 5. Translation Swami G. 1937b.
Commentary on ChU. Text *The Works of Sri Sankaracharya*, 1910, volumes 6–7. Translation Swami G. 2003.
Commentary on TU. Text *The Works of Sri Sankaracharya*, 1910, volume 6. Translation Swami G. 1937a.
Commentary on BĀU. Text *The Works of Sri Sankaracharya*, 1910, volumes 8–10. Translation Swami M. 1950.
Commentary on BS. Text *The Works of Sri Sankaracharya*, 1910, volumes 1–3. Translation Swami G. 1965; Thibaut 1890.
Commentary on BhG. Text *The Works of Sri Sankaracharya*, 1910, volumes 11–12. Translation Swami G. 2012.
Śabara. Commentary on MS. Text Abhyankar and Joshi 1929. Translation Jha 1933.
Śālikanātha. *Ṛju-vimalā* commentary on Prabhākara's *Bṛhatī*. Text Ramanatha Sastri 1934.
Śrīkaṇṭha. Commentary on BS. Text Śrīnivāsāchārya 1903. Translation Chaudhuri 1959.

Śrīnivāsa. *Vedānta-kaustubha* commentary on the BS. Text Brahmacārin 1904. Translation Bose 2004.
Śvetāśvatara Upaniṣad. Text and translation Olivelle 1998.
Sudarśana Sūri. *Śruta-prakāśikā* commentary on Rāmānuja's *Śrībhāṣya*. Text Śāstri 1916.
Sureśvara
Vārttika on Śaṅkara's commentary on *Bṛhad-āraṇyaka*. Text Āpte 1892.
Vārttika on Śaṅkara's commentary on *Taittirīya*. Text and translation Balasubramanian 1984.
Someśvara. *Nyāya-sudhā* commentary on Kumārila's *Tantra-vārttika*. Text Gosvāmī 1984.
Vallabha. *Aṇu-bhāṣya* commentary on BS. Text Telivala 2005.
Vācaspati Miśra. *Bhāmatī* commentary on Śaṅkara's *Brahma-sūtra-bhāṣya*. Text Śāstri and Śāstrācārya 1938. Translation of the first four *sūtra*s Suryanarayana Sastri and Kunhan Raja 1933.
Vijñānabhikṣu. *Vijñānāmṛta* commentary on the BS. Text Trīpāṭhī 1979.
Viṣṇu Purāṇa. Text Upreti 2003.

Editions, Translations, and Secondary Literature

Abhyankar, K. V. and Joshi, G. A. (eds.) (1929) *Mīmāṁsādarśanam, with the Śabarabhāṣya of Śabara, Prabhā of Śrī Vaidyanāthaśāstri, Tantravārttika and Ṭupṭikā of Kumārila Bhaṭṭa*. In 7 Volumes. Poona: Ānandāśrama Press.
Adams, G. C. Jr. (1993) *The Structure and Meaning of Bādarāyaṇa's Brahma Sūtras*. Delhi: Motilal Banarsidass.
Āgaśe, K. Ś. (ed.) (1934) *Bhagavad-Gītā-Bhāṣya of Śaṅkara, with the Ṭīkā of Ānandagiri*. Poona: Ānandāśrama Press.
Aklujkar, A. (2011) "Unity of the Mīmāṁsās: How Historiography Hides History," in *Vācaspativaibhavam: A Volume in Felicitation of Professor Vacaspati Upadhyaya*. New Delhi: D.K.Printworld (P) Ltd., pp. 821–900.
Anantha Rangacharya, N. S. (ed.) (2005) *Vedanta Deepa. Commentary on the Vedanta Sutras by Bhagavad Ramanujacharya*. In 2 Volumes. Bangalore: Sri Rama Printers.
Arnold, D. (2005) *Buddhists, Brahmins, and Belief: Epistemology in South Asian Philosophy of Religion*. New York: Columbia University Press.
Āpte, M. C. (ed.) (1892) *Bṛhadāraṇyakopaniṣadbhāsyavārtikam of Sureśvara*. In 3 Volumes. Poona: Ānandāśrama.
Balasubramanian, R. (1984) *The Taittirīyopaniṣad-Bhāṣya-Vārtika of Sureśvara*. Madras: Radhakrishnan Institute for Advanced Study in Philosophy, University of Madras.
Barnes, J. (1987) *Early Greek Philosophy*. London: Penguin Books.
Belvalkar, S. K. (1918) "The Multiple Authorships of the Vedānta Sūtras," *Indian Philosophical Review*, 2, pp. 141–54.

Belvalkar, S. K. (1927) "Jaimini's Śārīraka-Sūtra," in Julius von Negelein (ed.), *Aus Indiens Kultur: Festgabe Richard von Garbe dem Forscher und Lehrer zu seinem 70. Geburtstag dargebracht von seinen Freunden, Verehrern und Schülern*. Erlangen: Palm & Enke.

Belvalkar, S. K. (1929) *Shree Gopal Basu Mallik Lectures on Vedānta Philosophy*. Poona: Bilvakuñja Publishing House.

Bhatkhande, S. M. (1982) *The Chāndogya Upaniṣad and the Brahmasūtras of Bādarāyaṇa (A Comparative Study)*. Bombay: University of Bombay.

Bhattacharya, V. (1989) *The Āgamaśāstra of Gauḍapāda*. Delhi: Motilal Banarsidass.

Bilimoria, P. (1990) "Hindu Doubts About God: Towards a Mīmāṁsā Deconstruction," *International Philosophical Quarterly*, 30, pp. 481–99.

Bilimoria, P. (2013) "Towards an Indian Theodicy," in McBrayer, J. P. and Howard-Snyder, D. (eds.), *The Blackwell Companion to the Problem of Evil*. Chichester, West Sussex: Wiley-Blackwell, pp. 281–95.

Biswas, B. (1996) *The Concept of Upadeśa in Sanskrit Grammar*. Allahabad: Padmaja Prakashan.

Bodewitz, H. W. (1996) "The Pañcāgnividyā and the Pitṛyāna/Devayāna," in Goswami, A. K. and Chutia, D. (eds.), *Studies on Indology: Professor Mukunda Madhava Sharma Felicitation Volume*. Delhi: Sri Satguru Publications, pp. 51–7.

Bose, R. (2004) *Vedānta-Pārijāta-Saurabha of Nimbārka and Vedānta-Kaustubha of Śrīnivāsa: English Translation*. In 3 Volumes. Delhi: Munshiram Manoharlal.

Brahmacārin, N. (ed.) (1904) *Brahma-Sūtra with Vedānta-Pārijāta-Saurabha of Nimbārka, Vedānta-Kaustubha of Śrīnivāsa, and Vedānta-Kaustubha-Prabhā of Keśava Kāśmīrī*. Vrindavana.

Brereton, J. (2004) "Bráhman, Brahmán, and Sacrificer," in Griffiths, A. and Houben, J. E. M. (eds.), *The Vedas: Text, Language & Ritual*. Groningen: Egbert Forsten, pp. 325–44.

Brick, D. (2006) "Transforming Tradition into Texts: The Early Development of Smṛti," *Journal of Indian Philosophy*, 34, pp. 287–302.

Bronkhorst, J. (2007) *Greater Magadha: Studies in the Culture of Early India*. Leiden and Boston: Brill.

Bronkhorst, J. (2014) "Mīmāṃsāsūtra and Brahmasūtra," *Journal of Indian Philosophy*, 42, pp. 463–9.

Buchta, D. (2016) "Devotion and Karmic Extripation in Late Vedānta: Viṭṭhalanātha and Baladeva Vidyābhūṣaṇa on Brahmasūtra 4.1.13–19," *The Journal of Hindu Studies*, 9, pp. 29–55.

van Buitenen, J. A. B. (1956) *Vedārthasaṁgraha*. Poona: Deccan College.

van Buitenen, J. A. B. (1981) *The Bhagavad-Gītā in the Mahābhārata*. Chicago and London: University of Chicago Press.

van Buitenen, J. A. B. (1988) *Studies in Indian Literature and Philosophy*. Delhi: Motilal Banarsidass.

Carman, J. B. (1974) *The Theology of Rāmānuja: An Essay in Interreligious Understanding*. New Haven and London: Yale University Press.
Chattopadhyay, R. (1992) *A Vaiṣṇava Interpretation of the Brahmasūtras: Vedānta and Theism*. Translated by K. Chattopadhyay. Leiden, New York, and Köln: E.J. Brill.
Chaudhuri, R. (1959) *Doctrine of Srikantha, Vol. II: First English Translation of Srikantha-Bhasya or Commentary of Srikantha on the Brahma-sutras*. Calcutta: Pracyayani.
Chaudhuri, R. (1962) *Doctrine of Srikantha, Vol. I: Doctrine of Srikantha and Other Monotheistic Schools of Vedānta*. Calcutta: Pracyayani.
Clooney, F. X. (1988) "Devatādhikaraṇa: A Theological Debate in the Mīmāṁsā-Vedānta Tradition," *Journal of Indian Philosophy*, 16(3), pp. 277–98.
Clooney, F. X. (1989) "Evil, Divine Omnipotence, and Human Freedom: Vedānta's Theology of Karma," *The Journal of Religion*, 69(4), pp. 530–48.
Clooney, F. X. (1990) *Thinking Ritually: Rediscovering the Pūrva Mīmāṁsā of Jaimini. Vienna: Institute for Indology*. Leiden and Vienna: University of Vienna & Commission Agents, E. J. Brill.
Clooney, F. X. (1992) "Binding the Text: Vedānta as Philosophy and Commentary," in Timm, J. R. (ed.), *Texts in Context: Traditional Hermeneutics in South Asia*. Albany: State University of New York Press, pp. 47–68.
Clooney, F. X. (2003) "Restoring 'Hindu Theology' as a Category in Indian Intellectual Discourse," in Flood, G. (ed.), *The Blackwell Companion to Hinduism*. Oxford: Blackwell Publishing, pp. 447–77.
Clooney, F. X. (2020) "On the Style of Vedānta: Reading Bhāratītīrtha's Vaiyāsikanyāyamālā in Light of Mādhava's Jaiminīyanyāyamālā," in Maharaj, A. (ed.), *The Bloomsbury Research Handbook of Vedanta*. New York: Bloomsbury Academic, pp. 341–66.
Cohen, S. (2018) *The Upaniṣads: A Complete Guide*. New York: Routledge.
Copleston, F. S. J. (1993a) *A History of Philosophy. Volume I: Greece and Rome*. New York: Image Books, Doubleday.
Copleston, F. S. J. (1993b) *A History of Philosophy. Volume II: Medieval Philosophy*. New York: Image Books, Doubleday.
Couture, A. (2018) "*Avatāra*," *Brill's Encyclopedia of Hinduism Online*. Edited by K. A. Jacobsen et al. Leiden: Brill.
Dasti, M. (2013) "Asian Philosophy," in Taliaferro, C., Harrison, V. S., and Goetz, S. (eds.), *The Routledge Companion to Theism*. New Haven and London: Routledge, pp. 23–37.
Dasti, M. and Phillips, S. (2017) *The Nyaya-Sutra: Selections with Early Commentaries*. Indianapolis: Hackett Publishing.
Davis, R. H. (1991) *Ritual in an Oscillating Universe*. Princeton: Princeton University Press.
Deussen, P. (1908) *The Philosophy of the Upanishads*. Edinburgh: T. & T. Clark.

Deussen, P. (1912) *The System of the Vedanta*. Chicago: The Open Court Publishing Company.
Doniger O'Flaherty, W. (ed.) (1980a) *Karma and Rebirth in Classical Indian Traditions*. Berkeley, Los Angeles and London: University of California Press.
Doniger O'Flaherty, W. (1980b) *The Origins of Evil in Hindu Mythology*. Berkeley, Los Angeles and London: University of California Press.
Doniger O'Flaherty, W. (1981) *Rig Veda*. London: Penguin Books.
Duquette, J. (2014) "Reading Non-Dualism in Śivādvaita Vedānta: An Argument from the Śivādvaitanirṇaya in Light of the Śivārkamaṇidīpikā," *Journal of Indian Philosophy*, 44, pp. 67–79.
Dvivedin, P. V. P. (ed.) (1915) *Brahmasūtra with A Commentary by Bhāskarāchārya*. Benares: Chowkhamba Sanskrit Book Depot.
Edelman, J. (2013) "Hindu Theology as Churning the Latent," *Journal of the American Academy of Religion*, 81(2), pp. 427–66.
Elkman, S. M. (1986) *Jīva Gosvāmin's Tattvasandarbha: A Study on the Philosophical and Sectarian Development of the Gauḍīya Vaiṣṇava Movement*. Delhi: Motilal Banarsidass.
Faddegon, B. (1923) "The Chapter (III, 3), the Method of Exegesis, in the Vedānta-Sūtra," *Acta Orientalia (Netherlands)*, 1, pp. 105–13.
Fort, A. O. (1990) *The Self and Its States: A States of Consciousness Doctrine in Advaita Vedānta*. Delhi: Motilal Banarsidass.
Fort, A. O. (1998) *Jīvanmukti in Transformation: Embodied Liberation in Advaita and Neo-Vedanta*. Albany: State University of New York Press.
Fort, A. O. and Mumme, P. V. (eds.) (1996) *Living Liberation in Hindu Thought*. Albany: State University of New York Press.
Garge, D. V. (1952) *Citations in Śabara-Bhāṣya*. Poona: Deccan College.
Gethin, R. M. L. (2001) *The Buddhist Path to Awakening*. Oxford: Oneworld Publications.
Ghate, V. S. (1926) *The Vedānta*. Poona: Bhandarkar Oriental Research Institute.
Gonda, J. (1950) *Notes on Brahman*. Utrecht: J.L. Beyers.
Gopālakṛṣṇācārya (ed.) (1900) *Śrīmad-Brahmasūtrāṇi, Śrīmaj-jagannātha-yati-kṛta-ṭippaṇī-saṁvalita-śrīman-madhva-bhāṣya-sametāni*. Madras: The Grove Press.
Gosvāmī, M. (ed.) (1984) *The Mīmāṁsā Darśana of Maharṣi Jaimini. With Śābarabhāṣya of Śabaramuni, Tantravārtika by Kumārila-Bhaṭṭa with its Commentary Nyāyasudhā of Someśvara-Bhaṭṭa, Bhāṣyavivaraṇa of Govindāmṛtamuni and Bhāvaprakāśikā by Dr. Mahāprabhulāla Gosvāmī*. In 4 Volumes. Varanasi: Tara Printing Works.
Griswold, H. D. (1900) *Brahman: A Study in the History of Indian Philosophy*. New York: The Macmillan Company.
Gupta, R. (2007) *The Caitanya Vaiṣṇava Vedānta of Jīva Gosvāmin: When Knowledge Meets Devotion*. London and New York: Routledge.

Gupta, R. M. and Valpey, K. (2017) *The Bhāgavata Purāṇa: Selected Readings*. New York: Columbia University Press.

Halbfass, W. (1991) *Tradition and Reflection: Explorations in Indian Thought*. Albany: State University of New York Press.

Halbfass, W. (1992) *On Being and What There Is: Classical Vaiśeṣika and the History of Indian Ontology*. Albany: State University of New York Press.

Harikai, K. (1994) "On the Three-fold Clasification of the Arthavāda," in Dwivedi, R. C. (ed.), *Studies in Mīmāṁsā: Dr. Mandan Mishra Felicitation Volume*. Delhi: Motilal Banarsidass, pp. 299–311.

Hartshorne, C. (1969) *The Divine Relativity: A Social Conception of God*. New Haven: Yale University Press.

Herman, A. L. (1993) *The Problem of Evil and Indian Thought*. Delhi: Motilal Banarsidass.

Hick, J. (2010) *Evil and the God of Love*. London: Palgrave Macmillan.

Hickson, M. W. (2013) "A Brief History of the Problem of Evil," in McBrayer, J. P. and Howard-Snyder, D. (eds.), *The Blackwell Companion to the Problem of Evil*. Chichester, West Sussex: Wiley-Blackwell, pp. 3–18.

Hock, H. H. (2002) "The Yājñavalkya Cycle in the Bṛhad Āraṇyaka Upaniṣad," *Journal of the American Oriental Society*, 122(2), pp. 278–86.

Hoffman, J. and Rosenkrantz, G. (2020) "Omnipotence," in Zalta, E. N. (ed.), *The Stanford Encyclopedia of Philosophy*. Spring 2020. Metaphysics Research Lab, Stanford University. Available at: https://plato.stanford.edu/archives/spr2020/entries/omnipotence/ (Accessed January 11, 2022).

Holdrege, B. A. (1994) "Veda in the Brāhmaṇas: Cosmogonic Paradigms and the Delimitation of Canon," in Patton, L. L. (ed.), *Authority, Anxiety, and Canon: Essays in Vedic Interpretation*. Albany: State University of New York Press, pp. 35–66.

Ilievski, V. (2020) "The 'Whence' of Evil and How the Demiurge Can Alleviate Our Suffering," *Religions*, 11(3).

Ingalls, D. H. H. (1954) "Śaṁkara's Arguments Against the Buddhists," *Philosophy East and West*, 3(4), pp. 291–306.

Ingalls, D. H. H. (1967) "Bhāskara the Vedāntin," *Philosophy East and West*, 17, pp. 61–7.

Jacobi, H. (1911) "The Dates of the Philosophical Schools of the Brahmans," *Journal of the American Oriental Society*, 31(1), pp. 1–29.

Jakubczak, M. (2004) "Living Liberation (jīvan-mukti) in Sāṁkhya and Yoga," in Balcerowicz, P. and Mejor (eds.), *Essays in Indian Philosophy, Religion and Literature*. Delhi: Motilal Banarsidass, pp. 363–71.

Jha, G. (ed.) (1896) *Tattva-kaumudī (Sāṅkhya) of Vācaspati Miśra: An English Translation with the Sanskrit Text*. Bombay: Tookaram Tatya, F.T.S., for the Bombay Theosophical Publication Fund.

Jha, G. (1907) *Ślokavārttika. Translated from the Original Sanskrit with Extracts from the Commentaries of Sucarita Miśra (the Kāśikā) and Pārtha Sārathī Miśra*. Calcutta: Asiatic Society of Bengal (Bibliotheca Indica).

Jha, G. (1933) *Shabara-Bhāshya*. In 3 Volumes. Baroda: Oriental Institute.
Jha, G. (1983) *Tantravārttika of Kumārila Bhaṭṭa: A Commentary on Śabara's Bhāṣya on the Pūrvamīmāṁsā Sūtras of Jaimini*. In 2 Volumes. Delhi: Sri Satguru Publications.
Jha, G. (1984) *The Nyāya-sūtras of Gautama. With the Bhāsya of Vātsyāyana and the Vārttika of Uddyotakara*. In 4 Volumes. Delhi: Motilal Banarsidass.
Karmarkar, R. D. (1919–20) "Comparison of the Bhasyas of Sankara, Ramanuja, Kesavakasmirin and Vallabha on Some Crucial Sutras," *Annals of the Bhandarkar Oriental Research Institute*, 1(2), pp. 105–27.
Karmarkar, R. D. (1920–21) "Comparison of the Bhasyas of Sankara, Ramanuja, Kesavakasmirin and Vallabha on Some Crucial Sutras: Part II," *Annals of the Bhandarkar Oriental Research Institute*, 2(1), pp. 23–61.
Karmarkar, R. D. (1921) "The Relation of the Bhagavadgītā and the Bādarāyaṇa Sūtras," *Annals of the Bhandarkar Oriental Research Institute*, 3(2), pp. 73–9.
Karmarkar, R. D. (1925) "The Devayāna and the Pitryāna," *Proceedings and Transactions of the Third Oriental Conference*, pp. 451–64.
Karmarkar, R. D. (ed.) (1959–1964) *Śrībhāṣya of Rāmānuja. University of Poona Sanskrit and Prakrit Series*. In 3 Volumes. Poona: University of Poona.
Kataoka, K. (2011) *Kumārila on Truth, Omniscience, and Killing. Part 2: An Annotated Translation of Mīmāṁsā-Ślokavārttika ad 1.1.2 (Codanāsūtra)*. Wien: Verlag der Österreichischen Akademie der Wiessenschaften.
Kato, T. (2011) *The First Two Chapters of Bhāskara's Śārīrakamīmāṁsābhāṣya: Critically Edited with an Introduction, Notes and an Appendix*. Philosophischen Fakultät der Martin-Luther-Universität Halle-Wittenberg.
Kaufman, W. R. P. (2005) "Karma, Rebirth, and the Problem of Evil," *Philosophy East and West*, 55(1), pp. 15–32.
Khanna, A. B. (1998) *Bhāskarācārya: A Study With Special Reference to His Brahmasūtrabhāṣya*. Delhi: Amar Granth Publications.
Krishnamacharya, P. V. and Narasimha Ayyangar, M. B. (eds.) (1979) *Vedāntasāra of Bhagavad Rāmānuja. With English Translation*. Madras: The Adyar Library and Research Centre.
Kṛṣṇadasa Baba (ed.) (1965) *Śrī-brahmasūtra-govindabhāṣyam. Śrī-baladevavidyābhūṣaṇa-viracitam*. Kusuma Sarovara: Gaura Hari Press.
Kumar, S. (1983) *Sāṁkhya Thought in the Brahmanical Systems of Indian Philosophy*. Delhi: Eastern Book Linkers.
Larson, G. J. (1979) *Classical Sāṁkhya*. Santa Barbara: Ross/Erikson.
Lipner, J. (1986) *The Face of Truth*. Albany: State University of New York Press.
Mackie, J. (1982) *The Miracle of Theism: Arguments for and against the Existence of God*. New York: Oxford University Press.
MacLeod, M. and Rubenstein, E. M. (no date) "Universals," *Internet Encyclopedia of Philosophy*. Available at: https://iep.utm.edu/universa/ (Accessed January 11, 2022).

Mainkar, T. G. (1972) *Sāṁkhya-Kārikā of Īśvarakṛṣṇa, with the Commentary of Gauḍapāda: Translated into English with Notes*. Poona: Oriental Book Agency.

Marfatia, M. (1967) *The Philosophy of Vallabhācārya*. Delhi: Munshiram Manoharlal.

Matilal, B. K. (1992) "A Note on Śaṁkara's Theodicy," *Journal of Indian Philosophy*, 20, pp. 363–76.

McBrayer, J. P. and Howard-Snyder, D. (eds.) (2013) *The Blackwell Companion to the Problem of Evil*. Chichester, West Sussex: Wiley-Blackwell.

McCrea, L. (2000) "The Hierarchical Organization of Language in Mīmāṁsā Interpretive Theory," *Journal of Indian Philosophy*, 28, pp. 429–59.

McCrea, L. (2012) "Rationalisation and Sincerity in Mīmāṁsā Hermeneutics," in Balcerowicz, P. (ed.), *World View and Theory in Indian Philosophy*. Delhi: Manohar, pp. 119–35.

McCrea, L. (2013) "The Transformations of Mīmāṁsā in the Larger Context of Indian Philosophical Discourse," in Franco, E. (ed.), *Periodization and Historiography of Indian Philosophy*. Wien: Institut für Südasien-, Tibet- und Buddhismuskunde der Universität Wien, pp. 127–43.

McCrea, L. (2014) "Appayyadīkṣita's Invention of Śrīkaṇṭha's Vedānta," *Journal of Indian Philosophy*, 44, pp. 81–94.

McCrea, L. (2015) "Freed by the Weight of History: Polemic and Doxography in Sixteenth Century Vedānta," *South Asian History and Culture*, 6(1), pp. 87–101.

Minkowski, C. (2011) "Advaita Vedānta in Early Modern History," in O'Hanlon, R. and Washbrook, D. (eds.), *Religious Cultures in Early Modern India: New Perspectives*. New Delhi: Routledge, pp. 73–99.

Modi, P. M. (1943) *A Critique of the Brahmasutra (III.2.II-IV). Part I: Interpretation of the Sūtras*. Bhavnagar: Mahodaya P. Press.

Modi, P. M. (1956) *A Critique of the Brahmasutra (III.2.II-IV). Part II: System of the Sūtras*. Baroda: Ramvijay Printing Press.

Nakamura, H. (1974) "The Historico-Social Attitude of the Brahma-sūtras," in S. K. Chatterji, V. Raghavan, R. N. Dandekar, Vishna Bandhu, A. D. Pusalkar, and Satya Vrat Shastri, *Charudeva Shastri Felicitation Volume*. Delhi: Charu Deva Shastri Felicitation Committee, pp. 373–8.

Nakamura, H. (1983) *A History of Early Vedānta Philosophy*. Volume 1. Delhi: Motilal Banarsidass.

Nakamura, H. (2004) *A History of Early Vedānta Philosophy*. Volume 2. Delhi: Motilal Banarsidass.

Nicholson, A. J. (2010) *Unifying Hinduism: Philosophy and Identity in Indian Intellectual History*. New York: Columbia University Press.

Nicholson, A. J. (2020) "Making Space for God: Karma, Freedom, and Devotion in the Brahmasūtra Commentaries of Śaṅkara, Rāmānuja, and Baladeva," in Maharaj, A. (ed.), *The Bloomsbury Research Handbook of Vedānta*. New York: Bloomsbury Academic, pp. 227–53.

Nietzsche, F. (2006) *Thus Spoke Zarathustra*. Translated by A. Del Caro. Cambridge: Cambridge University Press.

Okita, K. (2014a) *Hindu Theology in Early Modern South Asia*. Oxford and New York: Oxford University Press.

Okita, K. (2014b) "Hindu Theology and the Question of Qualification," *International Journal of Hindu Studies*, 18(2), pp. 153–79.

Olivelle, P. (1993) *The Āśrama System: The History and Hermeneutics of a Religious Institution*. Oxford and New York: Oxford University Press.

Olivelle, P. (1997) "Orgasmic Rapture and Divine Ecstasy: The Semantic History of ānanda," *Journal of Indian Philosophy*, 25(2), pp. 153–80.

Olivelle, P. (1998) *The Early Upaniṣads*. Oxford and New York: Oxford University Press.

Olivelle, P. (2000) *Dharmasūtras: The Law Codes of Āpastamba, Gautama, Baudhāyana, and Vasiṣṭha. Annotated Text and Translation*. Delhi: Motilal Banarsidass.

Olivelle, P. (2005) *Manu's Code of Law: A Critical Edition and Translation of the Mānava-Dharmaśāstra*. Oxford and New York: Oxford University Press.

Oppy, G. (2013) "Rowe's Evidential Arguments from Evil," in McBrayer, J. P. and Howard-Snyder, D. (eds.), *The Blackwell Companion to the Problem of Evil*. Chichester, West Sussex: Wiley-Blackwell, pp. 49–66.

Pandey, S. L. (1983) *Pre-Śaṁkara Advaita Philosophy*. Allahabad: Darshan Peeth.

Pandit, Ś. (ed.) (1891) *Vaiyāsika-nyāya-mālā*. Poona: Ānandāśrama Press.

Parpola, A. (1981) "On the Formation of Mīmāṁsā and the Problems Concerning Jaimini: With Particular Reference to the Teacher Quotations and the Vedic Schools," *Wiener Zeitschrift für die Kunde Süd- und Ostasiens und Archiv für indische Philosophie*, 25, pp. 145–77.

Parpola, A. (1994) "On the Formation of Mīmāṁsā and the Problems Concerning Jaimini: With Particular Reference to the Teacher Quotations and the Vedic Schools (Part II)," *Wiener Zeitschrift für die Kunde Süd- und Ostasiens und Archiv für indische Philosophie*, 38, pp. 293–308.

Pollock, S. (1997) "The 'Revelation of Tradition': Śruti, Smṛti, and the Sanskrit Discourse of Power," in Lienhard, S. and Piovano, I. (eds.), *Lex et Litterae: Studies in Honour of Professor Oscar Botto*. Torino: Edicioni Dell'Orso, pp. 395–417.

Pollock, S. (2006) *The Language of the Gods in the World of Men: Sanskrit, Culture, and Power in Premodern India*. Berkeley: University of California Press.

Radhakrishnan, S. (1960) *The Brahma Sūtra: The Philosophy of Spiritual Life*. London: George Allen & Unwin LTD.

Rai, G. S. (ed.) (1993) *Ślokavārttika of Śrī Kumārila Bhaṭṭa, With The Commentary Nyāyaratnākara of Śrī Pārthaṣārathi Miśra*. Varanasi: Ratna Publications.

Ramanatha Sastri, S. K. (ed.) (1934) *Bṛhatī (on the Mīmāṁsāsūtrabhāṣya of Śabarasvāmin), With the Ṛjuvimalāpañcikā of Śālikanātha (Tarkapāda)*. Madras: The University of Madras.

Ram-Prasad, C. (2007) *Indian Philosophy and the Consequences of Knowledge: Themes in Ethics, Soteriology, and Metaphysics*. Hampshire: Ashgate.

Renou, L. (1957) *Vedic India*. Calcutta: Susil Gupta Limited.

Śāstri, A. and Śāstrācārya, B. Ś. (eds.) (1938) *The Brahmasūtra Śāṅkara Bhāṣya, with the Commentaries Bhāmatī, Kalpataru and Parimala*. Bombay: Nirnaya Sagar Press.

Śāstri, H. (1979) *Vedānta-darśanam-bhāgavata-bhāṣyopetam*. Vrindavan: Shri Gadadhar Gaurahari Press.

Sastri, K. (ed.) (1984) *Brahmasiddhi. With Commentary by Śaṅkhapāni*. Delhi: Sri Satguru Publications.

Śāstri, S. (ed.) (1916) *Śrībhāṣyam. With Sudarśana Sūri's Śruta-prakāśikā and Raṅgarāmānuja's Bhāva-prakāśikā*. Vrindavan: Shri Shrinibas Press.

Sen, C. (1978) *A Dictionary of Vedic Ritual: Based on the Śrauta and the Gṛhya Sūtras*. Delhi: Concept Publishing Company.

Sharma, B. N. K. (1962) *Philosophy of Śrī Madhvācārya*. Bombay: Bharatiya Vidya Bhavan.

Sharma, B. N. K. (1986) *The Brahmasutras and Their Principal Commentaries*. In 3 Volumes. New Delhi: Munshiram Manoharlal.

Sharma, B. N. K. (1997) *Madhva's Teachings in His Own Words*. Mumbai: Bharatiya Vidya Bhavan.

Sharma, R. N. (2000) *The Aṣṭādhyāyī of Pāṇini. Volume II: English Translation of Adhyāya One with Sanskrit Text, Transliteration, Word-boundary, Anuvṛtti, Vṛtti, Explanatory Notes, Derivational History of Examples, and Indices*. New Delhi: Munshiram Manoharlal Publishers Pvt. Ltd.

Shastri, J. L. (ed.) (1983) *Bhāgavata Purāṇa of Kṛṣṇa Dvaipāyana Vyāsa with Sanskrit Commentary Bhāvārthabodhinī of Śrīdhara Svāmin*. Delhi: Motilal Banarsidass.

Slaje, W. (2007) "Yājñavalkya-brāhmaṇas and the Early Mīmāṁsā," in Bronkhorst, J. (ed.), *Mīmāṁsā and Vedānta: Interaction and Continuity*. Delhi: Motilal Banarsidass, pp. 115–58.

Smith, D. (1996) *The Dance of Śiva: Religion, Art and Poetry in South Asia*. Cambridge: Cambridge University Press.

Sprung, M. (ed.) (1973) *The Problem of Two Truths in Buddhism and Vedānta*. Dordrecht: D. Reidel Publishing Company.

Srinivasa Chari, S. M. (2002) *The Philosophy of the Upanisads: A Study Based on the Comments of Śaṁkara, Rāmānuja and Madhva*. New Delhi: Munshiram Manoharlal Publishers Pvt. Ltd.

Srinivasa Chari, S. M. (2008) *The Philosophy of Viśiṣṭādvaita Vedānta: A Study Based on Vedānta Deśika's Adhikaraṇa-Sārāvalī*. Delhi: Motilal Banarsidass.

Śrīnivāsāchārya, L. (ed.) (1903) *The Brahma-mīmāṁsā with Śrīkaṇṭhāchārya's Commentary*. Mysore: Government Branch Press.
von Stietencron, H. (2006) *"Theology," The Brill Dictionary of Religion*. Leiden and Boston: Brill.
Subba Rau, S. (1904) *The Vedanta-Sutras with the Commentary of Madhwacharya*. Madras: Thompson and Co.
Subramania Iyer, K. A. (1965) *Vākyapadīya of Bhartṛhari with the Vṛtti, Chapter I. English Translation*. Poona: Deccan College.
Subramania Iyer, K. A. (ed.) (1966) *Vākyapadīya of Bhartṛhari, with the Commentaries Vṛtti and Paddhati. Kāṇḍa 1*. Poona: Deccan College.
Sukthankar, V. S. (ed.) (1927) *The Mahābhārata; for the First Time Critically Edited by Vishnu S. Sukthankar et al.* In 19 Volumes. Poona: Bhandarkar Oriental Research Institute.
Suryanarayana Sastri, S. S. and Kunhan Raja, C. (1933) *The Bhāmatī: Catussūtrī*. Madras: Theosophical Publishing House.
Suthren Hirst, J. G. (2005) *Śaṁkara's Advaita Vedānta: A Way of Teaching*. London and New York: RoutledgeCurzon.
Swami, G. (1937a) *Eight Upaniṣads: Volume One (Īśā, Kena, Kaṭha, Taittirīya). With the Commentary of Śaṅkarācārya*. Calcutta: Advaita Ashrama.
Swami, G. (1937b) *Eight Upaniṣads. Volume Two (Aitareya, Muṇḍaka, Māṇḍūkya & Kārikā, Praśna). With the Commentary of Śaṅkarācārya*. Calcutta: Advaita Ashrama.
Swami, G. (1965) *Brahma-Sūtra-Bhāṣya of Śrī Śaṅkarācārya*. Kolkata: Advaita Ashrama.
Swami, G. (2003) *Chāndogya Upaniṣad With the Commentary of Śaṅkarācārya*. Kolkata: Advaita Ashrama.
Swami, G. (2012) *Bhagavadgītā With the Commentary of Śaṅkarācārya*. Kolkata: Advaita Ashrama.
Swami, M. (1950) *The Bṛhadāraṇyaka Upaniṣad with the Commentary of Śaṅkarācārya*. Mayavati: Advaita Ashrama.
Taber, J. (1992) "What did Kumārila Bhaṭṭa Mean by Svataḥ Prāmāṇya?," *Journal of the American Oriental Society*, 112(2), pp. 204–21.
Taber, J. (2007) "Kumārila the Vedāntin?," in Bronkhorst, J. (ed.), *Mīmāṁsā and Vedānta: Interaction and Continuity*. Delhi: Motilal Banarsidass, pp. 159–84.
Telivala, M. T. (1918) *Discuss How Far Sankaracharya Truly Represents the View of the Author of the Brahmasutras*. Bombay: Nirnaya Sagar Press.
Telivala, M. T. (ed.) (2005) *Aṇubhāṣya on the Brahmasūtra, With the Commentary Bhāṣyaprakāśa and the Super-commentary Raśmi on the Bhāṣyaprakāśa*. In 4 Volumes. Delhi: Akshaya Prakashan.
Thakur, A. (ed.) (1997) *Nyāyabhāṣyavārttika of Bhāradvāja Uddyotakara*. New Delhi: Indian Council of Philosophical Research.
The Works of Sri Sankaracharya. In 20 Volumes (1910) Srirangam: Sri Vani Vilas Press.

Thibaut, G. (1890) *The Vedānta-Sūtras, with the Commentary of Śaṅkara*. In Two Parts. Oxford: Clarendon Press.
Thibaut, G. (1904) *The Vedānta-Sūtras, with the Commentary of Rāmānuja*. Oxford: Clarendon Press.
Trīpāṭhī, K. (ed.) (1979) *Vijñānabhikṣu's Vijñānāmṛta-bhāṣyam on Brahmasūtras*. Varanasi: Banaras Hindu University.
Turcan, R. and Tomassi, C. O. (2005) *"Apotheosis," Encyclopedia of Religion*. Volume 1. 2nd edn. Edited by L. Jones. Detroit: Macmillan Reference USA, pp. 437–40.
Upreti, T. (ed.) (2003) *Viṣṇumahāpurāṇam of Maharṣi Vedavyāsa. With Sanskrit Commentary "Ātmaprakāṣa" of Śrīdharācārya*. In 2 Volumes. Delhi: Parimal Publications.
Uskokov, A. (2018a) "Brahma Sūtras (Vedānta Sūtras)," in Jain, P., Sherma, R., and Khanna, M. (eds.), *Hinduism and Tribal Religions*. Dordrecht: Springer Netherlands, doi:10.1007/978-94-024-1036-5_579-1.
Uskokov, A. (2018b) "Brahman," in Jain, P., Sherma, R., and Khanna, M. (eds.), *Hinduism and Tribal Religions*. Dordrecht: Springer Netherlands, doi:10.1007/978-94-024-1036-5_579-1.
Uskokov, A. (2018c) *Deciphering the Hidden Meaning: Scripture and the Hermeneutics of Liberation in Early Advaita Vedānta*. PhD Dissertation. University of Chicago.
Uskokov, A. (2019) "A Mīmāṁsaka Reading Kṛṣṇa's Song: Pārthasārathi Miśra and the Bhagavad-gītā," *Journal of Vaishnava Studies*, 28(1), pp. 197–221.
Uskokov, A. (2020) "The Soteriology of Devotion, Divine Grace, and Teaching: Bhagavadgītā and the Śrīvaiṣṇavas," in Theodor, I. (ed.), *The Bhagavad-gītā: A Critical Introduction*. London: Routledge, pp. 68–79.
Uskokov, A. (2022) "The Black Sun That Destroys Inner Darkness: Or, How Bādarāyaṇa Became Vyāsa," *Journal of the American Oriental Society*, 142, pp. 63–92.
Vasu, S. C. (2002) *The Vedāntasūtras of Bādarāyaṇa, with the Commentary of Baladeva*. Delhi: Munshiram Manoharlal Publishers Pvt. Ltd.
Vattanky, J. (1993) *Development of Nyāya Theism*. New Delhi: Intercultural Publications.
Veezhinathan, N. (1972) *The Saṁkṣepaśārīraka of Sarvajñātman*. Madras: Centre for Advanced Study in Philosophy, University of Madras.
Venkataramiah, D. (1948) *The Pañcapādikā of Padmapāda*. Baroda: Oriental Institute.
Venkatkrishnan, A. (2015) *Mīmāṁsā, Vedānta, and the Bhakti Movement*. Doctoral Dissertation. Columbia University.
Vrajlal, J. M. (1964) *A Critical Study of Aṇubhāṣya of Śrī Vallabhācārya*. PhD Dissertation. Dwarka: Institute for Research in Indology.
Webster, D. (2005) *The Philosophy of Desire in the Buddhist Pali Canon*. New York: RoutledgeCurzon.
Wiltshire, M. G. (1990) *Ascetic Figures Before and in Early Buddhism*. Berlin & New York: De Gruyter.

Index